CHINA: TWENTY YEARS OF ECONOMIC REFORM

CHINA: TWENTY YEARS OF ECONOMIC REFORM

Ross Garnaut and Ligang Song

(editors)

Australian
National
University

E PRESS

ANU
E PRESS

Published by ANU E Press
The Australian National University
Canberra ACT 0200, Australia
Email: anuepress@anu.edu.au
This title is also available online at http://epress.anu.edu.au

National Library of Australia Cataloguing-in-Publication entry

Title: China : twenty years of economic reform / Ross Garnaut and
             Ligang Song, editors.

ISBN: 9781922144454 (pbk.) 978192214461 (ebook)

Notes: Includes bibliographical references and index.

Subjects: China--Economic conditions--1976-
             China--Economic policy--1976-

Other Authors/Contributors:
             Garnaut, Ross.
             Song, Ligang.
             Australian National University. National Centre for Development Studies.

Dewey Number: 330.951

First published by Asia Pacific Press, 1999
This edition © 2012 ANU E Press

Contents

Tables and figures

Figures

The following symbols are used

	not available
..	not available
-	zero
.	insignificant
n.a.	not applicable

Abbreviations

APEC	Asia-Pacific Economic Cooperation
AusAID	Australian Agency for International Aid
CBE	commune and brigade enterprise
CCP	Chinese Communist Party
CFETS	China Foreign Exchange Trading System
CHIBOR	China interbank rate
CITIC	China International Trust and Investment Corporation
EEFSU	Eastern Europe and the former Soviet Union
FDI	foreign direct investment
FEC	Foreign Exchange Certificate
FK	foreign capital
GATT	General Agreement on Tariffs and Trade
GDE	Guangdong Development Enterprises
GDP	gross domestic product
GITIC	Guangdong International Trust and Investment Corp
GNP	gross national product
HRS	household responsibility system
LK	local capital
MLD	mean logarithmic deviation
MOFTEC	Ministry of Foreign Trade and Economic Cooperation
NBFIs	non-bank financial institutions
OECD	Organisation for Economic Cooperation and Development
OLS	ordinary least squares
R&D	research and development
RMB	renminbi
S&P	Standard and Poor's
SAFE	State Administration of Foreign Exchange
SIC	State Information Council
SOE	state-owned enterprise
SSB	State Statistical Bureau
STAQS	Securities Trading Automated Quotation System
TFP	total factor productivity
TIC	trust and investment corporation
TVE	township and village enterprise
TVP	township, village and privately-owned enterprise
WTO	World Trade Organization

Contributors

Ross Garnaut
Director, Asia Pacific School of Economics and Management, The Australian National University, Canberra, Australia

Michael Hasenstab
Research Scholar, National Centre for Development Studies, Asia Pacific School of Economics and Management, The Australian National University, Canberra, Australia

Yiping Huang
Fellow, Asia Pacific School of Economics and Management and The Research School of Pacific and Asian Studies, The Australian National University, Canberra, Australia

Xin Meng
Fellow, Asia-Pacific School of Economics and Management and The Research School of Pacific and Asian Studies, The Australian National University, Canberra, Australia

Zhao Renwei
Professor, Institute of Economics, Chinese Academy of Social Sciences, Beijing, China

Li Shi
Professor, Institute of Economics, Chinese Academy of Social Sciences, Beijing, China

Ligang Song
Fellow, Australia-Japan Research Centre, Director, China Economy and Business Program, Asia Pacific School of Economics and Management, The Australian National University, Canberra, Australia

Xiaolu Wang
Deputy Director and Senior Research Fellow, National Economic Research Institute (NERI), China Reform Foundation, Beijing, China

Yongzheng Yang
Fellow, National Centre for Development Studies, Asia Pacific School of Economics and Management, The Australian National University, Canberra, Australia

Twenty years of economic reform and structural change in the Chinese economy

Ross Garnaut[*]

On 22 December 1978, the Eleventh Central Committee of the Chinese Communist Party completed its third plenary meeting. There was no contemporary recognition in the West of the significance of the meeting.

The twentieth anniversary of the third plenum received far more attention. In the intervening years, China, and its relations with the international community, have been transformed. China's economy has expanded by five times, and its foreign trade by twelve. It has greatly increased consumption levels of what had been about half of the world's people in poverty. Then an isolated, autarchic economy, China through the mid and late 1990s absorbed about half of the direct foreign investment flows to developing economies. From having no trade or investment ties with Taiwan and the Republic of Korea, it is now the first or second export destination of one and the third of the other.

Even greater has been the transformation of the Chinese mind. Tens of millions of Chinese are now part of an international community of ideas and information. Personal security is provided significantly by the value of people's labour and produce in the market place, in the stead of an intrusive and overwhelming state. With the expanded role of the market has come a substantial widening in the sphere of personal freedom—to travel and communicate with others.

Changes of this dimension and at this extraordinary speed are unsettling, and potentially destabilising. Yet for all the disruption of change, and the many new problems that it has generated, most Chinese welcome the transformation. Certainly the large increase in living standards and the expanded sphere of personal freedom are appreciated enough to provide a base for continuity in political leadership and institutions despite the immense stress and dislocation.

Reform in China has not and could never have been a smooth or a painless process. There have been challenges at every step, some bumps in the road, detours, and dead ends. Reform faced its greatest danger in the traumatic aftermath of the Beijing massacre in May 1989 which compounded the risks of an inflationary boom and a major effort to bring it under control. The financial and economic crisis in neighbouring East Asian economies since 1997 is the great challenge of the late 1990s.

The distance travelled: ideas and policy

Twenty years ago, Deng Xiaoping and his supporters took decisive control of the Central Committee of the Chinese Communist Party. This ended what Deng himself once described in my presence as two years of indecisive economic strategy and policy after the death of Mao Zedong. During those two years, policies embodying pragmatic acceptance of a large role for domestic and international market exchange were in continual contest with the Maoist commitments to local and national autarchy, central planning, state-owned enterprises in the cities and people's communes in the countryside.

Deng and his key supporters were victims of the Cultural Revolution, and the anarchy of that decade was their political launching pad. They were not in any sense political or economic liberals. Deng and his senior supporters had been the managers of the early periods of Communist Party success, in the 1950s before the Great Leap Forward, and in the brief interlude between the recognition of failure in that first lethal experiment in unworldly application of Maoist theory, and the anarchy of the second. They harked back to earlier success, when markets had been allowed to play substantial roles at least in the countryside, within a system in which central planning was supported by a firm administrative order.

The reformist leaders of December 1978 were aware that the world had changed from the earlier, naive days of partial success. They were aware of China's military vulnerability, as an economically weak and technologically backward society. They were deeply conscious that

China shared the world's longest border with an apparently economically successful, technologically advanced and politically expansionist authoritarian state, the world's second military superpower. Some of them were aware as well that their rivals from the Chinese Civil War across the Taiwan Strait, their compatriots in colonial Hong Kong, and their cold war enemies in southern Korea were enjoying sustained economic success that raised deeply challenging questions about China's own continuing backwardness.

It was the strategic vulnerability that had caused and allowed Premier Zhou Enlai to champion the modernisation of industry, agriculture, science and technology and national defence in the early 1970s, after the armed clashes on the Heilongjiang. The intensification of the Sino-Soviet conflict, and the four modernisations, provided the context for diplomatic rapprochement with the United States, and for Deng Xiaoping's temporary rehabilitation as Vice Premier in the early 1970s. China's national policy lurched dangerously as competing ideas and political forces struggled over the tiller of state. The ultimate directions were settled by the People's Liberation Army's arrest of the 'Gang of Four' after the death of Mao, although policy continued to wobble until Deng Xiaoping's ascendancy in 1978.

Important steps were taken to lay a base for future growth in the period of indecisive policy. The awesome denial of formal education during the Cultural Revolution ended, with the return of competitive entry into the great universities in 1978. China's state enterprises experimented with the purchase of exotic new technologies from abroad. But there were cross-currents and counter-currents, continued ideological contests over high policy, and uncertainty as subordinate leaders watched for the emergence of a clear national direction.

Since December 1978 there has been no turning back.

It is not that Deng and his colleagues obtained endorsement for an elaborate, comprehensive new economic policy or plan. There was no blueprint for China's economic reform and internationalisation—even less than there had been in Taiwan and Korea at the beginnings of their sustained, rapid growth one and a half decades earlier.

But after the 1978 Plenum there was acceptance that domestic and international exchange through markets was a necessary and acceptable component of a national development strategy. There was pragmatic acceptance that institutions and policies that raised national economic output had a valid place in China—summed up in Deng's rehabilitation of an early Maoist exhortation to 'seek truth from facts'. These strands were drawn together in the 1987 Party Congress' acceptance of General Secretary Zhao Ziyang's definition of China as a backward country in the 'primary stage of socialism', in which the first national objective had to be the strengthening of the national economy.

The new political environment after 1978 saw foreign trade, direct foreign investment, and the utilisation of external technological co-operation and capital in all forms become acceptable components of national policy. Local experiments with new forms of organisation of agricultural production were legitimised, leading within a few years to the virtually complete replacement of the people's communes with the immensely more productive household responsibility system. Markets became important for exchange for the rapidly expanding agricultural output.

The absence of a comprehensive reform strategy, the eclecticism of economic policy and the gradualism of change have been criticised by foreign observers from time to time over the past two decades. But the absence of a blueprint was an inevitability of China's circumstances, and in practice a virtue.

It was an inevitability because there was no conceptual basis for a market-oriented economy. A few leaders, and a few intellectuals around the edges of policy, had absorbed some of the elements of internationally-oriented growth in Japan, Korea, Taiwan and Hong Kong. But the main understanding grew out of the new patterns of economic development themselves, through observations of the operation of markets within China, and increasing contact with foreign experience and ideas.

Nor was there an ideological basis in the early years for articulation of a model of development based on the operation of markets, deeply integrated into an international economy. Deng Xiaoping's political control of the Chinese Communist party and the People's Liberation Army was strong but not unconditional. It was built partly on others' confidence that he stood firmly for continued Communist Party political dominance, and commitment to some undefined minimum core of socialist principles and objectives.

The absence of a blueprint was a virtue because any theoretical model of reform of the centrally planned economy in China would have been deeply flawed. The rapid unwinding of a centrally planned economy, dominated by state enterprises in the cities and communes in the countryside, is fraught with risk of massive dislocation—a reality which was imperfectly understood before the unhappy later experience of Eastern Europe and the former Soviet Union. Some of the great strengths of the Chinese economy in the era of reform came as surprises to Chinese and foreign observers alike and would have been given an inadequate place in a program of reform built upon the received theory and experience of others. First amongst the surprises was the extraordinary dynamism of industrial production in the township and village enterprises that grew from the remnants of the disintegrating people's communes.

Deng Xiaoping used to describe economic reform in China as crossing the river by feeling for stones at each step. Hu Yaobang described reform to Australian Prime Minister Bob Hawke as an experiment without precedent. In the uncertain months following the dismissal of Hu Yaobang from his office of General Secretary of the Chinese Communist Party, Deng alluded uncharacteristically to the Chinese classics in a conversation with the Secretary General of Japan's Liberal Democratic Party, Noboru Takeshita, and compared the path of reform to the mission of Guan Yu, who had had to cross five passes and cut down six generals to achieve his noble objective.[1]

These metaphors contain important insights. Chinese reform required transformations in ideology, in ideas about economic development and policy, in law and regulatory systems and in economic institutions. Above all, it required the accumulation of new knowledge and wisdom in a billion Chinese minds, as the Chinese people learned to do new things in an economic and social world that was fundamentally changed.

These transformations in ideology, ideas, policy, law, institutions, knowledge and experience occurred alongside each other, reinforcing each other. Each created problems for others when it ran into trouble itself.

It took great courage, and faith in some abstract and thinly formed ideas, for the Chinese collective leadership to wade into the river of reform. Courage and faith, and a clear view of the reality—that the maintenance of the *status quo* in centrally planned China in the aftermath of the Cultural Revolution meant continued backwardness, vulnerability and eventually instability in a rapidly developing East Asia and changing world.

Upon establishing his pre-eminence in the exercise of political power, Deng Xiaoping identified as his agents in the reform of the Party, and of the State and economy, Hu Yaobang and Zhao Ziyang. As General Secretary of the Communist Party, Hu led the task of replacing the huge cadre of beneficiaries of the Cultural Revolution with others able to lead and support reform. Zhao was the leader of the practical business of policy reform. Each made extraordinary contributions of leadership and intellect, managing change on a scale and at a pace that was rare in human experience. Each was informed by experience to the view that successful economic reform and development would require a widening of the scope for open discussion of policy, for dissent within the limits set by the imperatives of continued Communist Party rule, and for reform of the political system to make policy somewhat more open to pressures from the rapidly changing society beyond the central leadership. Deng eventually came to doubt the will or the capacity of each to secure and enforce the authority of the Chinese Communist Party, causing the dismissal of Hu in early 1987 after the Shanghai student demonstrations, and of Zhao, then Party General Secretary, in the Party crisis over the management of the Beijing student demonstrations in May 1989.

The succession after the reform leadership crisis of 1987–89, selected by Deng Xiaoping and until his last years sustained by him, placed a higher premium on stability, and on defining and narrowing the boundaries of discussion of political system change. As it turned out, economic reform and change had its own momentum, that carried along continued social and political change in the local sphere. Li Peng's decade-long Premiership, and the Jiang Zemin leadership of the Party, now approaching the completion of its tenth year, are remarkable for the stability and continuity that they reflect. This stability, in turn, reflected the wider leadership's consciousness of the risk of instability, especially in the period bridging the death of Deng Xiaoping. The emergence of a more activist, reformist Premier in 1998, Zhu Rongji, indicates a return to a sense of urgency in reform and structural change.

In the early years of reform, courage and faith, and a clear view of the futility of standing still, were required in leadership of all state institutions. In the great universities, ageing professors, often with pre-revolutionary experience of academic institutions in the West, were called from the disgrace of the Cultural Revolution to the massive and depressing replacement of half a generation lost to disciplined education. Some leaders of pre-revolutionary business who had opted to make their lives in the mainland, and who had mostly been rewarded by humiliation in the years before reform, accepted invitations to lead market-oriented new state businesses, as examples for the huge and cumbersome enterprises that had grown within the framework of central planning. Loyal servants of the state were called to new tasks for which their education and experience had provided no preparation at all.

In one of the boldest of early reform decisions, many tens of thousands of young people were sent or allowed abroad as students—to America, Australia, Japan, Europe and Hong Kong. They became windows of information and of change when they returned to live and work, or more commonly when they returned to visit or simply kept in touch with home.

The conceptual gap that had to be bridged in the course of reform was immense, extending into every corner of economic policy.

To take one corner, the idea that a country can maximise the value of its production and incomes through open trade, relying on imports for goods and services in which the economy has comparative disadvantage, is not intuitively obvious to Chinese any more than to other components of the human species. Even where the logic of comparative advantage is accepted by policymakers, its full reflection in policy is resisted by vested interests that expect to be damaged by it. In China, the usual resistances to specialisation according to comparative advantage were reinforced by the heavy emphasis on autarchy in Communist central planning, by the special Maoist exhortation to 'self reliance', and by the overlay of security concerns about dependence on foreign trade. Inside and outside China there were doubts about the capacity and willingness of the rest of the world to adjust to much higher levels of Chinese exports.

The acceptance of the idea that there are gains in specialisation according to comparative advantage came slowly. Each major sector of the economy became a battleground over acceptance of the concept. The idea gained enough ground for policy change to allow the beginnings of rapid expansion of labour-intensive manufactures balanced by rapid growth in imports of a range of capital-intensive and technologically sophisticated manufactured goods, and of industrial raw materials. The gains from trade then made their own eloquent case for going further. An important milestone was General Secretary Zhao Ziyang's articulation of a coastal economic strategy in early 1988, under which coastal China would expand its export-oriented manufactured export base, building on its relative abundance of labour, and drawing raw materials from international markets.

Resistance to liberalisation remains strong in some sectors, nowhere more so than in grain. But even in grain, the objective has recently been stated by the Ministry of Agriculture as 95 per cent, rather than complete, self-sufficiency. The difference would represent about 10 per cent of world trade in grain.

Reform was constrained by the legacy of Chinese Communist Party ideology—specifically, the elements of ideology associated variously with Marx, Lenin, Stalin, and Mao. The ideological legacy of Mao turned out to be the least constraining for economic reform, once the Party had delivered its verdict that Mao was 70 per cent right and 30 per cent wrong. The 70 per cent was the contribution of the early Mao to building the supremacy of the Communist Party, a strong Chinese state, and the early policy which had been developed with the co-operation of Deng Xiaoping and the other, older leaders of the reform period. The excesses of the Great Leap Forward and the Cultural Revolution comprised much of the 30 per cent, including the elevation of ideological purity above the requirements of economic development. On the legacy of Marx, the theoretical distance of classical Marxism from the practical decisions of state, and its denial of the possibility of socialism in a backward country, weakened the constraint that it placed on reform. Some intellectual gymnastics were required in the mid 1980s to render the operation of a labour market consistent with the labour theory of value. What then remained was a commitment to avoid the extremes of income inequality that the Chinese leadership associated with capitalist developing countries, and a view that the state should continue to own the largest enterprises in key economic sectors. The Leninist legacy of firm Communist Party that control through 'democratic centralism' remained a cardinal principle of Deng Xiaoping, has not been successfully challenged and remains a premise of the current leadership. The Stalinist legacy of central planning has had little continuing ideological resonance, at least in the 1990s.

Beyond ideology and policy, there have been immense problems of a highly practical kind, especially in reforming the system of central planning. The practical challenge was how to build the regulatory system, the institutions and the human knowledge and skills to implement reform policy and to make the partially reformed system work. Amongst the most difficult tasks has been the building of an institutional framework to implement monetary and therefore macroeconomic stabilisation indirectly, as is necessary in a market economy. Through the first one

8

and a half decades of reform, weaknesses in this area had generated a cycle in growth, inflationary and balance of payments pressure that seemed to be widening over time (Garnaut and Ma 1993a). The apparent 'soft landing' after the inflationary boom of 1993–95 is suggestive of progress, although the role that continued to be played by costly direct controls on investment during this episode qualifies the success. By the mid 1990s it was clear to the government that sustained stable growth required the completion of the reform of state-owned enterprises, allowing, finally, enforcement of hard budget constraints. The 1997 Party Congress and 1998 National People's Congress laid a base for rapid progress, which has as yet been only partially utilised.

At the end of the 1990s, the practical problems centred on the threat of contagion from the East Asian crisis. This was—and indeed still is—a massive challenge, threatening stability and growth.

The larger perspective is that the reform and internationalisation of the Chinese economy is an undertaking of such immense dimensions, and unusual character, that it is inevitably challenged in ways that are potentially dangerous to its successful conclusion. The contemporary challenge is dangerous, but not especially large compared with the passes that have already been crossed, and in particular the barriers of ideology, ideas, policy, institutions and practical difficulties that faced the reformers at the beginning.

The distance travelled: economic change

China's real economy expanded strongly with reform. Over these two decades, China has emerged as the most dynamic large player in the world economy. Growth in output and in external economic relations has been as rapid in China as in any of the East Asian economies in their own periods of strong growth, although China happens to have been excluded from the World Bank's ill-fated *East Asian Miracle* (World Bank 1993a).

Figures 1.1 to 1.7 summarise the story of growth and structural change in output and foreign economic relations in a series of charts, taken from the standard data accepted and published by the international agencies.

Can we believe the statistics? This question was asked with more urgency as China claimed success in maintaining growth near 8 per cent through the East Asian crisis in 1998.

The external trade and investment data are broadly confirmed from other countries' records of the same transactions. The main questions focus on the domestic output data. There are some conceptual problems with the conventions of the standard national accounts. They measure increases in stocks as valuable production, even when the discounted present value of future sales is low. This is not only a problem in China—it arises in advanced market economies in recession. But it is a larger problem when stocks held by government-supported state enterprises are rising rapidly. There are problems of valuing non-marketed services in all economies, and a larger problem in economies like China where this sector is large, leading

Figure 1.1   Proportionate increase in real output, 1978–98
(per cent)

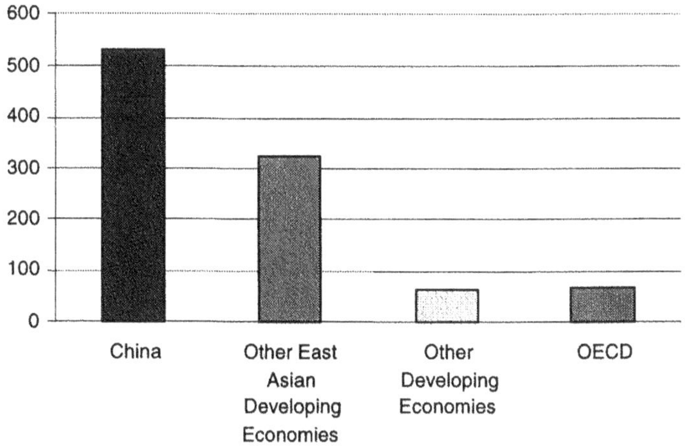

Sources: Author's calculations based on data compiled from World Bank, 1997. *World Development Indicators*, World Bank Publications, Philadelphia [CD-ROM]; International Monetary Fund, (various years). *World Economic Outlook* (various issues), International Monetary Fund, Washington, DC; International Economic Databank, The Australian National University, Canberra.

Figure 1.2 Structural changes in China, 1978–97 (industrial output by ownership, per cent of total, total = 100)

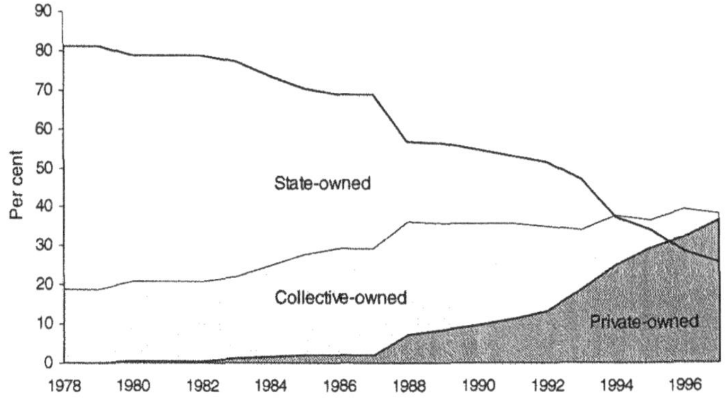

Source: State Statistical Bureau, (various years). *Statistical Yearbook of China*, China Statistical Publishing House, Beijing.

Figure 1.3 Employment in township and village enterprises, 1978–97

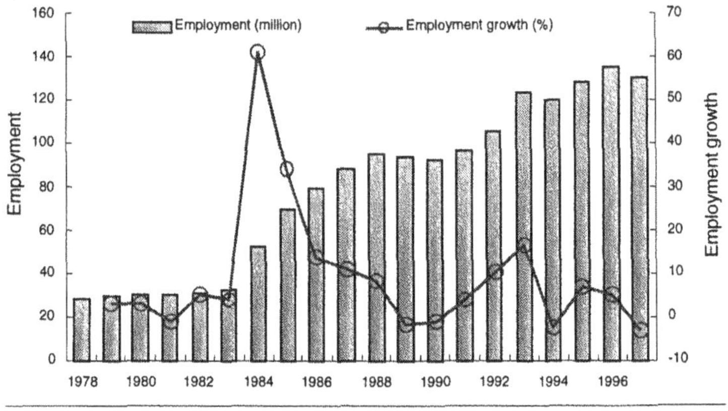

Source: State Statistical Bureau, (various years). *Statistical Yearbook of China*, China Statistical Publishing House, Beijing.

Figure 1.4 Exports of large developing countries and Australia, 1978–98 (US$billion)

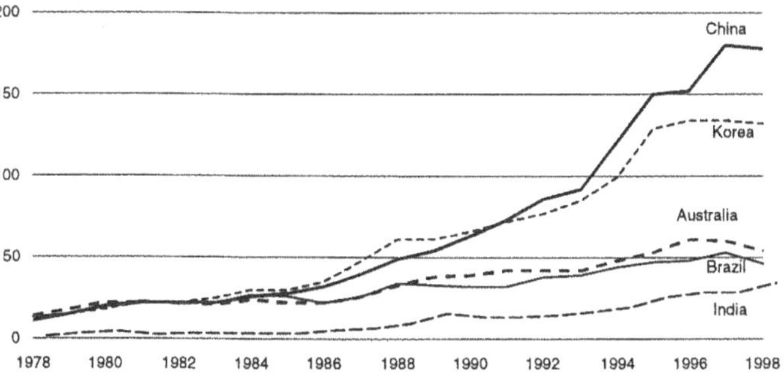

Source: Author's calculations based on data compiled from United Nations COMTRADE database, International Economic Databank, The Australian National University, Canberra.

Figure 1.5 Proportionate growth of exports (constant prices), 1978–98 (per cent)

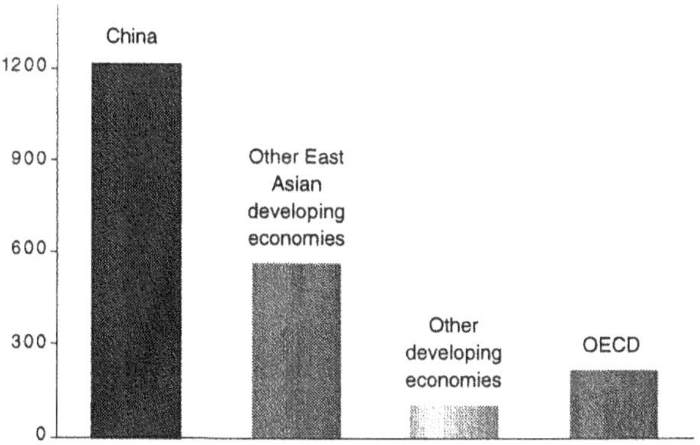

Source: Author's calculations based on data compiled from United Nations COMTRADE database, International Economic Databank, The Australian National University, Canberra.

Figure 1.6   China: changes in composition of exports, 1978–96
(per cent)

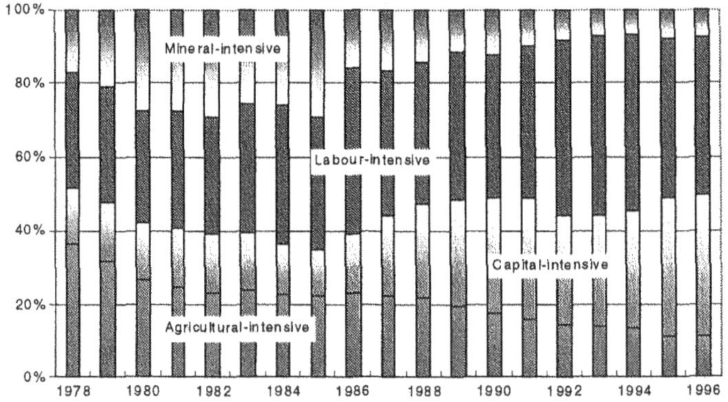

Source: Author's calculations based on data compiled from United Nations COMTRADE database, International Economic Databank, The Australian National University, Canberra.

Figure 1.7   Developing economy shares of world exports in labour-intensive manufactures, 1978–96 (per cent)

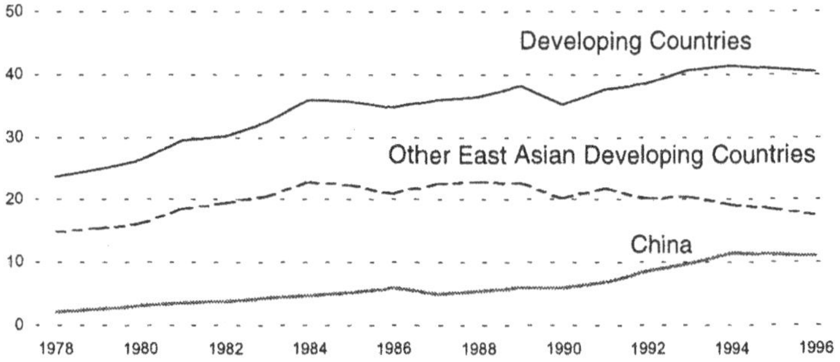

Source: Author's calculations based on data compiled from United Nations COMTRADE database, International Economic Databank, The Australian National University, Canberra.

to underestimation of the level, although not necessarily the growth, in output. In all economies there are problems in bringing natural resource depletion and environmental degradation or enhancement to account in assessment of the growth of valuable economic output, and this is especially important in low income developing economies experiencing rapid industrialisation.

The professional quality of China's statistical collections has improved greatly since the early years of reform. Nevertheless, there are continuing problems in China beyond those that are present in all national accounts. One is a difficulty in valuing output in the township and village enterprises. The weight of informed professional opinion suggests that this may lead to over-estimation of real growth on average by up to 2.5 per cent per annum over the reform period. For example, Maddison (1998) measures the over-estimation at 2.4 per cent or 0.1 per cent, depending on the sectoral weights that are applied. The Maddison logic suggests that the over-estimation would be less important at times of low-inflation, such as the present.

There is a difficulty in reconciling reported data on levels of output over time with reported growth rates, and observed levels of consumption, use and trade in a wide variety of commodities in China and in other developing economies. Garnaut and Ma (1993b) examined this issue and concluded that the standard national accounts, converted into foreign currencies at official exchange rates, undervalued Chinese output relative to other developing economies with low and middle incomes by a factor of three. The large real appreciation of the renminbi since early 1994 and especially through the East Asian crisis would have reduced the relative overvaluation substantially.

The overall story is that, leaving aside the general conceptual problems of the national accounts in all countries, the Chinese data substantially understate the size and average incomes of the Chinese economy, moderately overstate output growth rates, and give a reasonable picture of the scale and growth of China's interaction with the international economy.

There is a separate issue concerning the relationship between GDP as measured in the national accounts, and the purchasing power of GDP. The standard national accounts data underestimate the purchasing power of lower relative to higher income countries. This simply reflects the lower valuation in the national accounts of labour and non-tradable goods and services in a low-income economy.

This is the reason why China looms much larger in the 'purchasing power parity' estimates of economic size, than it does in the national accounts data. The difference in relative incomes and size resulting from this influence alone is typically a factor of two or three in low income countries. This relative undervaluation of the volume of goods and services produced in low income countries disappears as labour becomes more valuable in the course of economic development. The phasing out of the relative undervaluation explains a general tendency for rapidly growing developing economies to catch up with the world economic frontiers more rapidly than the initial income differences and the growth rate differentials would suggest.

China and the East Asian crisis

China's growth and structural change in the reform era has had much in common with other East Asian economies at corresponding periods of their own development. This was once a comfort, when there was none amongst the East Asian economies that had grown fast enough to double output in a single decade, that had failed to sustain strong growth until it had been lifted to the frontiers of world productivity and average incomes. Growth slowed in Japan from the mid 1970s, and in Hong Kong and Taiwan in the 1990s, but only after these economies' average incomes had entered the range of advanced industrial economies.

Now the question is being asked, whether the crisis in the economies of many of China's neighbours suggests that China can be expected to enter a period of economic instability and slower growth.

Certainly the East Asian crisis is the greatest external challenge of the past twenty years to stability and growth in China. So far China has had a relatively good crisis, sustaining growth at high levels (although down on the twenty-year average) in the second half of 1998 through massive fiscal expansion, and winning much international kudos for this and for holding the pre-crisis US dollar value of the renminbi.

At the time of the twentieth anniversary of reform, and still in early 1999, a view was emanating from the foreign community in Beijing and the business community in Hong Kong that China had not really done so well through the crisis, or that it would run into deep trouble in the near future. This view had its origin in incredulity that China, with structural flaws in its financial system as large as any in the region, could avoid the problems that had defeated apparently stronger economies.

15

The East Asian crisis has certainly been a large blow for mainland China. The East Asian economies that are currently in recession, including China's Northeast Asian neighbours, Korea, Hong Kong and Japan, account for half China's exports and three-quarters of its direct foreign investment. The East Asian orientation of China's trade and investment was an advantage when the rest of the region was growing strongly. In 1998 it was a large drag on performance, with East Asian imports from the world as a whole declining by 17.3 per cent in 1998 (Figure 1.8).

In these circumstances, even if China held its share in total imports of other East Asian economies—not an easy task given the heightened competitiveness of others—it would have to expand exports beyond East Asia well above 30 per cent per annum if total exports were to continue to grow at a rate near the average of the reform period. This is simply impractical, if only because of the protectionist response it would generate. In fact, China's export growth slumped through 1998, going strongly and at first sight dangerously into negative territory from October (Figure 1.9). At the same time, the weak real exchange rates of other East Asian economies through the crisis reduced pressure and capacity for direct foreign investment, including to China.

China stood up well to the East Asian crisis, at least through its first year and a half, because its macroeconomic fundamentals were strong at the onset of crisis. Inflation was low in response to the corrective policies applied mid-decade. The current account of the balance of payments, and export momentum were strong. A recent history of high levels of direct foreign investment and reform was generating considerable productivity growth in the export industries. High levels of capital inflow were mainly in the form of direct foreign investment, with controls on capital movement inhibiting inflows of speculative portfolio capital. Foreign exchange reserves were high—second only to Japan in global terms—and rising.

These strengths at the onset of the crisis allowed China to implement a massive fiscal expansion to offset the recessionary impulses from the external sector. This was cutting in powerfully from the third quarter of 1998.

China chose early in the crisis to maintain the US dollar value of the renminbi, at least through 1998, and perhaps indefinitely. In late 1998, leaders of the government and of the People's Bank of China stated firmly that China intended to maintain the rate at least through 1999.

The motive of the exchange rate policy was primarily domestic: to avoid the inflation and pressure on financial and other businesses that had accompanied massive depreciation elsewhere in East Asia. The maintenance of growth and the old exchange rate parity reduced the pressure on the weak financial system. China's policy of maintaining the exchange rate and supporting growth with fiscal expansion was favourable to eventual stabilisation and recovery elsewhere in the region. China's imports from other East Asian economies held up reasonably well through 1998 (Figure 1.10). Favourable international feedback encouraged China to persist with the policy.

Figure 1.8   Growth in East Asian imports, 1985–98
(per cent per annum)

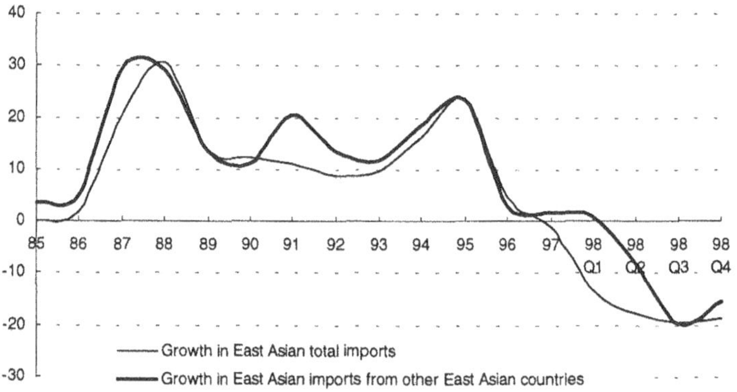

Note: Quarterly data represent change on corresponding period of previous year.
Source: Author's calculations based on data collected from International Monetary Fund, (various years). *Direction of Trade*, International Monetary Fund and International Bank for Reconstruction and Development, Washington; China, (various years). *China Monthly Statistics*, China. Statistical Information and Consultancy Service Centre, Peiching; various country sources.

Can this approach be maintained? Or does the sharp downturn in exports from October 1998 portend an eventual depreciation, abandonment of fiscal expansion, and recession, with the contraction of the economy being intensified greatly by these factors' interactions with a chronically weak financial system?

China could not sustain for many years fiscal deficits on the scale of 1998 and that proposed for 1999. Nor could it sustain indefinitely an appreciation of its real effective exchange rate on the scale of early 1998, against its East Asian trading partners and competitors. This was the reason for its pressure on Japan when the yen was at its weakest point in mid 1998. Eventually the unmanageably large decline in competitiveness can be corrected by declining costs and prices in China, inflation in other countries, faster productivity growth in China than in trading partners and competitors, and by recovery in the economies and re-appreciation in the exchange rates of other East Asian countries.

Figure 1.9   Growth in China's exports, 1985–98 (per cent)

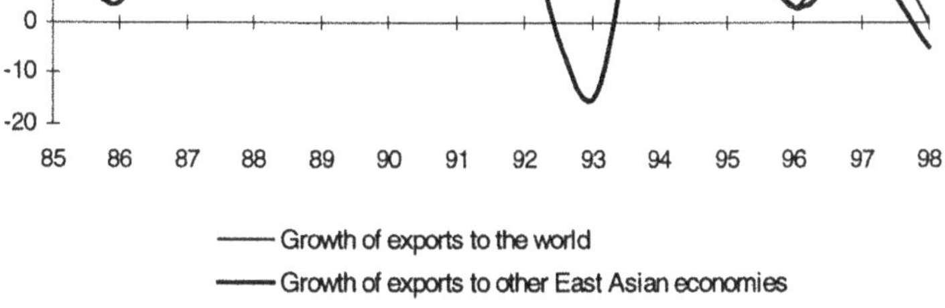

Growth of exports to the world
Growth of exports to other East Asian economies

Sources: Author's calculations based on data collected from State Statistical Bureau, (various years). *Statistical Yearbook of China*, China Statistical Publishing House, Beijing; China, (various years). *China Monthly Statistics*, China Statistical Information and Consultancy Service Centre, Peiching; International Monetary Fund, (various years). *International Financial Statistics*, International Monetary Fund, Washington; various country sources.

There are recent signs of favourable movement in several of these parameters. Figure 1.11 sets out the data for China's average real exchange rate.

Financial markets in the East Asian economies in recession have been stronger since late September 1998. This in itself takes pressure from the Chinese exchange rate and economy, and indicates expectations of recovery in at least some economies. So long as these expectations come to be realised in 1999, China will be able to hold on to its late 1998 strategy.

That is not to say that the weakness of China's financial institutions can be seen as anything other than major potential threats to growth, requiring firm correction. This problem is less urgent in China because the state stands unequivocally behind the banks that it owns, turning a potential financial crisis into a potential budget problem. The Chinese fiscal system seems able to handle the load in the immediate

Figure 1.10   Growth in China's imports, 1985–98 (per cent per annum)

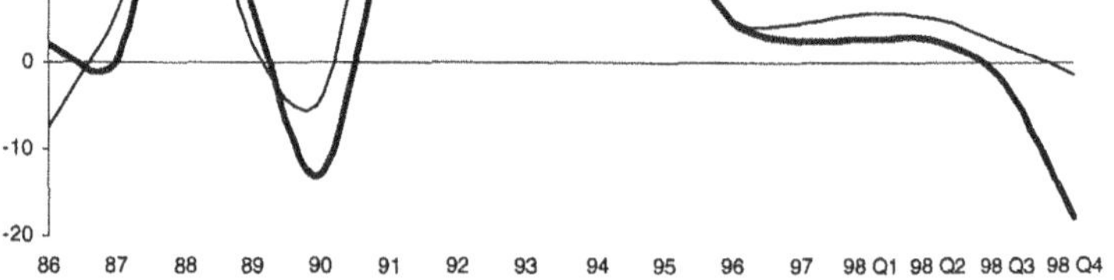

Note: Quarterly data represent change on corresponding period of previous year.
Sources: Author's calculations based on data collected from International Monetary Fund, (various years). *Direction of Trade*, International Monetary Fund and International Bank for Reconstruction and Development, Washington; China, (various years). *China Monthly Statistics*, China Statistical Information and Consultancy Service Centre, Peiching.

future, but not indefinitely without correction of the underlying weaknesses.

The Chinese authorities have learned the main lesson of the East Asian crisis—that the strengthening of the regulatory and institutional framework of the banking system is of high national importance and that in China this requires early completion of the reform of state-owned enterprises. They have learned another lesson as well—that free capital flows carry risks, and that capital convertibility should be placed on hold. The reflection of this apparent lesson in policy in itself may not impose large costs, but it will do so if capital controls reduce the urgency that is applied to financial sector reforms.

While the exchange rate and fiscal policy responses to the crisis have so far been well judged, the exchange rate may not and the fiscal expansion will not be sustainable much beyond 1999. So 1999 is a year in which the authorities have some space to undertake much of the analytic work and some of the policy action in the financial sector that is necessary to support growth into the long-term future.

Already some of the policy actions taken in support of the fixed exchange rate are damaging to growth, including the restoration of much of the earlier large role of state enterprises in grain marketing and price management, and the tolerance of price-fixing cartels to resist falls in prices in a number of sectors in which state-owned enterprises play important producer roles.

One of the objectives of contemporary work on financial reform should be to build the institutions that are necessary smoothly to replace the pegged exchange rate with a floating rate regime. In the first six months of the East Asian crisis there was upward pressure on the foreign exchange value of the renminbi, with foreign exchange reserves rising. The pressure is now strongly downward, with large speculative outflows of capital despite the capital controls. The current downward pressure may intensify, becoming a large problem for domestic economic performance. To move the peg downwards by a discrete amount in

Figure 1.11 China in the East Asian crisis, competitiveness index, 1990=100

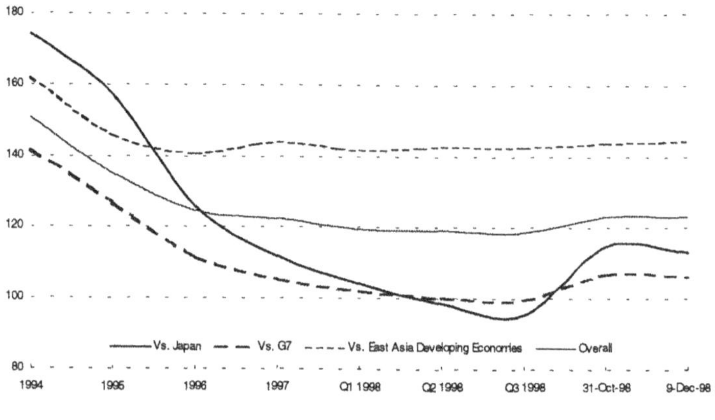

Note: The competitiveness index is a trade share weighted average real exchange rate. It is calculated based on the following formula

$$RER_t^i = \sum_j^n \alpha_{ijt} \left(\frac{e_t^i}{e_t^j} \right)_{index} \cdot \left(\frac{P_t^j}{P_t^i} \right)$$

where RER_t^i denotes country i's real exchange rate at time t, superscripts j denotes trade partner country, α_{ijt} stands for the share of country i's exports to country j in country i's total exports at time t. e_t is country i or j's nominal exchange rate against US$ at time t. P_t is country i or j's consumer price index at time t. The ratio of nominal exchange rate between country i and j is indexed (1990=100) in order to remove the effects of difference in currency units.
Source: Data for trade shares are collected from *Direction of Trade*, International Monetary Fund (IMF). Data for nominal exchange rate and consumer price index are collected from *International Financial Statistics* (IMF) and various country sources; Asia Pacific Economics Group, 1998. *Asia Pacific Profiles 1998*, FT (Asia Pacific), Singapore.

response to any such development would risk misjudgment and the intensification of uncertainty.

The best course now would be to let it be known that the authorities were working on the institutional reform that was necessary for a floating exchange rate to be successful. The authorities could then credibly state that the next move in the exchange rate against the US dollar would be a float, and not a discrete devaluation. The authorities could provide assurances that the next move would not take place in 1999, and may not take place soon after. The market would be asked to judge upon both the direction and the extent of any change in parity. A mechanism would be on hand to allow flexibility without loss of policy credibility should circumstances over the next few years require it.

Where is growth going and when will it end?

The experience of East Asia in the past half century, and of China in the two decades of reform, tells us that sustained, rapid economic growth is no 'miracle'. Rather, it is a normal part of the human condition in a poor country, which meets a number of conditions for growth.

Rapid economic growth in the postwar East Asian style is a process of catching up with the world's advanced economies, from a low base. It involves catching up technologically, by drawing on the knowledge and techniques of advanced economies through a range of mechanisms. It involves catching up in the amount of capital available for each worker to use, through high savings and investment and through the use of foreign capital. The accumulation of human capital through education and experience is important to the process. Economic growth involves the allocation of capital and labour to more and more productive uses, through the use of markets at home and open trade that allows international specialisation in line with comparative advantage as it changes over time. All of these conditions require economic policy to deliver a reasonable degree of economic stability.

When the policy conditions allow it, economic growth can proceed more rapidly in a poor country, because a wider technological gap from the world's frontiers allows more rapid technological improvement. Growth can proceed more rapidly in a densely populated poor country because the gains from trade are greater in a country whose resource endowments are very different from the advanced economies.

Rapid economic growth is a stressful process. It forces changes in the industries and locations in which people are employed and the way jobs are done. It churns and re-orders economic and political élites. It can destabilise the political order that is responsible for the policies that sustain it unless the political order itself evolves with the economic structure. At the same time, the capacity to support rising living standards that are generated by economic growth is a salve to the stress of structural change if its benefits are distributed widely. The dispersion of the distribution itself is affected by some factors that are beyond the control of governments. Importantly, a wide distribution of the benefits of internationally-oriented economic growth is facilitated in a densely populated country in which employment and labour incomes grow exceptionally as it opens to foreign trade. This helps China, as it helped other East Asian economies before it. But China's size, poor internal transport and communications, and wide variation in the natural and human resource base for development increase the challenge of maintaining an acceptably broad distribution of the benefits of growth. Acceptable dispersion of the gains from growth in China, more so than in other East Asian economies, is therefore significantly reliant on sound policy choice.

Perfect policy is not a necessary condition for rapid economic growth to proceed. Protectionist policies that reduce the gains from trade, market imperfections that keep some resources in relatively unproductive uses, periods of economic instability that inhibit the accumulation of capital, inadequate public investment in education and infrastructure—all of these hold growth back from attainable levels, but, depending on their extent, may not be inconsistent with rapid growth. As growth proceeds, and the frontiers of world technology and living standards are approached, the tolerance of growth to weaknesses in policy and institutions declines. In particular, the costs of poor policies affecting income distribution become larger over time.

Because it is so stressful, rapid economic growth does not proceed unless the view is widely held in society that it is a prime objective. Growth attained this status in 1978 in China, and has retained it since.

Rapid growth is easier to sustain than to initiate. Rising incomes are more effective in allaying doubts and allaying resistance to change when they are a current reality rather than a hope and a promise. Savings rates rise with rapid growth, supporting the growth process.

Nevertheless, the old as well as the new experience of East Asia, and the older experience of industrialisation in the West, tell us that growth and modernisation do not proceed in logarithmic straight lines. There is a strong tendency for them to proceed until the world's economic frontiers are reached, but they can be broken temporarily or permanently by adverse developments of several kinds. Booms and manias, followed by economic collapse, are ever-present risks of market economies and sometimes result in major lurches in policy that block a return to growth. Poor policy—resulting from professional weakness or political manifestations of resistance to change—can block the continual re-allocation of resources to more productive uses. A failure of the political institutions to adjust to the changing structure and aspirations of the community can undermine social and political cohesion around the objective of growth.

Any one of these risks could emerge to block China's modernisation and continued growth. It is not likely that these risks will crystallise in China into a collapse of growth as in the East Asian crisis, for reasons that I have already set out. But there will be plenty of other risks and challenges, some arising when China is less well placed to handle them than in 1997.

There is another possibility, that is more closely consistent with the experience of the past twenty years. Within this prospect, ideas about policy, policy itself, institutions, and the knowledge of Chinese people, evolve with the experience of rapid growth, in ways which sustain it. The rapid growth which has been concentrated amongst a few hundred million people in the coastal provinces, spreads inland, as regulatory and infrastuctural barriers to internal trade are removed. It is unlikely, and at odds with the experience of others, that there would be no setback to rapid growth—no recessionary end to a market mania, no large misjudgment of macroeconomic policy, no failure of leadership nerve or judgment on continued market reform. But is it possible that for a long period ahead, as in these past twenty years, the realisation of the national and personal benefits of growth, and awareness of the conditions that sustain it, will be sufficiently widespread and strong to return China to a growth path whenever it is temporarily knocked from it?

Within this prospect, which the experience of the reform period suggests is more likely than not, the average growth of the last two decades will be sustained for several decades more. Output will double each decade. In another two decades, China will be the world's second largest economy by conventional national accounts measures in output and foreign trade, or third if the European Union by then is seen as a single entity. By the end of these two decades, the dynamic coastal provinces—several hundred million people—will enjoy living standards broadly at the level of Taiwan today.

Economic growth can always end with political convulsion that removes the primacy of the growth objective. This would become a greater risk in China if policy were ineffective in allowing the spread of economic growth into the vast inland. This is an avoidable outcome, with awareness of the issue and good policy.

Economic growth in China will not end in global famine, as has been contended famously. Global markets can handle the growing demand for food that rising incomes in China would generate.

It will not end in national environmental catastrophe. Rising incomes are bringing both the will and the capacity to do something about the environmental degeneration that has been associated with urbanisation and industrialisation in China. China's sustained, rapid growth raises larger, global environmental issues, but not just for China.

In two decades, China will face a huge challenge of demographic transition, when the one child family is entering middle age and the number of young workers is shrinking sharply. This will be much on the minds of leaders if there is a 19th Party Congress in 2017, as a threat to the longer term dynamism of Chinese society and economy.

But two decades hence would be an unlikely place for the growth process that began with reform to end. The modernisation of the vast inland of China will be in its early years. It is more likely that Chinese society, aware as never before of the pain and costs of growth, will choose to push ahead. It will be a natural and in no way a miraculous outcome if the growth of China's past two decades continues until most of China's people enjoy living standards and productivity levels close to those in the world's most advanced economies.

Notes

* I am grateful to Xu Xinpeng for assisting me in putting together the statistical material for this chapter, and to Song Ligang for helpful comments on an earlier draft. This paper was delivered to the Australian China Business Council, Melbourne, 25 November 1998.

[1] When Takeshita visited the Australian National University in November 1998, I reminded him of the 1987 conversation, reported at the time in the Chinese press. He remembered it more for Deng Xiaoping's imprecision in the numbers and details of economic policy than for his classical allusion!

Economic growth over the past twenty years

Xiaolu Wang

China has experienced rapid economic growth over the past twenty years of reform. Official statistics show that the average growth rate of GDP increased from 6.1 per cent during the pre-reform period (1953–78) to 9.7 per cent for the reform period of 1979–98 (State Statistical Bureau 1998; *Economic Daily*, January 1999). Growth of per capita GDP was around 7.8 per cent (World Bank 1996a, 1997a).[1]

What contributed to the acceleration of economic growth? Was the rapid growth input-driven and short-term, or sustainable over the long run?[2]

An engine of economic growth: institutional change and rural industrialisation

Development of China's rural industrial and other non-agricultural sectors—the township and village enterprises (TVE) sector[3]—played an important role during the reform period (Garnaut and Ma 1996). Employment in this sector increased by more than 100 million workers, from 28 to 130 million (1978–97), and accounted for 19 per cent of China's total labour force and 28 per cent of the rural labour force in

27

1997. During the period 1978–97, the share of GDP contributed by TVE increased from 4 per cent to 28 per cent, contributing to one-third of economic growth. The rapid growth of the TVE sector was mainly a result of institutional change that removed restrictions on factor allocation among rural sectors. Although commune and brigade enterprises (CBEs, the predecessors of TVEs) were encouraged by central policy during the pre-reform period (1958–78), development of rural industrial enterprises was under various institutional restrictions including

* production was restricted to a few agriculture-related areas
* rural enterprises had to be collectively owned; private enterprises were prohibited
* important inputs and bank funds were controlled and only guaranteed for state-owned enterprises
* geographic migration was restricted, not only from rural to urban, but also among different rural areas
* the collectives could not transfer their labour, capital, or land to non-agricultural use without fulfilling the state quota for agricultural production (LBSC 1987).[4]

These institutional restrictions were put in place so that agricultural products could be obtained at below-market prices to support the 'heavy industry priority' development strategy (Dong 1988; Lin *et al.* 1996a), and to protect the central-planning system from the threat of free-market competition.

Table 2.1 Comparison of growth performance in the pre-reform and reform periods (per cent)

Average growth rates	1953–78	1979–97
GDP	6.1	9.8
Agriculture	2.1	5.0
Industry and construction	11.0	11.9
Services	5.5	10.6
GDP per capita	4.0	8.4
Foreign trade	9.5	15.6
Exports	10.0	16.7
Imports	9.1	14.5

Source: State Statistical Bureau, 1998. *Statistical Yearbook of China*, China Statistical Publishing House, Beijing.

Under these restrictions rural non-agricultural activities were seriously under developed in the pre-reform period. However, with the scarcity of arable land and water, labour productivity in the agricultural sector was very low.

Early agricultural reform—the introduction of the household responsibility system (HRS) in 1979–82, and abolition of the people's commune system in 1982–83—transformed the agricultural sector from collective to household-based production. Farmers had more freedom in allocating their labour to non-agricultural activities.

Another important change that occurred from 1984 onwards was an easing of discriminative policies against non-state enterprises. Most barriers to entry were removed. The ban on rural private enterprises was lifted. There was also a significant reduction in the level of central control over industrial inputs and outputs, particularly government quotas on agricultural output.

The development of TVEs accelerated significantly following institutional and policy changes. TVE employment increased by more than 12 million workers per year from 1984 to 1988. Transfer of rural labour slowed but remained at a level of four million workers per year during the period 1989–97.

Table 2.2 Contribution to GDP by sectors (billion yuan, current prices)

	1978 Value	Share[a] (%)	1997 Value	Share[a] (%)	1979–97 Growth rate (%)	1979–97 Share in growth[b] (%)
Urban sectors	235	65	3,800	51	8.4	52
State sector[c]	195	54	2,160	29	6.3	26
Urban non-state[c]	40	11	1,640	22	13.8	26
Rural sectors	127	35	3,677	49	10.4	48
Agriculture	102	28	1,397	19	5.0	10
TVE	14	4	2,074	28	21.8	35
Others	11	3	206	3	9.2	3
GDP	362	100	7,477	100	9.8	100

Notes: [a]Sector's share of total GDP (GDP in the corresponding year = 100).
[b]Average economic growth rate as 100 per cent.
[c]Author's estimations based on various sources from State Statistical Bureau.
Source: State Statistical Bureau, 1998. *Statistical Yearbook of China*, China Statistical Publishing House, Beijing.

Associated with the massive transfer of rural labour, there was also a reallocation of capital, technology and human capital from other rural and urban sectors to the TVE sector. There was a large productivity gap between the TVE and agricultural sectors. Both the average and marginal product of labour in the TVE sector were three to four times that in agriculture (Wang 1997a). Therefore, transfer of labour increased total factor productivity (TFP) in the economy, significantly accelerating economic growth. Preliminary estimations suggest that institutional changes, and labour and capital reallocation between the agricultural and TVE sectors accelerated economic growth by 1.4 percentage points between 1980 and 1992— a net contribution to economic growth of 14 per cent (Table 2.3).[5]

The remainder of TFP growth in the two sectors could have been the result of institutional changes that increased producers' efficiency at the firm or household level. In Table 2.3 the two effects are indicated separately. From the point of view of sectors, the contribution of factor

Table 2.3 **The net contribution of rural factor reallocation to economic growth** (average growth rate, 1981–92, per cent)

Contributors	Contribution to output growth [a]	Contribution to GDP growth [b]	Share of the contribution
The economy	11.7	9.7	100.0
The rural sectors	6.0	5.0	51.0
Contribution by natural growth of factors	2.9	2.4	25.0
Contribution by factor reallocation	1.7	1.4	14.0
TFP growth in the agriculture and TVE sectors	1.4	1.2	12.0

Notes: [a]Average growth rate of gross output.
[b]Approximately converted from the contribution to gross output growth.
Sources: Calculated from State Statistical Bureau, (various years). *Statistical Yearbook of China*, China Statistical Publishing House, Beijing. Wang, X., 1997a. What contributed to China's rapid rural industrial growth during the reform period?, PhD dissertation, The Australian National University, Canberra.

reallocation is the same as the contribution of factor growth. Only at the aggregated economy level does this effect exhibit increases in TFP. At this level the two effects—factor reallocation between sectors and TFP growth within sectors—together positively contributed to economic growth by 2.6 percentage points during the period 1981–92, as a net increase in TFP. They accelerated economic growth from 7.1 per cent to 9.7 per cent.

After twenty years of reform, the major institutional restrictions that hindered factor reallocation have been removed, and the economic benefits of reallocation of factors between rural sectors have been largely realised. The rate of agricultural labour transfer to the TVE sector has begun to decrease. Employment growth in the TVE sector was 11.1 per cent on average between 1981 and 1992, but decreased to 4.2 per cent during 1993–97. With consideration of the different natural growth rates of rural labour, employment growth in the TVE sector that was induced by cross-sector transfer of rural labour was 7.6 and 3.7 per centage points for the two sub-periods, respectively (SSB 1996:388, 1998:387, 420).

Taking this fact into account, the contribution of factor reallocation as a share of economic growth diminished from 14 per cent in the first sub-period to 8 per cent in the second sub-period. During the entire period of 1979–97 it comprised about 11 per cent of economic growth.

Similarly, excluded TFP growth in the agricultural and TVE sectors was also lower in the period 1993–98, due to the diminishing institutional effect (Wang 1997a). According to this trend, we can assume that its contribution to economic growth fell from 12 per cent in the first sub-period (Table 2.3) to between 7 and 8 per cent in the second sub-period (therefore, between 9 and 10 per cent over the period 1979–98). Thus, at the aggregate economy level, TFP growth—from both factor reallocation and increased firm efficiency—contributed 20 per cent to economic growth over the last two decades, lifting the growth rate by close to two percentage points.

Development of the TVE sector was uneven. In many east coast areas rural industries were well developed, but development in the central and west regions was lower and progressed more slowly. It is not likely to accelerate in the immediate future due to limitations in the supply of human capital and infrastructure. In general, the effect of institutional reform on rural industrialisation—and therefore on economic growth—is diminishing.

The TVE sector had absorbed 130 million of a total 450 million workers from the agricultural sector by 1998. Another 60–70 million migrated to cities, mainly in the 1990s, either permanently or temporarily (Wang forthcoming). However, there is still a large agricultural workforce—250–260 million—sharing only 95 million hectares of farming land and with low labour productivity. Further reallocation of this labour is a potential source of economic growth in the future.

China's urbanisation is well below the world average. Its urban population only accounts for 30 per cent of the total population, lower than the average of other countries of the same income level by 10–15 per cent (SSB 1998). Due to lack of urban infrastructure and the heavy budgetary burden of urban residents' welfare provisions, the government encouraged rural industrialisation rather than urbanisation in the earlier stages of economic reform. Restrictions on rural-urban migration began to be eased only gradually since the late 1980s. Further reduction of institutional barriers to labour mobility, policy promotion of urban infrastructure construction and urbanisation will be the stimulus for continued economic growth in the twenty-first century.

Domestic savings and investment

High domestic saving and investment rates have been an important source of economic growth in China. During the pre-reform period, total savings increased from 21 per cent to 38 per cent of GDP. They further increased during the reform period, to 41 per cent in 1997 (SSB 1998). Under the central planning system, the major source of investment was government revenue. The low efficiency of government investment restricted its contribution to economic growth. However, there have been three major changes in the investment pattern since reform. First, enterprises and individuals received a greater share of income. Government budgetary expenditure as a share of GDP declined from 31 per cent in 1978 to 22 per cent in 1985, and 12 per cent in 1997 (SSB 1998).[6] Government investment decreased, but state and non-state enterprise investment, either funded by banks or self-funded, increased dramatically. Second, the structure of budgetary expenditure changed, with provincial and local governments constituting a greater share. The share of central government in total budgetary expenditure declined from 47 per cent in 1978 to 40 per cent in 1985, and 27 per cent in 1997 (SSB 1998). Provincial and local governments are more market-oriented in their investment behaviour. Third, rapid increases in disposable incomes brought about a rise in household savings. There was a rise in savings rates of urban and rural residents in the reform period (Table 2.5). Banks replaced the government budget as the major suppliers of investment funds, and household savings became the major source of bank credit. Household savings accounted for only 25 per cent of total bank deposits in 1985, but this figure increased to 56 per cent in 1997 (Table 2.4).

High savings sustained high investment. Domestic investment in fixed assets (the major part of total domestic investment) is highly correlated with domestic savings (Figure 2.1). As a result of increases in the savings rate and market-oriented changes in the investment mechanism, the growth rate of total investment in fixed assets significantly increased in the reform period. It was 5.3 per cent on average in 1954–78 with large fluctuations, but accelerated to an average of 11.4 per cent in 1979–97 (both deflated to constant prices by the author).

A comparison of GDP growth rate with the growth rate of domestic investment in fixed assets in 1954–97 shows a close relationship between the two, suggesting that high levels of investment bring about high economic growth (Figure 2.2).

Table 2.4 Change in sources of bank funds

Year	Total bank deposit (100 million yuan)	Treasury and govt agency deposit (%)	Enterprise deposit (%)	Household deposit (%)
1985	4,273	16.2	48.5	24.8
1990	11,645	8.5	44.6	34.3
1992	18,891	4.9	36.1	45.9
1993	23,230	5.2	33.0	48.2
1994	40,502	4.2	32.8	53.1
1995	53,882	3.6	32.2	55.0
1996	68,596	3.3	32.7	56.2
1997	82,390	-	34.8	56.2

Note: The different sources of deposit are as a percentage of total bank deposits. Data for 1993 and earlier years are that of the state banks.
Source: Calculated from State Statistical Bureau, various years. *Statistical Yearbook of China*, China Statistical Publishing House, Beijing.

In future years, the savings rate is likely to decrease due to changing consumption patterns of the younger generation and the increasing ratio of aged dependency (the proportion of aged people in the total population). However, a high investment rate is likely to be sustained in the coming decades, since there are no signs of domestic savings declining in the short run. High savings have led to a contraction in consumer demand in the late 1990s. This is explained by economists as a result of increasing uncertainty in people's future employment status, income and pensions, and increasing expenditures on housing, medical services and children's education. For urban residents, uncertainty has resulted from incompleteness of the reform of the employment, pension, housing, medical and education systems. The new systems may need a number of years to be completed, and may still provide less certainty than the old ones. For rural residents, uncertainty arises from large fluctuations in grain prices and the increasing burden of various unregulated fees and charges collected by local governments. Further reforms of the grain trade and government finance systems are needed, and the effectiveness of anti-corruption campaigns needs to be raised in the intermediate and long run.

Table 2.5 Savings rates of rural and urban residents

	Urban residents			Rural residents		
	Income (yuan)	Savings (yuan)	Saving rate	Income (yuan)	Savings (yuan)	Saving rate
1978	..	..	..	134	116	13.4
1980	..	..	..	191	162	15.2
1981	500	457	8.6	223	..	..
1985	739	673	8.9	398	317	20.4
1990	1,510	1,279	15.3	686	585	14.7
1994	3,496	2,851	18.4	1,221	1,017	16.7
1995	4,283	3,538	17.4	1,578	1,310	17.0
1996	4,839	3,919	19.0	1,926	1,572	18.4
1997	5,160	4,186	18.9	2,090	1,617	22.6

Notes: Income for rural residents is average net income per capita (for 1985 and earlier it is total income per capita); for urban residents it is average disposable income per capita. All are in current prices. The consumer price index in 1997 was about 350 per cent of 1978.
Source: Household surveys, in State Statistical Bureau, 1998. *Statistical Yearbook of China*, China Statistical Publishing House, Beijing.

Figure 2.1   Domestic savings and investment in fixed assets as percentages of GDP

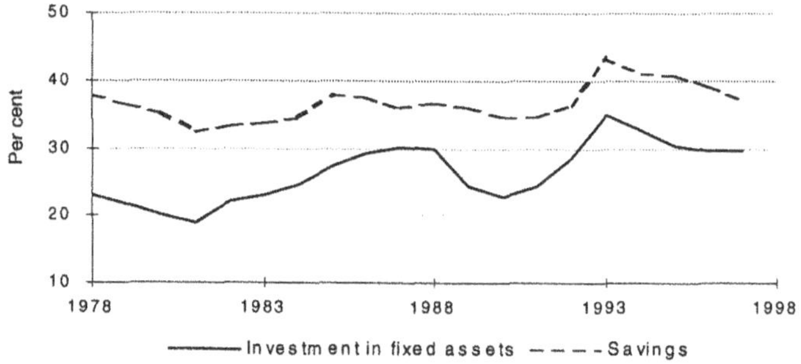

Note: Domestic investment in fixed assets = total investment in fixed assets – foreign investment in fixed assets. Saving rates are based on GDP calculated using the expenditure method.
Source: Calculated from State Statistical Bureau, various years. *Statistical Yearbook of China*, China Statistical Publishing House, Beijing.

Figure 2.2   Growth rates of GDP and domestic investment, 1954–97 (per cent)

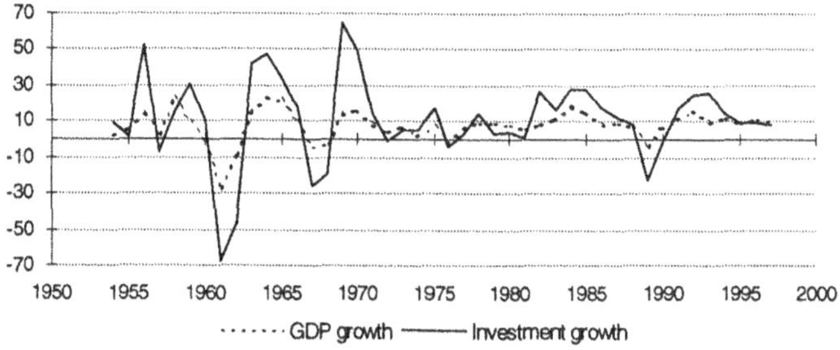

Note: Growth rates are calculated using 1980 constant prices as a base. The deflator used is a weighted combination of the producer price indexes of industrial products and the retail price indexes (weights = 0.5 and 0.5).
Source: Calculated from State Statistical Bureau, various years. *Statistical Yearbook of China*, China Statistical Publishing House, Beijing.

Total factor productivity growth

Numerous studies showed positive TFP growth in the industrial and agricultural sectors during the period of economic reform (World Bank 1985, 1997b; Chen *et al.* 1988a; Jefferson *et al.* 1992). Comparative studies of TFP changes between the pre-reform and reform periods have been done, and economic growth rates and TFP changes decomposed. Capital stock for the period of 1953–97 is derived based on: gross investment in fixed assets, decomposed by state and non-state sectors; capital formation ratios,[7] and price indices of investment in fixed assets.

Results of the calculation of total capital stock, domestic capital stock, and the total employment and GDP data for the period 1953–97 are provided in Appendix Table 2.2. Growth rates of factors and GDP are shown in Appendix Table 2.1.

Estimation results using a Cobb-Douglas production function and Cochrane-Orcutt for auto-correction, suggest that the capital and labour elasticities of GDP 0.52 and 0.48, respectively (Appendix Table 2.3). The estimation results also indicate positive and significant effects from foreign direct investment, in addition to total capital, and a negative effect of inflation on economic growth. The regression suggests higher TFP growth in the reform than pre-reform period, but this could not be confirmed due to the statistic insignificance. The model specification and the results are provided in Appendix Table 2.3.

Due to a shortage of information about human capital accumulation, technical inputs, and effective measures for overall institutional changes, their effects on economic growth could not be directly estimated from the model.[8] However, using estimated values of α and β, the effect of capital and labour on economic growth (input-driven growth) can be calculated. TFP growth can then be derived as the residual when the input-driven growth rate is subtracted from the actual economic growth rate, yielding

$$g_t = \hat{Y}_t - \hat{Y}_t^F(K_t, L_t) = \hat{Y}_t^F - \alpha\hat{K}_t - (1-\alpha)\hat{L}_t$$

where Y_t, K_t, L_t, and Y_t^F are growth rates of GDP, capital stock, employment, and fitted input-driven growth rate at year t, respectively; g_t is the TFP growth rate at year t. They are instantaneous growth rates, and are converted into annual growth rates later. α is the elasticity of capital.

The TFP growth rate, g_t, is broadly defined since it includes all the effects of human capital accumulation, technological progress—including new technology introduced through foreign direct investment (FDI)—and efficiency changes brought about by institutional and policy changes. Part of the effects of human capital growth and technical changes, excluding their spillover effect, could be defined as input-driven growth, as they result from investment in human capital and research and development.

The last column of Appendix Table 2.1 shows the calculated TFP changes for each year in the period 1954–97. The average growth rates of inputs, GDP and TFP for the pre-reform and reform periods are provided in Table 2.6. The table indicates a clear acceleration of TFP growth during the reform period, increasing from 1.8 to 2.5 percentage points.[9] The growth rate of net capital stock increased dramatically, from an average of 4.2 per cent during the pre-reform period to 10.7 per cent after (Table 2.6). Labour growth increased by half a per cent due to high fertility rates in the pre-reform period. These two factors drove up the average economic growth rate by 3.5 percentage points. Actual GDP growth increased by 4.2 percentage points, to 9.5 per cent,[10] with an 0.7 percentage point increase in TFP.

In this study the calculated growth rate of capital for the pre-reform period is significantly lower than some other calculations. It appears that this is the result of using the actual capital formation ratios for the calculation. The capital formation ratio was only 67 per cent on average in 1958–77, but increased to an average of 76 per cent in 1978–97. This indicates lower efficiency in capital investment in the pre-reform period. Thus, higher capital accumulation during the reform period not only resulted from an increase in savings, but also from more efficient use of investment funds. Institutional changes were also a contributing factor. The higher savings rate was partly due to institutional effects—changing incentive mechanisms for individuals' and firms' saving and investment behaviour.

Total factor productivity growth accounted for 27 per cent of the average growth rate in 1979–97 (Table 2.6). According to the estimations in Table 2.3, factor reallocation between the agricultural and TVE sectors contributed to 12 per cent of economic growth. Together with the excluded TFP growth in the two rural sectors, about 20 per cent of the TFP contribution—the major part—was from the rural sector.

The remaining 6 per cent share of TFP in economic growth is likely attributable to the urban non-state sector, since the state sector was found to have either slight positive TFP growth, or none at all. In comparison to the TVE sector, the urban non-state sector is smaller, with a lower growth rate, but it experienced dramatic growth after 1992, particularly as a result of FDI. In contrast, the situation in the state sector worsened (Jefferson *et al.* 1992; Woo *et al.* 1994a).

The difference between actual GDP growth and fitted input-driven growth is the growth in TFP indicating large fluctuations in economic growth and an unstable TFP growth rate, particularly during the pre-reform period (Figure 2.3 and Appendix Table 2.1). The major growth fluctuations are explained by policy changes and political instability (see Table 2.7). For example, fluctuations in TFP growth were significant and positive in 1978–80, 1983–85 and 1992–94, when reform was accelerated, particularly in the rural sectors, but became negative in 1989–90, when the reform process was suspended. This indicates that TFP growth was mainly an effect of economic reform (institutional change induced rural industrialisation). Technological progress and human capital accumulation would have yielded a more stable trend in TFP growth, if they had been the major contributors to the higher economic growth rate.

The lower employment and output growth rate of the TVE sector in the 1990s show that the effect of institutional change on rural industrialisation is diminishing. Rural industrialisation will still be an important contributor to economic growth in the short to medium term,

Table 2.6 Input-driven growth and TFP changes in the pre-reform and reform periods (per cent)

Year	Capital growth	Labour growth	Actual GDP growth	Input-driven growth	TFP growth
1954–78	4.22	2.55	5.29	3.42	1.80 (1.78)
1979–97	10.69	2.93	9.51	6.90	2.46 (2.43)
Acceleration	6.47	0.38	4.22	3.48	0.66 (0.65)

Note: Average TFP growth rates in parentheses are instantaneous growth rates; others are annual growth rates.

however technological progress and human capital accumulation will become increasingly important means of sustaining high economic growth in the long run.

Contribution of economic openness to growth performance

China's economic growth performance also benefited from the economic openness of the market approach. During the reform period, the old self-sufficiency policy and the 'heavy industry priority' development strategy were replaced by an 'open-door policy'—predominantly export-orientation based on China's comparative advantage of cheap labour, and the introduction of foreign investment and technology from abroad. Exports, the majority of which were labour-intensive goods, increased from US$18 billion to 183 billion in 1980–97 (SSB 1998:621). Imports and exports accounted for only 9.8 per cent of GDP in 1978, whereas in 1997, this figure was 36 per cent. The current account has been in surplus since 1990 (except 1993). Net exports accounted for 1.6 per cent of GDP on average in 1990–97 (see Table 2.8). In cases of

Figure 2.3   Actual GDP growth and input-driven growth, 1953–1997 (per cent)

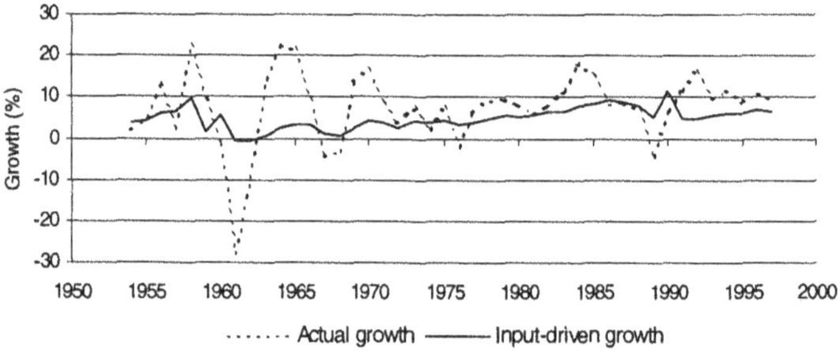

Actual growth ——— Input-driven growth

Source: Data from Appendix Table 2.1.

Table 2.7 The impact of policy changes and political instability on economic growth

Year	Policy	Direction of short run impact on growth
1956	Introduction of 156 large investment projects from the former Soviet Union	+
1957	'Anti rightwing' campaign	-
1958–59	'Great Leap Forward'	+
1960–62	Disastrous failure of 'Great Leap Forward'	-
1963–65	Recovery from the disaster	+
1967–68	Beginning of 'Cultural Revolution'	-
1969–70	Recovery from the early stages of 'Cultural Revolution'	+
1976	'Refuting Deng' campaign	-
1981	Contractionary macro policy	-
1983–85	Liberalisation of the rural non-state sectors	+
1989–90	Policy changes towards re-centralisation	-
1992–93	Restoring market-oriented reform	+

Sources: Ma, H., Liu, Z. and Lu, B. (eds), 1998. *Report of China's Macroeconomic Policy*, China Finance and Economics Press, Beijing; Zhou, T.H., Wu, Z., Fu, F.X. and Gao, S.Q. (eds), 1984. *Economic System Reform in Contemporary China*, China Social Sciences Press, Beijing.

Table 2.8 Net exports as percentage of GDP (billion yuan)

Year	Exports	Imports	Net exports	GDP	Net exports/GDP (%)
1990	299	257	41	1,855	2.2
1991	383	340	43	2,162	2.0
1992	468	444	23	2,664	0.9
1993	529	599	-70	3,464	-2.0
1994	1,042	996	46	4,676	1.0
1995	1,245	1,105	140	5,848	2.4
1996	1,257	1,156	102	6,859	1.5
1997	1,516	1,182	335	7,477	4.5
Average					1.6

Note: In current prices.
Source: State Statistical Bureau, 1997, 1998. *Statistical Yearbook of China*, China Statistical Publishing House, Beijing.

insufficient domestic demand, net exports contributed as much as 1.6 percentage points to the economic growth rate. This figure could have been even higher in 1997 and 1998, as net exports accounted for a significantly higher percentage of GDP.

FDI was another important contributor to economic growth in the 1990s. It increased rapidly, from US$1.3 billion in 1984 to 4.4 billion in 1991, and then 45 billion in 1997. In Table 2.9, the calculated capital stock is provided and decomposed into local capital and foreign capital (from FDI); their contribution to capital growth and economic growth have been calculated. Foreign capital accounted for 5.5 per cent of total capital stock in 1991, and increased to 11.1 per cent in 1997.

Using the estimated elasticity of capital ($\alpha = 0.5$), the direct contribution of foreign capital to the economic growth rate is derived as 0.2 and 0.5 percentage points in the two sub periods 1979–92 and 1993–97, respectively. For the entire period, it accelerated economic growth by an average of 0.3 percentage points (see Table 2.9).

The production function estimation also suggests that an additional 1.3 percentage points is contributed to the economic growth rate by every 10 per cent share of foreign capital in total capital stock (see coefficient γ in Appendix Table 2.3). This partly arises from better technology brought by FDI, and partly from the spillover effects on technology, management skills, and the pressure of market competition on local firms to increase efficiency (this may be called a spillover effect of institutional reform). For simplicity, these effects are together called the spillover effect. The estimated spillover effect may be further confirmed, however, it is significant at the one per cent level. According to this estimation, its contribution to the economic growth rate was minor in the 1980s and early 1990s: only 0.3 percentage points in 1979–92 on average, but increased rapidly to 0.9 on average in 1993–97, higher than its direct contribution (see Table 2.9). As the sum of its direct contribution and the spillover effect, total contribution of foreign capital to the economic growth rate in the two sub-periods was 0.5 and 1.4 percentage points, respectively. Its total contribution could reach 2.2 percentage points in 1997, a share of 24 per cent of economic growth.

Due to the East Asian financial crisis and the lower economic growth rate in China, capital inflow will be slower in the near future. In 1998, FDI in China remained at 1997 levels. If this trend continues over the next three to four years, the contribution of foreign capital to the economic growth rate will fall by 0.2–0.3 percentage points each year, and will diminish from three to two percentage points.

Conclusion

China's economic growth significantly accelerated during the last two decades of economic reform, reaching an average of 9.5 per cent. Growth was predominantly due to a higher rate of capital formation. Growth of capital and labour contributed 6.9 percentage points, or 73 per cent of total economic growth, during the period 1979–97. The higher growth of capital was due to higher savings and investment, the results of decentralisation in income distribution and market-oriented changes to create greater incentives to invest. The capital formation ratio increased from an average of 67 per cent in the pre-reform period to 76 per cent. This means more efficient use of investment funds, particularly in the non-state sector. FDI played an important role, but only after 1992.

Table 2.9 Contribution of foreign capital to economic growth

	Total capital	Contribution to capital stock and growth		Economic growth	Contribution to economic growth by foreign capital	
		Local capital[1]	Foreign capital[1]		Direct effect	Spillover contribution
Stock (billion yuan, 1980 prices)						
1978	534	100	-	..	..	..
1992	2,141	95.1	4.9	..	..	..
1997	3,679	90.7	9.3	..	´..	..
Growth (%)						
1954–78	4.2	4.2	-	5.3	-	-
1979–97	10.7	10.1	0.6	9.5	0.3	0.6
1979–92	10.4	10.0	0.4	9.2	0.2	0.3
1993–97	11.4	10.4	1.0	10.3	0.5	0.9

Notes: [1]Local capital and foreign capital (formed from FDI) are calculated as percentages of total capital stock and the percentage points contribution to the growth rate of total capital. Direct contribution of foreign capital to economic growth is calculated on the assumption that foreign capital is indifferent from local capital. Any possible contribution from higher technology and the spillover of technology and management skill are included under 'spillover effect'.
Source: Calculated from Appendix Table 2.1 and State Statistical Bureau, various years. *Statistical Yearbook of China*, China Statistical Publishing House, Beijing.

Changes in TFP were the other important source of economic growth, constituting the remaining 2.6 percentage points, or 27 per cent of total economic growth. Compared with the pre-reform period, TFP growth increased from an average of 1.8 per cent to 2.5 per cent.

A major reason for TFP growth was institutional change, mainly those that encouraged rural industrialisation. This effect contributed 14 per cent to economic growth over the period 1979–92, but fell to 8 per cent during 1993–97. Together with the excluded TFP changes in the rural sectors, rural development contributed to about 20 per cent of economic growth and was the major part of TFP contribution.

Technological progress and efficiency increases at the firm level played a minor role in TFP changes from 1979 to 1992, but have become more important in recent years. Nine per cent of changes in TFP came from FDI due to better technology and spillover effects. The remaining 11 per cent was likely due to short-run effects, part of which may be the result of overstatement of economic growth rate.

The role of FDI is becoming increasingly important. FDI accounted for 15 per cent of total investment in fixed assets in 1996 and 1997

Table 2.10   Decomposition of economic growth by contributors (per cent)

	Share of total contribution			Contribution to growth rate
	1979–92	1993–97	1979–97	1979–97
GDP growth rate	9.2	10.3	9.5	9.5
Share of contribution				
Input-driven	77	63	73	6.9
Labour	19	6	15	1.4
Capital	58	57	58	5.5
Foreign capital	2	5	3	0.3
TFP	23	37	27	2.5
Rural factor reallocation	14	8	11	1.0
Technology and efficiency	9	29	16	1.5
Foreign capital	3	9	6	0.7
Total contribution	100	100	100	9.5

Sources: Tables 2.3, 2.6 and 2.9, and Appendix Tables 2.1 and 2.2.

(calculated using current exchange rate). As a source of both input-driven and TFP induced growth, foreign capital contributed to 14 per cent of economic growth in 1993–97, but 24 per cent in 1997. Recently FDI has replaced the TVE sector as the main engine of economic growth.

Foreign trade, particularly exports, was another important contributor to economic growth, especially in the 1990s. It has been important for maintaining economic growth in the short term since aggregate demand in the domestic market has been insufficient in recent years. In the long run a relatively large foreign trade sector will enable the economy to maintain its competitiveness in the world market, and allow transfer of new technologies to the domestic sector (Feder 1983). The East Asian financial crisis caused FDI and export growth to stagnate.

The three most important engines of growth—domestic investment and capital formation, rural industrialisation and FDI—will continue to play important roles in the future, although the latter two may not maintain the strong performance of recent years. A relatively high economic growth rate can be sustained in the coming decades, although without new sources of growth, this rate will be lower than in the past 20 years.

In the future, three factors may become more important in China's economic growth. The first is the acceleration of urbanisation, which will continue to bring China's abundant rural labour into non-agricultural sectors, with increasing efficiency in factor allocation. Economic efficiency will also be improved through economies of scale and urban externalities. The second factor is further industrial reform and structural adjustment, which will increase firms' efficiency and create incentives for technical innovation and adoption. Finally, but perhaps most important in the long run, is research and development (R&D) and education. Realisation of some or all of these potential growth factors will see China's high economic growth continue for another two decades.

Appendix Table 2.1 Input-output growth and TFP growth, 1954–97 (per cent)

Year	Capital	Labour growth	GDP growth	Input driven	TFP growth
1953	5.61	3.06	..	4.33	..
1954	5.92	2.19	1.90	4.04	-2.05
1955	6.09	2.27	4.89	4.16	0.70
1956	8.97	3.09	12.97	5.99	6.58
1957	9.71	3.27	2.36	6.44	-3.84
1958	7.37	11.90	22.13	9.61	11.43
1959	8.92	-5.36	9.12	1.53	7.47
1960	8.95	2.81	-1.79	5.84	-7.21
1961	-0.53	-1.12	-27.94	-0.82	-27.34
1962	-2.43	1.25	-9.24	-0.61	-8.69
1963	-1.12	2.82	14.04	0.83	13.10
1964	0.85	4.11	22.42	2.47	19.47
1965	3.81	3.37	21.30	3.59	107.10
1966	2.52	3.96	9.18	3.24	5.75
1967	-1.09	3.39	-4.37	1.12	-5.43
1968	-2.10	3.57	-2.96	0.69	-3.63
1969	0.59	4.10	13.72	2.33	11.12
1970	5.29	3.63	16.48	4.46	11.51
1971	4.30	3.45	8.47	3.87	4.43
1972	4.05	0.66	3.99	2.34	1.61
1973	6.31	2.23	7.41	4.25	3.03
1974	5.33	1.96	2.03	3.63	-1.55
1975	6.61	2.14	7.22	4.35	2.75
1976	4.62	1.74	-2.08	3.17	-5.09
1977	6.44	1.40	6.64	3.89	2.65
1978	7.78	1.97	9.13	4.83	4.10
1979	8.76	2.17	9.52	5.41	3.89
1980	6.94	3.26	8.43	5.08	3.19
1981	7.73	3.22	6.25	5.45	0.76
1982	9.26	3.59	7.96	6.39	1.48
1983	10.53	2.52	11.29	6.45	4.54
1984	12.17	3.79	18.33	7.90	9.67
1985	13.31	3.48	14.95	8.28	6.16
1986	16.50	2.83	8.45	9.45	-0.91
1987	14.60	2.93	8.99	8.61	0.35
1988	12.96	2.94	6.82	7.83	-0.94
1989	8.71	1.83	-4.15	5.21	-8.90
1990	8.07	15.51[b]	6.45	11.72	-4.72
1991	8.10	1.39	11.56	4.69	6.56
1992	8.77	1.17	16.16	4.90	10.74
1993	9.85	1.25	9.75	5.46	4.06
1994	11.02	1.24	11.97	6.02	5.61
1995	11.38	1.11	8.89	6.12	2.61
1996	12.98	1.33	11.11	6.99	3.85
1997	11.99	1.09	9.87	6.40	3.26
Average rate 1954–97	6.97	2.72	7.10	4.82	2.17(2.15)[a]

Notes: [a] Instantaneous growth rate; [b] High employment here is the result of data adjustment by the State Statistical Bureau according to 1990 national census.
Source: Calculated from Appendix Table 2.2 and the estimated values of α and β.

Appendix Table 2.2 Capital, employment and GDP, 1952–97

Year	Investment in fixed assets Billion yuan 1980 prices	Capital formation ratio Investment = 1	Total capital stock Billion yuan 1980 prices	Domestic capital stock Billion yuan 1980 prices	Total employment Million persons	GDP Billion yuan 1980 prices
1952	::	0.820	180	180	207	::
1953	23.3	0.813	190	190	214	105
1954	25.5	0.862	201	201	218	107
1955	25.9	0.754	214	214	223	112
1956	39.6	0.934	233	233	230	127
1957	36.7	0.748	255	255	238	130
1958	42.2	0.692	274	274	266	158
1959	55.2	0.688	299	299	252	173
1960	60.6	0.745	325	325	259	169
1961	19.5	0.790	324	324	256	122
1962	10.5	0.819	316	316	259	111
1963	15.0	0.828	312	312	266	126
1964	22.1	0.936	315	315	277	155
1965	29.7	0.704	327	327	287	188
1966	34.9	0.506	335	335	298	205
1967	25.9	0.459	332	332	308	196
1968	20.9	0.527	325	325	319	190
1969	34.4	0.653	327	327	332	216
1970	51.5	0.544	344	344	344	252
1971	58.1	0.557	359	359	356	273
1972	58.2	0.687	373	373	359	284
1973	61.4	0.634	397	397	367	305
1974	64.6	0.639	418	418	374	311
1975	75.9	0.589	445	445	382	334
1976	72.7	0.714	466	466	388	327
1977	74.6	0.743	496	496	394	349
1978	85.3	0.837	534	534	402	380
1979	87.9	0.762	581	581	410	417
1980	91.1	0.825	622	622	424	452
1981	95.9		670	667	437	480

continued....

1982	123.0	0.776	732	724	453	518
1983	143.2	0.794	809	795	464	577
1984	180.9	0.767	907	888	482	682
1985	231.0	0.719	1,028	1,003	499	784
1986	273.0	0.809	1,197	1,164	513	851
1987	307.5	0.763	1,372	1,328	528	927
1988	335.2	0.735	1,550	1,491	543	990
1989	262.2	0.810	1,685	1,614	553	949
1990	258.0	0.853	1,821	1,740	639	1,010
1991	300.9	0.793	1,968	1,877	648	1,127
1992	376.9	0.719	2,141	2,036	656	1,309
1993	481.6	0.660	2,352	2,222	664	1,437
1994	568.7	0.662	2,611	2,437	672	1,609
1995	630.8	0.678	2,908	2,682	679	1,752
1996	694.3	0.753	3,285	3,000	689	1,947
1997	743.1	0.751	3,679	3,340	696	2,139
Growth (%)						
1953–78	::	::	280	280	190	360
1978–97	::	::	690	620	170	560
1953–97	::	::	1940	1760	330	2040

Notes: 1. Capital stock is calculated from total investment in fixed assets. Total investment data for 1953–79 are estimated from state sector investment in fixed assets and the shares of the state sector in the economy. In 1953–56, before the nationalisation of private sectors, state sector investment was assumed to be 50 per cent of total investment, whereas in 1957–79 it was assumed to be 80 per cent. The scale of investment was far smaller in this period than in later periods (1980–97), therefore errors caused by the assumptions would not seriously affect the calculated results of capital stock in the reform period. 2. Total investment data are deflated using 1980 prices and converted into capital formation by using the capital formation ratios of each year, with a deduction for capital depreciation (using a rate of 5 per cent) from the previous year. The deflator is price indices of investment in fixed assets (supplemented by the producer price indices of industrial products and retail price indices when data unavailable). 3. Capital stock is accumulated through capital formation, with initial capital stock in 1952 estimated at 180 billion yuan (1980 prices) based on the size of the economy at that time. This estimation was found to be acceptable since other estimations yielded growth rates of capital stock beyond reasonable bounds, particularly for the years immediately following 1952.

Source: Author's calculations; State Statistical Bureau, various years. *Statistical Yearbook of China*, China Statistical Publishing House, Beijing.

Appendix Table 2.3 **Estimation result** (Cochrane-Orcutt regression)

Variable	Coefficient	Value	Std Err	T	P>ItI
kl	a	0.5204	0.2683	1.940	0.060
F	g	13.028	4.8710	2.675	0.011
p	d	-0.9608	0.2314	-4.153	0.000
T_1	g_1	0.0257	0.0077	3.328	0.002
T_2	g_2	0.0031	0.0275	0.111	0.912

Number of obs = 42
F (5, 36) = 58.75
Prob > F = 0.0000
Dependent variable: yl   Adj R² = 0.8757

Notes: yl = lnY-lnL, kl = lnK-lnL, and p=lnP.
Estimation of production function
The effects of different factors on economic growth are estimated by the
following assumed production function

$$Y = A_0 e^{g_1 T_1 + g_2 T_2} K^{\alpha} L^{1-\alpha} e^{\gamma F} P^{\delta}$$

To take the logarithm form and impose the restriction of constant returns to
scale, the model becomes

$$\ln Y - \ln L = \ln A_0 + g_1 T_1 + g_2 T_2 + \alpha(\ln K - \ln L) + \gamma F + \delta \ln P$$

where Y, K, L, P are GDP, capital stock, employment, and inflation rate (initial
year =1) respectively; F is the ratio of foreign capital to total capital; T_1 and T_2
are two time trends for the entire (pre-reform and reform) period and the
reform period respectively (T_1 = 0, 1, 2, 3..., and T_2=0, 0, 0,...1(s), 2,...;
where s is the first year of economic reform, 1978). A_0 is initial TFP; g_1 and
g_1+g_2 are TFP growth rates for the pre-reform and reform periods,
respectively. α is the capital elasticity of GDP. Data are for the period 1953–97.
To rectify the auto-correction, the model is estimated using the Cochrane-
Orcutt iterative process.
Sources: Estimation result; data calculated from Appendix Table 2.2 and
State Statistical Bureau, 1998. *Statistical Yearbook of China*, China Statistical
Publishing House, Beijing.

Notes

[1] Some economists suggest an overstatement of the economic growth rate by one to two percentage points in the reform period (World Bank 1997d). This is possible, however the reasons may be more complex than which deflator was chosen. The author used the method suggested by the World Bank (1997d) and obtained an only slightly lower growth rate than the official statistics. Further investigation is needed. Even if the growth statistics for the reform period were overstated, economic performance was far better than during the pre-reform period, in which growth figures were at least equally overstated.

[2] See Solow (1956), Lucas (1988) and Romer (1986) for growth theories, and World Bank (1993b), Krugman (1994) and Martellaro (1996) for the current debates on East Asia and China's economic growth.

[3] The TVE sector includes nearly the entire rural non-agricultural sector with a major part being industry (60 per cent of TVE employment in 1997). It also includes a negligible agricultural contribution (1.5 per cent of TVE employment in 1997).

[4] This was also true at the early stages of the reform period. Using 1980–82 data from a case study, Chang (1993) found a negative and significant relationship between the share of TVE employment in rural labour and per capita state quota for grain production. In the study, this relationship became insignificant in 1983–85.

[5] Gross contribution of a sector to economic growth is simply the sector's share in economic growth, but a net contribution means it accelerates economic growth. If two sectors have the same marginal product of a factor, reallocating this factor from one sector to another would increase the gross contribution of one sector to growth but decrease it in another and the net contribution could be zero.

[6] There were increases in the non-budgetary revenues and expenditures of local governments, which more or less moderated the declining trend of government share of GDP.

[7] The capital formation ratio for year t is the ratio between the value of newly formed fixed assets and total investment in fixed assets at year t. Before 1980 it was calculated for the state sector as a weighted average for the state and non-state (collective) sectors for 1980–94, and for the overall economy afterwards. The capital formation ratio was higher in the reform than the pre-reform period. It has also increased more in the non-state sector than the state sector sine the late 1980s (see Appendix 2.2).

[8] The World Bank (1997d) suggests a positive contribution of workers' schooling to economic growth. However, the historical data for schooling are limited. Using the same method as the World Bank, the author obtained an insignificant result for schooling.

[9] The World Bank (1997d) estimated higher TFP growth for a similar period. This is likely to be the result of different estimations of capital stock and its growth rates.

[10] GDP growth rate is derived from current price data and deflated into constant price data using a weighted deflator (see note in Figure 2.2). It is slightly lower than the growth rate provided by the State Statistical Bureau.

Agricultural reform

Yongzheng Yang [*]

China's reform began in agriculture. To be precise, it began in farming, where reform has universally been acclaimed a success. In the first seven years of reform (1978–84), grain output increased by 5 per cent per annum, 1.5 percentage points higher than for the pre-reform period, 1949–78. Even more rapid than the growth of grain output was the growth in the output of other agricultural commodities. During the pre-reform period the growth of grain output had been at the expense of these commodities. Over the longer period of reform from 1978 to 1996, gross agricultural output grew at 5.5 per cent per annum in real terms.

The most remarkable aspect of China's agricultural reform was its 'spillover' effect. Non-agricultural activities in rural China sprung up immediately after the reforms began. According to official statistics, the gross output value of township and village enterprises (TVEs) grew at 24 per cent per annum from 1978 to 1995 and employment grew at 9 per cent per annum (SSB 1996).[1] Chinese farmers benefited enormously from the rapid growth of TVEs. In the earlier years of reform, the main source of farm income growth was the combination of increased grain output and the price increases instituted by the government. Per capita net farm income grew by 20 per cent per annum from 1978 to 1984. This was clearly unsustainable. In the years following 1984, per capita income grew by 4 per cent per annum. TVEs have contributed to much of this growth. Rural poverty has been reduced dramatically. According to the UNDP (1996), the number of people in poverty fell from 250 million in 1978 to 80 million in 1995.

The impact of agricultural reforms

These achievements are unprecedented in Chinese history. What has made agricultural reform so successful? And why has the success of urban reform not matched it, judging by the financial difficulties currently being experienced by state-owned enterprises (SOEs)?

To understand the success of agricultural reform requires an examination of the pre-reform era and the reasons for the failure of the commune system. The commune system was premised on two propositions. First, if farmers collectively own and manage their land, and if income is distributed according to labour contribution, they must have greater incentives to work than existed under the old landlord-tenant system. The communist mentality was that public ownership would unleash the enormous 'enthusiasm and creativity' of the people. Second, the communes would be able to achieve economies of scale in farming.

The first condition in the first proposition was fulfilled, but the second failed miserably. Income was never distributed according to labour contribution; it would never have been possible under the commune system. The enthusiasm and creativity of the people thus never emerged. In a commune of a few thousand people, there was the inevitable problem that one could never accurately assess how much a member of the commune had contributed to the collective effort. A rigorous supervision system may have helped, but farmers often worked individually on different tasks at different times. No efficient supervision system was thus possible. Economic incentives were not allowed; only rewards of political nature (such as 'model farmers') were possible and they were few. In a commune, it was even difficult to identify the principals from the agents. Commune cadres might be regarded as the principals and the farmers as the agents. These cadres had few incentives to maximise profits as the most senior ones were paid by the state and their promotion depended more on their relationships with county officials than on their performance.

The principal-agent problem created a free-rider problem. The earnings of a commune member did not depend on how much he or she contributed. He could benefit from other members' efforts. Rational behaviour for an individual farmer who could not control output outcomes would be to minimise work input. In the end, it was a negative-sum game—a result of the prisoners' dilemma. Everyone was made worse off by free-riding.

The problem was made much worse by the political situation. Mao's 'utopianism' dictated that the contribution of farmers to their communes should not be assessed only by their work contribution, but also by their 'revolutionary' spirit. Thus one could make no economic contribution to his commune, but was still rewarded with income, perhaps more than those who were not so 'revolutionary'. The son of a former landlord who was forced to work long hours would earn much less than a 'revolutionary' farmer would. To make the situation even worse, the communists decided at the beginning of rural collectivisation that the leaders of the communes must be 'poor and lower-middle peasants'. Those who seized power in the communes tended to have little experience in farming and management.

The second proposition, concerning economies of scale, was right in principle, but there were probably few economies of scale in Chinese farming at the time and if they did exist it was not as a result of the communist regime. Wan and Cheng (1999) show that even in today's Chinese agriculture, there is little evidence of economies of scale. There were probably economies of scale and externalities in rural infrastructure projects, such as irrigation and pest control, but the enormous losses resulting from the poor planning and implementation of such projects overwhelmed these potential gains. Poor planning and implementation were inevitable under the commune system. Inexperience in management was partly to blame, but the fundamental problem was that no one took responsibility for the success or failure of projects—a situation that is not uncommon in SOEs today. Numerous reservoirs and dams were built in the pre-reform period, but many of them were a complete waste of money.[2]

By the late 1950s, the weaknesses of the commune system had already become apparent. For example, the restaurants run by the commune wasted an enormous amount of food as food was essentially free.[3] Work incentives were already lacking in many collectives. Unfortunately, the spectacular failure of the Great Leap Forward diverted attention away from the fundamental problems in the commune system, as official propaganda sought to blame the Soviet Union (for its demand of debt payments) and natural disasters for the failure. The problems of the commune system seemed to have been recognised by some Chinese leaders, especially then President Liu Shaoqi and his followers. In the early 1960s, the so-called *sanzi yibao* was introduced. Under this policy, free trade fairs—small plots of arable land for household farming—were allowed. The communes were encouraged to be responsible for their own profits and losses. The communes could contract farm output to households and households were allowed to retain output that exceeded the contracted amount. Under this policy, agricultural production recovered rapidly from the devastation inflicted by the Great Leap Forward in the period 1962–65. Unfortunately, the Cultural Revolution occurred in 1966; the commune system was kept alive until late 1983, when it was formally abolished.

The failure of the commune system had become obvious by the mid 1970s. Even though national grain output had increased since the Communists took power in 1949, starvation and malnutrition were widespread, especially in poor provinces such as Sichuan and Anhui. The communes crumbled. Chinese farmers knew what should be done. They first reduced the size of their communes, production brigades and production teams[4] and introduced piece-work points wherever possible.[5] Towards the late 1970s they introduced the production responsibility system. Its form varied from place to place, but its essence was to link work points earned to work outcomes. In practice, this meant that various farm tasks or plots of land were contracted to individuals, or groups of farmers. Based on their attainment of specified outcomes, farmers would be rewarded with a certain number of work points. Although it was a major step forward, the production responsibility system had a high transaction cost in terms of contract enforcement, and farmers' contributions to the communes were difficult to assess due to variations in the nature of different farm tasks. So farmers eventually divided up the land and introduced the household responsibility system, which quickly spread throughout the country. Under this household-based system, earnings (rather than the workpoints, whose worth still depended on the efforts of all commune members, even under the production responsibility system) were directly linked to the overall performance of the farm household.

The household responsibility system (HRS) largely solved the principal-agent and free-rider problems which had afflicted the communes. It was this system that unleashed the enormous enthusiasm and creativity of Chinese farmers. Under it, farmers took full responsibility for their farming activities and were profit-driven. Resources began to be used more efficiently. Fertilizer was no longer dumped in the fields and farm machinery no longer allowed to rust during winter. Leaking ditches were repaired. Urban workers were no longer needed to support their 'younger brother peasants' in busy seasons and school children did not have to leave their classes to help in the fields. As a result, there was an enormous increase in farm productivity in the earlier years of reform. Many studies have attributed this increase to institutional change (McMillan *et al.* 1989; Fan 1991; Lin 1992). Indeed, these productivity gains stemmed from the progressive changes in 'production relationships' within the commune (to use Marxist terminology), and culminated with the abolition of the commune system.

Agricultural reforms had extensive ramifications for the whole rural economy. As farmers were now allowed to retain their excess output (after satisfying their quota), there arose a need for markets. Rural trade fairs were restored across the country. This gave farmers room for specialisation in production, and productivity further increased. Agricultural commodities were not the only goods that entered the rural trade fairs. Farm inputs, handcrafted products, building materials and other goods needed by rural households became available. The success of rural reforms should not be assessed only by the increases in grain output or farm incomes. Freedom of choice and enriched lifestyles were also part of the achievement and represented a substantial improvement in living standards in rural China.

Perhaps the most far-reaching spillover effect of the agricultural reforms was the development of TVEs.[6] As labour productivity increased under the household responsibility system, surplus farm labour became available for non-agricultural activities. The rise in productivity meant that even in busy seasons labour shortages basically disappeared. Farmers already had some experience in the production of non-agricultural commodities as the commune system had forced them to be self-sufficient in many industrial products and farm tools. Further, rapid increases in farm incomes as a result of agricultural reform also enabled farmers to invest in non-agricultural activities. With the tremendous development of township and village enterprises, rural incomes increased much more rapidly than otherwise would have been possible.[7]

The timing of agricultural reforms was also fortunate for the rural people. While the agricultural sector was booming, urban reforms had just begun, albeit hesitantly. In the late 1970s and early 1980s, there were widespread shortages of consumer goods, and the SOE-dominated urban economy was slow to respond. TVEs seized upon this opportunity by expanding rapidly (Huang 1998a). An enormous amount of human capital and skills migrated from urban to rural areas.

The increased mobility of urban workers in response to the booming rural economy also helped the startup of TVEs.

So, what has made the agricultural reforms a success? Their success comes from following basic human instincts, allowing farmers to pursue their own interests at their own costs. Allowing market development, and reasonably stable rural institutions, enabled farmers to release their entrepreneurial skills. It must be noted that throughout the course of agricultural reform, farmers took the initiative, and the government responded by granting its consent, albeit with hesitation. Unfortunately, constraints on the further development of markets and rural institutions began to hamper the rapid growth of the rural economy.

What remains to be done?

The problems facing the farming sector and the rural TVE sector differ. In the farming sector, work incentives and responsible decision-making are no longer a problem. The problems lie in rural factor market policy, the agricultural marketing system, trade policy (both for internal and external trade) and rural institutions.

Land tenure

When the household-based farming system was introduced, farmers were given the right to use collectively-owned land for a specified number of years (normally 15), depending on the region and type of land (forestry land was allowed much longer leases). Now most land leases are due for renewal for another 30 years as stipulated by the government.[8] Thirty years of land lease is probably long enough for Chinese farmers to make long-term investment decisions, given that they have become used to uncertainty over property rights. However, there are problems. According to surveys conducted by the Ministry of Agriculture (Ding 1999; Chen 1998a), by the end of 1995 only 60 per cent of villages had extended land tenure, and of these villages, less than 20 per cent had extended land tenure for 30 years. Even though the central government proclaims land tenure policy, villages have control over the implementation of the policy as land is supposed to be collectively owned. Many villages have not extended land leases according to the official policy. In some villages, land contracts are renegotiated frequently; some don't even use contracts. There have been reports that village cadres have unilaterally terminated contracts in an attempt to obtain the benefits of farm investments (such as matured forests).

No legal framework is yet in place to regulate land transfer and its proper use. Farmers have been left to make their own arrangements, often at high political risk and transaction cost because of uncertainty. It is not uncommon for farmers who do not wish to continue farming because of off-farm employment opportunities to make little effort to improve land productivity; other farmers are willing to put in the effort required because they face lower opportunity costs. As a result, farmland is not used efficiently. The lack of a formal land market also tends to lead to inefficient use of land for non-agricultural purposes. Collective ownership of land means that village cadres are often under pressure to provide land for non-agricultural uses (such as housing construction) at a subsidised rate.

Grain marketing

The problems in the agricultural marketing system require more urgent attention than those in the factor markets. Reform in this area has been the least consistent and has led to volatility in agricultural production and prices (Chen 1998a). In 1985, bumper harvests in the previous years prompted the government to abolish the compulsory purchase system and effectively reduce state purchase prices for grain. But soon after, agricultural output declined and the policy was reversed. The so-called purchases contracts with farmers became *de facto* compulsory purchases under a different name. Further policy retrenchments occurred in 1988–89 when the government attempted to stabilise domestic grain prices and reduce inflation in general. After several years of slow change the government introduced more radical reforms in 1992–93, when planned rationing and procurement policies were abolished (Garnaut and Ma 1994). This period saw rapid commercialisation of grain trade and institutional reforms in the grain marketing system. The high inflation during 1994–95 prompted another round of policy retrenchment, when the so-called Provincial Governor Responsibility System was introduced. Under this regime, provinces had a primary responsibility of ensuring stable and adequate grain supply. Many provinces pursued grain self-sufficiency to fulfil their responsibility. Over time, however, controls over grain marketing have been loosened. Non-state marketing channels have grown and grain trade has increased substantially (Rozelle *et al.* 1998).

As market channels and participation in grain marketing have increased in recent years, the state grain marketing agencies have suffered large financial losses, which have become an increasing drain on the government budget. Under the central planning system, the government provided full subsidies to its grain-purchasing agencies because neither the purchase prices nor the sales prices (both for wholesaling and retailing) were market-determined. With the development of free grain markets, the non-state sector has posed strong competition to the state grain agencies. At the wholesale level, private enterprises and individuals increasingly resort to direct purchase from farmers. At the retail level, higher quality grain is becoming available on free markets. Farmers have incentives to sell lower quality grain to the state and higher quality grain on the free markets. The state grain purchasing agencies tend to give low grades to grain they purchase. This has often led to complaints by farmers. However, none of these have prevented the financial losses of the state grain agencies from increasing. Early in 1998, the government overhauled the grain marketing system in an attempt to provide a complete solution to the problems.

The new system works as follows. First, the state grain purchasing agencies have a complete monopoly over grain purchase at set prices. These prices were set to ensure a desired level of farm income. Second, to eliminate further financial losses to the grain agencies, they are allowed to sell grain at a price level that ensures full cost recovery. Third, the State Agricultural Development Bank of China provides bank loans to cover the full costs once the grain purchased is sold. The intention of this policy is twofold: it reduces the strain imposed on the state budget by the grain department, and guarantees adequate farm incomes.

Unfortunately, this policy is flawed and unlikely to achieve its objectives. Due to the development of rural markets over the past 20 years, it is now very difficult to monopolise grain purchase without extremely draconian policies. Non-state grain agencies are likely to continue to market grain and probably at a very competitive price as they tend to have lower overhead costs. With fixed state purchase prices, farmers have incentives to sell lower quality grain (such as grain that has been in storage for an excessive period of time) to the state grain agencies. Chinese farmers hold large grain stocks due to high food security consciousness (Ke 1999). In selling low quality grain, state grain agencies face strong competition from high quality grain available on the free market. The state grain agencies are now allowed greater grade margins to differentiate grain quality. However, with little in the way of checks and balances, the grain purchase agencies may abuse their monopolistic power. This is likely to happen as many agencies also run (directly or indirectly) profit-driven businesses.

More fundamentally, the grain state agencies are not efficiently run. This is hardly surprising as grain enterprises have long been subsidised by the government and have not been under as much pressure as other SOEs to improve their performance. As a result, state grain agencies find it difficult to compete with non-state agencies. Stockpiles of grain in state agencies lead to even greater financial losses. Because the state has given up its budget responsibility for the purchase of grain, the Agricultural Development Bank of China— as the designated bank—will have to shoulder the financial losses of the agencies. Given the current relationship between state-owned banks and the government, the latter will eventually have to bear the costs. According to surveys conducted by the Centre for Chinese Agricultural Development at the Chinese Academy of Agricultural Sciences, the new grain marketing system has already shown signs of collapsing, as state grain agencies are unable to sell their procurement at cost-recovery prices.

The poor design of this new marketing system highlights the problems with decision-making in the Chinese government. It has been suggested that the policy was formulated at the Commission of Economics and Trade under the direct leadership of Premier Zhu Rongji. It was alleged that there was no prior consultation with the Chinese government departments that are affected by, or that have the responsibility for, implementing the policy. Apparently the Ministry of Foreign Trade and Economic Relations was not consulted regarding the implications of the policy. Even the Ministry of Agriculture was not consulted and was caught by surprise when it was announced. There was no public debate and no opposing views were allowed to be expressed.[9] Apart from its market-unfriendly nature, this policy has significant international implications. Once the domestic grain market is fully monopolised, external trade has to be restricted to support the policy. This will affect China's position on the World Trade Organization

(WTO) accession negotiations and its potential participation in future rounds of multilateral trade liberalisation in agriculture.

Trade policy

China's agricultural trade policy itself has been subject to little rigorous debate. Many issues need to be discussed, but two stand out. The first is internal trade in agricultural commodities. Before the new grain marketing policy was introduced, the Provincial Governor Grain Responsibility System was a major concern. In 1995, in response to the sharp increases in grain prices, the central government made the governors of all provinces responsible for adequate grain supply at stable prices in their jurisdictions. As a result, each province began to pursue policies of increasing provincial production, without due consideration to regional comparative advantage in grain production. Rozelle *et al.* (1998) found that grain trade during the period 1994–95 was hampered by higher transaction costs. Given that China is a large country and regional endowments vary greatly, this policy is likely to have led to significant inefficiencies.

China's fiscal system tends to reinforce the incentive for provincial self-sufficiency. Because local governments are primarily responsible for subsidising local agriculture and food consumption by urban residents, grain surplus regions try to keep grain within their jurisdications, instead of selling it to other regions at their own budget costs. In addition, there is no legal instrument to stop regional protection. The lack of legal framework regulating internal trade tends to increase the risks associated with regional interdependency, and regional self-sufficiency becomes the preferred option for ensuring adequate food supply. Regional protection in overt or covert forms is widespread, and not only in agricultural trade. For example, Shanghai has replaced Daihatsu Charade with VW Santana for taxi transport because Charade is produced in Tianjin whereas Santana is produced locally. Peugeots are almost exclusively used for taxicabs in Guangzhou as they are produced there.

Recently, the Chinese government banned car manufacturers from price competition because they believe excessive competition will harm the profitability of the industry and hence China's own interests. Ironically, most of China's large car manufacturers are joint ventures. There are already too many car manufacturers: over 120, and yet their combined output is no more than that of a medium-sized company overseas (He and Yang 1998). Similar policies have been attempted in the electrical appliance and paper industries. Even though such government-created cartels may not work because of a free-rider problem, the government's actions serve to demonstrate the state of political economy in many markets, where consumer interests are completely ignored for the sake of protecting certain producer groups.

Internal trade in agriculture will become increasingly important to China as the structural changes in its economy accelerate. Coastal regions have lost much of their comparative advantage in land-intensive agricultural production. Grain production, for example, has relocated from these regions to inland and northeast regions where land is relatively abundant and labour costs lower. Policies which prevent these structural changes have far-reaching economic consequences. Most of China's grain feed is produced in the northeast and inland provinces while demand is growing most rapidly in the South (Tan and Xin 1999). Even though high transport costs at present may prevent large trade flows between the northeast and southeast of the country, the potential for trade is huge as infrastructure improves and policy impediments disappear. This will in turn have significant implications for China's feed and livestock industries and agricultural exports (see Qin and Tian 1999). China is unlikely to develop a competitive feed industry if it restricts grain imports. This in turn means that contrary to the government's intentions, China's livestock production will continue to be domestically oriented and will find it difficult to compete in the world market.

China appears to have committed itself to grain self-sufficiency, but public debate on this policy has been limited. The grain self-sufficiency policy is meant to safeguard food security and farm income, a policy objective not unlike that in many other countries. The official view takes grain security to mean grain self-sufficiency, even though China's own experience has shown that grain trade has helped China to cope with the consequences of natural disasters and policy failures, such as the Great Leap Forward. One of China's specific concerns over food security is the potential for a grain embargo by the West should China increase its grain exports in the future. However, the likelihood or consequences of such embargoes have never been rigorously assessed (Lu 1997).

On the farm income issue, some Chinese policymakers seem to have based their decisions on simplistic reasoning; since most industrial countries and industrialising East Asian economies tend to protect their agriculture, it must be a good policy. The belief is that if China allows freer trade in agriculture, not only will it harm farm interests but also reduce China's food security. In truth, China probably offers little effective protection for agriculture at present, and hence immediate liberalisation would have little overall impact on agricultural production and farm income (Yang 1996). With increasing diversification of the rural economy, non-agricultural production has become a major (if not the main) source of rural income in many regions, especially in the coastal regions. In the longer run, it is even more unlikely that Chinese farmers would lose from agricultural liberalisation. One can hardly imagine that Chinese farmers would be able to achieve living standards comparable to those enjoyed by urban residents in the future, with 0.2 hectares of arable land per rural person. Chinese farmers have already felt the pressure and begun to industrialise the rural economy. This has been a very important factor driving the growth of the TVE sector. Given the momentum of growth in the TVE sector, China's longer-term rural policy should be about the promotion of rural industrialisation.

China must take a more broad view with its agricultural trade policy. If China wishes to join the WTO and if agricultural liberalisation is again the subject of debate in the next round of WTO trade talks, one can hardly imagine that China will be able to insulate its agriculture from international competition. Studies have shown that China would benefit substantially from membership-induced trade liberalisation (Yang 1996; Anderson 1997). China's trade partners will be more likely to impose trade restrictions on goods in which China has a comparative advantage if China restricts grain imports. China must balance its food self-sufficiency objective with the resulting economic costs—costs that not only arise from agricultural protection itself, but also from potentially reduced market access for its manufactured exports. A protectionist policy for agriculture could jeopardise China's overall process of integration with the world economy.

Rural government

Despite the abolition of the communes, many aspects of central planning remain, and these are increasingly hindering the development of the rural economy. In fact, the commune was simply replaced by the township government in many respects, and continues to exercise administrative and political control over village leaders, who have replaced the leaders of the former production brigades and teams. The township is the lowest level of government and higher level (county) governments appoint all the important township cadres. Village leaders are supposed to be elected by farmers, but township governments usually have a strong influence on election results, or the final say on appointments.

One of the problems with this government structure is that township leaders report only to the county-level governments, and are rarely accountable to farmers. Leaders who do not perform well in their position can be reappointed in various townships year after year until retirement. Apart from its governing function, the township does provide some services to agricultural production through its rural extension stations, but it has been unable to provide adequate law and order and other social services. Corruption, illicit drug use and trafficking, illegal gambling and gang fighting have become increasingly serious social problems in rural China.

Many townships run their own enterprises. While many of these enterprises have been successful, their faults (not unlike those facing state enterprises) have become increasingly obvious. In most cases, especially where the enterprises are not contracted to individuals, the township appoints the directors, and nepotism is widespread. Enterprise profits have to be submitted to the township, and the directors have little incentive to maximise profits; instead, potential profits tend to be absorbed through costpadding (for example, extravagant banquets and travels) and distributed as bonuses to the workers. When enterprises make financial losses the township has to bale them out. Township officials face little political pressure in such circumstances, nor do they have strong incentive to ensure better management in the enterprises as their salaries are paid by the state. Worse still, output levels and growth are often used to assess the performance of township leaders. This creates a strong incentive to overstate the output of TVEs. It was alleged that for this reason, the State Statistical Bureau reduced its estimates of TVE output for years prior to 1997 by 20 per cent even though the Ministry of Agriculture was opposed to the revision (personal communications with China Agricultural University staff). The overstatement of TVE output has recently come under closer public scrutiny.

Many township governments are seriously overstaffed. Most of the township staff are paid through township revenues; only the salaries of core staff are paid by the state. Some townships are compelled to impose excessive fines for illegal actions in order to maintain their staffing levels. Despite numerous decrees issued by the central government banning excessive fines, this problem has persisted. Farmers are powerless to do anything because they do not have any say in the appointment of their township leaders.

In general, township governments should provide more than they currently do. With increasing privatisation of TVEs, township governments must focus their attention on the provision of social and economic institutions, in order to improve the efficiency of TVEs. They have a much larger role to play in protecting the environment, regulating work conditions in firms, providing adequate funds for education and reducing poverty. It is hoped that the administrative reforms which have already begun at the ministerial level will be extended to township governments.

Prospects for further reform and growth

Given the political economy of Chinese reform, it is unlikely that agricultural reform will proceed rapidly. In land reform, ideological constraints are significant. Policymakers have recognised the problems associated with uncertainty over land tenure. However, the 30 years land tenure policy, which was aimed at addressing the uncertainty problem, has not been properly implemented. Current collective land ownership is regarded as a cornerstone of China's socialism. It is feared that without such ownership in rural China, income disparity will deteriorate further and poverty will spread. According to official lines, this would contradict everything the Chinese Communists have fought for over the past decades. Subsequently, private ownership of land has been ruled out. Unfortunately the central government does not consider land reform to be an issue of urgency. Given that the current situation gives local officials maximum control over land, there are unlikely to be major grass-root level initiatives. Ongoing democratisation at the village level may weaken local control, but it will probably be a long time before it makes a significant difference.

In recent years, the so-called 'two farmland system' has been experimented with. Under this system, farmland in a village is divided into two categories—one for subsistence farming and the other for commercial farming. The former is distributed free of charge according to family size, while the latter is contracted out for a fee. This experiment is designed to increase farm size in order to exploit economies of scale and reduce land fragmentation. After several years of advocating this policy, the government has recently banned the experiment. The policy reversion was prompted by reports that many farmers were opposed to the system because many villages took back land from farmers for redistribution without compensation. This again highlights the lack of property rights and the extent of power abuse by local cadres due to a lax legal system and weak law enforcement. This situation is unlikely to change without radical institutional reform in rural China.

Urban interest groups are the main force behind grain marketing reform and trade policy reform in general. Because of the paramount importance attached to food security and the perceived link between food security and grain self-sufficiency, the government has been extremely cautious about grain and agricultural market reform. Segments of government ministries in charge of internal and external trade have strong vested interests as they want to continue to retain their monopoly over trade. There are obvious conflicts of interests in those ministries simultaneously running businesses and regulating the market (He and Yang 1998). These ministries, together with those who are opposed to trade liberalisation, stress the importance of increasing domestic supply both as a means of stabilising the market and increasing food security and farm income. Furthermore, they regard this approach as an effective way of reducing rural-urban migration which would in turn reduce potential social unrest in cities. This goes well with the urban perception that rural migrants take urban jobs and their migration out of agriculture reduces China's food security. In the process of policymaking, political weight is clearly skewed towards urban interests. Given the massive unemployment problem arising from SOE reform in urban China, these forces are likely to remain strong.

The growth prospects for China's agriculture and rural economy depend on the growth of inputs, as well as reforms. Of course, the former also depends on the latter as, for example, land tenure policy has significant implications for farm inputs. Over the past two decades, the inefficiencies resulting from the commune system seem to have largely been eliminated. It is therefore difficult to achieve large productivity gains with current technology. Price incentives are not going to be as strong as in the past two decades as domestic prices have approached or even passed border prices for many agricultural commodities. Even if China raises its border protection, there is a limit to the effect on domestic prices, unless China wishes to further raise domestic floor prices (Yang and Huang 1997). Given the large resource implication of higher floor prices, this policy option is unlikely to be pursued. Under such circumstances, private investment in agriculture would be expected to grow slowly. Public investment has experienced a steady decline over the past two decades. This may have partly resulted from the government's response to the increasing opportunity cost of agricultural investment as non-agricultural sectors grew rapidly, and partly from a decline in the influence of the agricultural sector in the political process. Abundant food supplies tend to reduce the attention given to agriculture and hence public investment in agriculture is not likely to grow rapidly.

The poor taxation capacity of the government means that even if greater support is given to agriculture in the future, it is more likely to take the form of border assistance. China may insist on high protection for agriculture out of fiscal considerations as well as food security and farm income. In the short run this may help agriculture, especially the grain sector. In the long run, however, labour productivity growth in agriculture is likely to be slower as more farmers stay in agriculture. Land productivity growth may also be slower as land fragmentation is likely to remain. Perhaps most importantly, there will be slower growth in the non-grain sectors, including rural industries and higher value-added agricultural sectors such as cash crops, fruits and vegetables.

The growth prospects for the rural economy also depend on urban reform. This linkage works not only in terms of resource competition between the rural and urban economies, but also in terms of the pace of urban reform affecting rural reform and the health of the rural economy. With government attention clearly focused on SOE reform, rural reforms have become somewhat less important. The more successful is urban reform, the greater the opportunity for farmers to seek urban employment. Even though the reform of SOEs reform will increase their competitiveness relative to rural enterprises, greater capital mobility is likely to benefit the rural economy. Widespread financial difficulties in the SOE sector have in recent years not helped rural enterprises; instead, they seem to have had a strong adverse impact on the rural economy as the debt problem has spread to TVEs.

Overall, there is not great optimism about the pace of rural reform and the growth of the rural economy. Much seems to depend on the reform of the SOE sector and the emergence of a clear vision for a long-term development strategy for the rural economy. Current political forces seem to resist rapid structural change and consistent and coherent policy formation, which is necessary to maintain the strong growth of the rural economy.

Lessons and implications of agricultural reform

The key to the success of agricultural reform was its resolution of the principal-agent problem, thus reducing the free-rider problem associated with collective farming. Even though clear property rights have not yet been fully established, a direct link between work efforts and rewards has been established. This is the single most important lesson of agricultural reform that policymakers should bear in mind in reforming the SOEs, even though the issue is far more complicated in the urban context.

The principal-agent problem in the TVE sector has not been resolved to the same extent as in agriculture. Many TVEs face the same problem as the SOEs. The problem arises from the remains of the commune regime. Many TVEs were established using investment by the communes, and the communes' replacements, the townships, run the TVEs in the same way the central ministries run the SOEs. Reforms that are now being implemented to small and medium-sized SOEs should also apply to TVEs. Meanwhile, reform to the rural institutions needs to be pursued rigorously to complement TVE and agricultural reform.

The so-called budget hardening under the current system is unlikely to work. This is why Chinese farmers did not approve the production responsibility system as the final destination of their reform; they reverted to household-based farming. Unlike SOEs in economies where a transparent political system exists, there is little political pressure for the townships to lift the performance of their enterprises. Given the current political institutions and widespread nepotism in the appointment of enterprise directors and staff, anything short of full privatisation/leasing/contracting out of these enterprises is unlikely to alter their behaviour. This will not resolve all the problems, but it would be a critical step forward.

While it is essential that the property rights problem be resolved both in agriculture and TVEs—particularly in TVEs—China must also focus on the development of the domestic market and the integration of its rural economy into the urban economy and indeed into the world economy. In the early stages of reform, it was in the farmers' own interests to introduce fundamental changes to the way in which agricultural production was organised. It was a matter of possible starvation, and there was a desperate sense of urgency. The least successful part of China's agricultural reform seems to have been the liberalisation of internal and external trade. The newly introduced grain marketing system represents a step backward. Unlike with agricultural reform, farmers cannot simply take initiative in trade reform, as an open, integrated domestic market and a liberal external trade regime cannot be established without the cooperation of other interest groups. The government must introduce coherent policies to accomplish this reform.

The inconsistency and slow pace of market liberalisation reflect the lack of vision on the part of Chinese policymakers. Even though they desire industrialisation of the rural economy, their policies have not been consistent with this objective. To eliminate poverty and raise the living standards of the still very poor rural population, China must give priority to the development of non-agricultural sectors to absorb large amounts of surplus rural labour. This may mean lower grain self-sufficiency, but it does not necessarily lead to lower food security. Policymakers must be open-minded in exploring the options for increasing food security. Important SOE reform should not be allowed to divert attention from rural reform, especially TVE reform. Both should be parts of the overall strategy for rapid and efficient industrialisation.

Notes

* The author wishes to thank Professor Weiming Tian of the China Agricultural University for his helpful comments.

[1] It has been revealed recently that there has been much overstatement of the levels and possibly growth rates of TVE output. Nevertheless, the TVE sector does seem to have grown rapidly since the reform.

[2] This is not to deny that China made significant progress in water conservation in the pre-reform era. Many of the water conservation projects continued to play an important role well into the reform period. The point is that there was also much waste. The reforms, however, made some of these projects much more valuable, and some of them would have become sunk costs without the reforms. One example would be that some abandoned reservoirs have been turned into fish ponds.

[3] The provision of food free of charge was partly based on the wildly overstated grain yields, which even today's scientists can only dream of. Some communes reported grain yield per *mu* (1/15 hectare) of up to several hundreds of thousands of kilograms. Strangely for someone who had worked on a farm, Mao believed these overstated yield levels.

[4] A typical commune consisted of several production brigades and each brigade had several production teams. A brigade was normally formed from an existing village. The reduction in the size of the production units was predictable given that in the early stages of reform the key issue was work incentives, as discussed earlier in the context of the principal-agent problem. Politically this was more defendable than more radical options, such as the subsequently introduced production responsibility system.

[5] As communes only paid work points, which at the end of the year would be converted into wages according to the total revenue of the commune, piece wages had to take their form as piece-work points. It must be noted that as piece-work points could not apply to all farm tasks, this incentive mechanism had its limitations. Subsequently, the next logical step in the reforms was the production responsibility system.

[6] For an extensive study of TVEs, see Findlay *et al.* (1994).

[7] TVEs were not without their problems. This will be discussed later in the chapter.

[8] The policy for land tenure renewal was first announced in 1993, according to Chen (1998a). The most recent reaffirmation of this policy was on 19 October 1998 in the *People's Daily*.

[9] A rumour alleges that Premier Zhu sacked a deputy governor of a province at a briefing on the new policy because the deputy governor voiced the potential difficulties in implementing the policy, while other provincial leaders remained silent.

Trade reform and development

Ligang Song [*]

Trade system reform has been an important component in the overall strategy of reforming the economic system in China. Tremendous progress has been made over the past twenty years, but much more needs to be done in setting up a more open, efficient and transparent trade system, in line with the requirements of the World Trade Organization (WTO).

Historical legacy

China's trade system was a highly centralised and controlled planned system during the pre-reform period (1958–78). The main features of this type of trade system were [1]

- foreign trade was conducted strictly according to central planning, which covered areas such as trade procurement, imports, exports and balance of foreign exchange—the State Planning Commission and Ministry of Foreign Trade were the key players in drawing up the plan for trade with an objective to fulfil the government's overall plan
- a centralised accounting system was run through the Ministry of Foreign Trade and the Ministry of Finance—under this system, producers and trading companies (handling both imports and exports) were not responsible for profits or losses incurred in their production and trading activities

- trade (both imports and exports) was handled exclusively by state trading companies with numerous local branches which were highly specialised and monopolised
- a planned price system was used for conducting foreign trade. It virtually broke the link between domestic and international prices— for example, the procurement of export goods, and domestic sales (distribution) of imported goods were conducted according to domestic planned prices whereas goods were exported and imported based on international prices
- the state managed, monitored and controlled trade activities largely through administrative means such as tariff protection and import controls
- foreign exchange transactions were also centrally controlled and handled exclusively by the Bank of China—trading companies handed over all their foreign exchange earnings to the state; demands for foreign exchange by domestic users for imports were met by allocating foreign exchange to these users according to the plan
- the government implemented a policy of balancing foreign exchange—the renminbi (RMB) exchange rate became an accounting tool for planning and its determination was not associated with the demand for and supply of foreign exchange. This tended to lead to an overvalued RMB exchange rate (Shi 1998:158).

The major shortcomings and potential consequences of this highly centralised trade system included

- by limiting competitive pressure on domestic producers, the old trade system tended to restrict the development of exports. At the same time, there were always tendencies for China to import more due to excessive demand for imported goods, leading to a persistent shortage of foreign exchange, subsequent exchange controls and an overvalued exchange rate
- since neither producers nor exporters (trading companies) were responsible for profits and losses, trading activities tended to be inefficient, not very innovative and there was a lack of incentives to reduce costs
- due to the lack of incentives for enterprises to reduce costs, the losses on exports became apparent and the government was continually required to provide subsidies and various kinds of trade protection measures; distortions occurred

- because goods were traded according to the plan, there were no policy settings aimed at boosting foreign trade, particularly exports, or exploring gains from trade through close integration with the world market
- because goods were traded through monopolised trading companies and based on distorted prices, enterprises suffered from a lack of exposure to competition and there was no quick feedback from world market in terms of changing market conditions for exports. (Subsequently enterprises had little incentive to upgrade their production facilities or change the composition of trade. This lack of connection between production and trade in turn hampered enterprises' prospects for competing in the world market.)
- a high degree of protectionism and an overvalued exchange rate jointly reflected China's adoption of import substitution strategies during the pre-reform period—inwardly-oriented development strategies in which 'trade and other incentives were biased in favour of production for the domestic market and against production for export' (Lardy 1992:7)
- the highly centralised trade system produced large numbers of groups with vested interests in controlling and monopolising production and trading activities—they became strong forces in resisting reform.

Realising the shortcomings of the old system and their consequences, China embarked on reform to its economic system, including the trade system, towards the end of the 1970s. Reform has substantially reduced the extent of anti-export bias and allowed the Chinese economy to become more deeply integrated with the world economy.

Stages of trade reform

In the context of the overall economic reforms and institutional changes that started in the late 1970s, the reform of the trade system in China has gone through four stages, each with its own emphasis and associated problems.[2] The reforms have moved from being experimental to being more in line with the requirements of the WTO, and the main aim of external reform has been 'to scale back the scope of trade planning and to shift to a reliance on market mechanisms for determining the pattern of imports and exports (Tseng *et al.* 1994:4).

Stage one: 1979–84

The first stage of trade system reform in China began at the same time as the general reform of the economy. The aim of this initial stage was to explore the possibility of reforming the highly centralised trading regime inherited from the Soviet-style central planning system. Various experiments were undertaken at this stage of reform including decentralisation of foreign trade authority by relinquishing the monopoly on foreign trade it had exercised since the mid 1950s (Lardy 1992:39). The right to conduct foreign trade was gradually granted to provinces, municipalities, industrial sectors and enterprises.

The government also experimented with more diverse forms of trade including processing trade, compensation trade and border trade.[3] As an experiment to introduce foreign capital into the economy and to gain the experience of conducting production (management), trade and other business activities in line with standard practice, special economic zones were established during this period. To manage the new forms of trade that were not covered by the state plan, the government adopted the import and export licensing system and a number of large enterprises were given the right to conduct foreign trade directly. Furthermore, the foreign exchange retention system was established to provide local governments and enterprises with greater incentives to export.

The reform experiment at this initial stage was successful in that it took the first but very important step of reforming the whole trade system. In particular, the foreign trade planning system began to be transformed and the monopoly power of the foreign trade corporations under the Foreign Trade Minister was gradually weakened (Li 1996:81). However, owing to resistance to the reforms, a lack of experience and human skills needed to manage the reforms, and the problems that emerged in the process (such as the emergence of chaotic trading activities resulting from uncoordinated approaches to reform), the reform program achieved only limited success.

One important outcome of this initial period of reform was that the experience made the government realise that reforming the trade system would be a long and painful process and that it might be necessary to take a step-by-step approach, closely monitoring the results of each step and then making policy adjustments accordingly. This approach was crucial for conceiving and designing subsequent reforms, not only in trade but also in other areas of the economy. However, a side effect of such an approach is that the elements of the traditional structure have, in many ways, frustrated and hampered the reform efforts.

Stage two: 1985–86

In the second stage of reform[4] the government adopted a reform program aimed at separating government functions from enterprises, simplifying administrative procedures for approving imports and exports, adjusting tariff rates to increase competition and further decentralising power to enterprises.

Under this program, experiments in reforming the planning and accounting system were also carried out and attempts were made to break the planning framework in order to create more direct links between production and trade. From the beginning of 1985, China also abandoned the internal exchange settlement rate, which was introduced in 1981. A 'managed floating' exchange rate system was established in which exchange rates were predominantly adjusted according to changes in both domestic and international prices.

To accommodate the need for changing the management of trade from direct administrative control to indirect means, China also established a system of export tax-rebates, a fund for encouraging exports and differential tariff rates for exports and imports. China's Tariff Law was comprehensively modified during this period (Shi 1998:162).

Due to these reform programs, China entered a stage where compulsory planning, indicative planning, and market adjustment mechanisms were all in place at the same time.

As had happened during the first stage of the reform program, the measures taken at the second stage represented one more step towards the liberalisation of the trade system. However, reform at this stage also encountered some difficulties. For example, enterprises could not be truly independent because of their close relationship with the government, and price signals could not fully function because of the operation of a two-tier price system. As a result, enterprises were not wholly responsible for profits and losses in conducting foreign trade.

What the government learned from this stage of reform was the importance of reforming the system in a comprehensive manner. But owning to various difficulties—particularly those existing in the relationship between the government and enterprises—and, more importantly, because of the benefits of the reform measures—namely a rapid increase in trade—the government decided to continue its step-by-step approach to reforming the trade system rather than implementing any sudden changes.

Up to this stage, the reform measures had predominantly been aimed at changing the basic structure of the old system and not at conforming to the requirements of the General Agreement on Tariffs and Trade (GATT). However, the government realised the potential benefits to the reform process of joining GATT and believed that the time had come for China to apply for re-entry. In July 1986, China officially launched its application. Subsequently, reforming the trade system in accordance with the requirements of GATT became the main task in the next stage of the reform program.

Stage three: 1987–90

The key reform measure adopted at this stage was the general implementation of the 'contract system' in both trading and production enterprises in the export sector. The contract system was also applied to the relationship between local and central governments from 1988. The system included contracts between enterprises, trading companies, local governments, and the central government, in the areas of foreign exchange earnings, quotas of foreign exchange earnings handed over to the state, the reduction of export subsidies and responsibility for export profits and losses.

Under the contract system, though obliged to fulfil the plan for exports, foreign exchange, and total profits and losses in relation to the central government, local governments had the autonomy to decide on commodity mix, quantities, prices for exports and means of conducting trade. The central government was still responsible for profits and losses incurred by those who traded within the central plan, however the local governments were accountable for those who traded outside the plan. Local general specialised trading companies no longer had direct links with central finance, but were associated with local finance (Shi 1998:163)

To reflect the changes to the trade operation system, commodities were divided into three broad groups: a few resource products that were handled by those specialised trading companies; commodities that were subject to licensing and quotas and dealt with through local trading companies; and commodities that were allowed to be traded freely (Shi 1998:164). This division helped clear confusion about policy settings in which particular commodities were subject to trade, but a certain proportion of commodities were still traded under planning and administrative controls. Thus, this division of commodities was abandoned by the government at the next stage of reform. By then, only a few key commodities were handled by the state and all other commodities were traded freely by various trading companies and producers.

Other changes implemented at this stage of reform included: the central government no longer providing subsidies for price differentials, increased proportions of foreign exchange being retained by local governments, and the government allowing trading companies and enterprises to trade their retained foreign exchange at market prices in foreign exchange swap markets.

These reform measures touched upon the issues of operational mechanisms within enterprises and the role of local governments in managing foreign trade. The reforms themselves, therefore, had important implications for the government's attempts to build up a modern enterprise system to be adopted at a later stage of its reform program.[5]

One result from this stage of reform was a rapid expansion of trade owing to the strong production and trading incentives for enterprises, trading companies, and local governments that resulted from the contract system. However, there were some problems associated with the reforms, the key one being that a favourable environment in which fair competition could be conducted had not been created. The other area in which reform had not made much progress was in the import system. These problems were addressed at the next stage of trade system reform.

Stage four: 1991–93

In line with the policy on the reform of SOEs, the main objective of the reform program at this stage was to allow enterprises to be fully responsible for their profits and losses in order to equip them with a mechanism for competing both domestically and internationally on a fair basis. The measures adopted included phasing out export subsidies, narrowing the regional differences in foreign exchange retention rates, giving more power to enterprises to use foreign exchange, and using exchange rates and tariff rates to adjust trade activities. Efforts had also been made to raise the quality of export products and adjust the commodity structure of China's imports and exports. The government's intention was to create a truly competitive environment for enterprises involved in foreign trade, similar to that in which firms in other countries operated.

China also speeded up its efforts to re-enter GATT by substantially reducing the volume of exports subject to planning, further improving the export-licensing system by increasing its transparency, and deepening reform of the enterprise system.

Another important reform that resulted from conforming to the requirements of GATT was the reform of the import system, which had lagged behind reform of the export system. The import system in China was highly centrally planned, using import planning, administrative approval, import licenses, import price determination, exchange controls, and import tariffs to control import activities. The general results of these measures were nontransparency in import transactions and overprotection of some domestic industries. The need to reform its import system became even more obvious when China set its sights on re-entering GATT.

China initiated the reform of its import system at the beginning of 1992 with a unilateral reduction of tariff rates for a wide range of commodities, abandonment of import adjustment taxes (effective from April 1992), reduction of the coverage of import licensing,[6] and a re-examination and subsequent abandonment of the internal documents for import management and control.[7] While reforming the old import system, China aimed to establish a modern import management system, characterised mainly by reliance on tariffs and exchange rates to adjust imports, compatible with normal practice in other countries and consistent with the rules of GATT. The measures undertaken to achieve this goal included further reduction of the coverage of mandate planning for imports, abandonment of the system of administrative approval for imports, and further improvement of the import-licensing system, which entailed increasing its transparency and fairness.

Compared with the reforms of the previous stage, the new reform program went one step further in reforming China's trade system. More importantly, the reforms made the trade system increasingly consistent with the requirements of GATT. However, structural problems existing at a deeper level remained. For example, the two-tier currency system, under which foreign exchange transactions were conducted according to both the official rate and the rate prevailing in so-called foreign exchange swap centres, was still in place. This system hindered further deepening of the reform of China's trade system.

In principle, the two-tier exchange rate system should have been abolished but in reality there were many difficulties associated with abolishing it. By creating more distortions the system tended to discourage exports and imports, induce a scarcity of foreign exchange, increase the secondary market price of foreign exchange, and lower real income (Martin 1990). The main difficulty in reforming the currency system was that the system itself was tied up with the old institutional framework to which the relationship between the government and enterprises was intrinsically linked. Another difficulty was that official exchange rates were far from market equilibrium level. This meant that there were some preconditions for taking the steps necessary to reform the exchange rate system.

Although there were pros and cons for domestic enterprises—for example, unified exchange rates could bring an end to the effective subsidy given to the state enterprises that were allowed to buy foreign currency at the cheaper official rate—the potential gains for the whole economy from abolishing the system could be substantial. Most important, the reform measures taken at previous stages of the reform process had laid the foundations for the government to take more drastic measures in reforming its trade system. Two examples stand out. One was that the majority of enterprises had been trading based on market rather than official exchange rates, reflecting that the bond between government and enterprises had further loosened. The other was that the government had adopted a series of measures in adjusting official exchange rates towards more market-determined equilibrium prices. This has been characterised by a gradual and steady depreciation of the RMB during the past 15 years.

These examples suggest that the aforementioned preconditions had been more or less satisfied after several rounds of reforms. Reformation of the two-tier currency system became one of the most important targets of trade system reform in 1994.

Stage five: 1994 onwards

The fifth stage of reform is ongoing.[8] Characterised by its comprehensiveness in reforming taxation, finance, and the currency system, this stage has been the most dramatic so far in reforming the trade system. The key measure adopted was the reform of the system of controlled exchange rates. Its aim was to create a system of managed floating exchange rates based on market forces and the gradual transformation of the RMB into a convertible currency. The government abandoned the former two-tier exchange rate system—the foreign exchange certificate (FEC)—and unified the RMB's exchange rates at the beginning of 1994 by cutting the official exchange by 33 per cent and beginning to phase out FECs in an effort to bring the system up to world standards.[9] This move, a positive step in China's application to rejoin GATT, was welcomed in foreign business circles. Previously, foreign investment was calculated in RMB at the official rate, while profits were repatriated at the swap market rate, which tended to follow the currency's black market value. After the merging of the exchange rates, the government also abolished the exchange retention system and the system of turning over foreign exchange earnings to the government.

The unified exchange rate is determined in an interbank market. In April 1994, the China Foreign Exchange Trading System (CFETS) in Shanghai, a nationally integrated electronic system for foreign exchange trading, became operational. As a national market, the CFETS has largely eliminated the fragmentation of the foreign exchange market that resulted from the tendency of local authorities to protect local holdings of foreign exchange (Tseng *et al.* 1994:8). The CFETS is also proof that China has formed a market-driven mechanism for determining RMB exchange rates.

To institutionalise the reformed trading practices and speed up its campaign to re-enter GATT, China issued its first trade law in May 1994, which was designed to fulfil the two basic demands of GATT: transparency and uniformity. The trade law emphasises market measures over administrative means for the management of trade. With the new trade law, a uniform, fair, and free trade policy is expected to take shape in China.

From December 1996, the RMB has been made convertible under current account. Under the new system, foreign exchange for trade transactions can be purchased from designated banks upon presentation of valid trading documents. This change, together with the exchange rate unification which took place two years earlier, led to a more market-based exchange rate system and contributed to the rapid development of exports and imports through more efficient use of resources and increased international competitiveness.

Reform in other areas continued and is ongoing. In particular, the government eliminated all remaining mandatory trade planning in 1994 and gradually established an indirect mechanism for managing foreign trade. More enterprises have gained rights for conducting direct trade.[10]

To realise the ultimate goal of establishing a trade registration system under which official approval for conducting trade would not be required, in February 1997 the Ministry of Foreign Trade and Economic Cooperation (MOFTEC) issued a regulation for implementing a registration system for enterprises operating in the special economic zones.[11] Furthermore, tariffs and the commodity scope of trade quotas and licensing continued to be reduced.

Achievements

Trade system reform over the past two decades has made great achievements in trade and more broadly.

Reducing anti-export bias

The success of trade system reform has provided convincing evidence that trade liberalisation contributes to trade expansion and improvements in welfare. Several multi-country studies, for example Harrigan and Mosley (1991) and Papageorgiou *et al.* (1991), offer some support for the view that liberalisation and exports are related. The main proposition behind these studies is that liberalisation reduces anti-export bias and thus provides an environment conducive to expansion.

Reducing anti-export bias in China has been achieved through a series of reform and trade policies aimed at eliminating the distortions that resulted from extensive government restrictions on trading activities. The reform programs have become increasingly comprehensive over time and have been implemented gradually.

Reducing anti-export bias has had an enormous effect on trade. Total trade increased from US$20.6 billion in 1978 to US$325.1 billion in 1997, with an average growth rate of 14.8 per cent per annum. Exports increased at an average annual rate of 15.8 per cent and imports at an average annual rate of 13.7 per cent during this period. Trade structure continued to shift in favour of manufactured commodities. The share of manufactures in total exports increased to 87 per cent in 1997 compared with only 49.7 per cent in 1980. Official foreign exchange reserves increased from US$0.8 billion in 1979 to US$140 billion in 1997. China has become the largest recipient of foreign capital among developing countries in recent years and became the 10th largest trading nation in the world in 1997, having risen from 29th in 1978. The Chinese economy has become deeply integrated with the world economy.

Changing role of the state

The centralised planning of imports and exports has been replaced by government guidance and indirect controls (Tseng *et al.* 1994:4).[12] Export incentive schemes characterised by a high degree of decentralisation (and government preferential treatments) were first applied to the special economic zones, then the coastal areas and later other parts of the country. By the mid 1990s, thousands of big SOEs had direct trading rights and non-state sectors, particularly foreign firms, are playing an increasing role in China's foreign trade. To prevent the adverse effects of the tariff structure on the export sector and provide more incentives for exports, the government also adopted a system of duty exemptions and tax rebates for exporters. As a result, an indirect trade management system is taking shape in China.

Table 4.1 Share of goods sold at state-fixed prices, 1978–93
(per cent)

Year	Retail commodities	Agricultural goods	Capital goods
1978	97	94	100
1992	10	15	20
1993	5	10	15

Source: World Bank, 1997e. *China Engaged: integration with the global economy*, World Bank, Washington, DC:Table 1.1.

Tariff reduction

Both tariffs and non-tariff barriers have been gradually reduced. For example, from the tariff reduction announced at the November 1995 meeting of the Asia Pacific Economic Cooperation (APEC), which became effective in 1996, tariff cuts reduced the trade-weighted average tariff from 28.1 per cent to 19.8 per cent and the unweighted average from 36 per cent to 23 per cent in 1996, and the latter was further reduced to 17 per cent in October 1997 as the government accelerated the pace of reform (World Bank 1997e:14).

As part of the liberalisation program, import licenses and quantitative import restrictions (QRs) have been removed from a wide range of commodities since the early 1990s. For those commodities still subject to import controls, such as machinery and electronic equipment, new regulations for their administration were implemented that narrowed the scope of controls and simplified import procedures (Tseng *et al.* 1994:10).

Price linkage

A link between domestic and international prices has been established through price system reforms (Chai and Sun 1993:5). Such a link was virtually nonexistent in China before 1978. Price reforms since the mid 1980s mean that domestic prices for more than 90 per cent of imported goods are now linked to (and affected by) world prices. This link may imply a narrowing of price differentials, although trade barriers and other costs continue to drive a wedge between the two (World Bank 1997e:8).

Comparative advantage

The self-sufficiency policy and associated distortions in the pre-reform period prevented China from exploiting its comparative advantage in the market, particularly in the area of labour-intensive products. The increasing degree of marketisation as a result of institutional changes and trade liberalisation led to the conformity of China's trade pattern to its comparative advantage (Zhang 1993; Song 1996a). Such conformity has been the main reason for the rapid changes in the commodity composition of China's foreign trade, in particular its exports of labour-intensive products.

Trade, investment and standard of living

Trade reform and liberalisation, accompanied by a shift of development strategy away from heavy industries, completely altered the relationship between foreign trade, investment and the standard of living. In the pre-reform period, foreign trade acted as a mechanism for transferring resources from the consumer goods sectors, including agriculture, to the industrial sector through the selling of agricultural and primary products and the purchase of manufactured goods. Because the increased output comprised mainly producer goods, the growth of foreign trade and investment was limited by the extent to which the standard of living could be lowered. Therefore, the sharp rises in investment and foreign trade at that time often proved unsustainable (Hsu 1989:15).

The economic climate is fundamentally different now. Investment—including foreign direct investment (FDI)—boosts foreign trade which in turn helps sustain an increased scale of investment and capital formation in the Chinese economy each year. More importantly, the link between and growth of trade and investment has been accompanied by an extraordinary improvement in the standard of living of the Chinese people. The significance of this for China's foreign trade and investment is evident.

Opening of financial services market

Gradual opening of its financial service market is China's commitment to liberalising its services trade and the government has been adopting measures to implement the liberalisation plans in recent years. For example, by 1997 the government had approved nine foreign banks to deal with RMB transactions in the Shanghai Pudong area, marking the beginning of a gradual opening of China's financial sector to foreign competition and a new phase of China's financial system reform. In July 1997, the government approved the first joint venture trading company in Shanghai and by the end of the same year there were four such trading companies operating in Shanghai and Shenzhen. Also in 1997, the government issued a regulation allowing foreign asset assessment institutions to set up joint ventures or joint cooperation for asset assessment in China (Zhao 1998:198).

Economic benefits

The economic benefits generated by the openness of the economy are enormous and can be summarised as follows. First, an increasing level of exports has loosened the foreign exchange constraint. This in turn has enabled China both to improve its balance of payments position and to absorb foreign resources including imports of capital goods. Second, greater contact with foreign competitors has exerted pressure on Chinese export industries to increase efficiency and to improve the quality of their products. Third, trade expansion has been conducive to greater resource utilisation in China: export growth has led to resources being reallocated to the most efficient sectors of the economy in which China has a comparative advantage. Finally, export growth has promoted the emergence of greater economies of scale for Chinese firms, which in turn tends to raise productivity (Wang 1993:73; Lardy 1992:8 and Song 1996b:194). Based on these points, it can be said that the rapid growth of exports has positively contributed to economic growth in China (see Figure 4.1).[13]

Emerging overseas investments

With trade reform and much deepened integration with the world economy, capital has started to chase investment opportunities offshore. Other factors that contribute to an increase in China's overseas investment include high levels of domestic savings and international reserves, China's comparative advantage in certain areas and competitive pressures on the world market. By the end of 1998, a total of 5666 enterprises had invested overseas, with contracted total investment reaching US$6.33 billion. Investment areas include manufacturing, trade, resource exploration, processing and assembly, transport, tourism and food (*People's Daily*, 1 March 1999:2).

In summary, trade reform over the past twenty years has played a dual role in the reshaping of the Chinese economy. First, trade liberalisation has, through the improved allocation of domestic resources, enlarged the external economy, raised the standard of living and strengthened the national economy. Second, trade reform and liberalisation have, through the requisite changes to the domestic economy, become an impelling force to domestic reform.

Trade reform has been accompanied by a gradual reduction of domestic distortions, although continued distortions still limit the scope and extent of further improvement in the allocation of domestic resources. The result is a better utilisation of production resources.

The process of trade liberalisation has been periodically disrupted by macroeconomic instabilities (mainly in the form of excess demand, high inflation and the imposition of government controls over trade) in the 1980s and the early 1990s. A policy implication is that a prerequisite for a successful trade liberalisation program is the maintenance of macroeconomic stability.

Finally, trade reform had been both incremental and *ad hoc* in the 1980s (Lardy 1992:3). But the gains from the transition to a more open economy are evident. Deeper and increased participation in the world economy gradually paved the way for the introduction of more comprehensive reform programs, illustrated by the reform measures taken in the mid 1990s.

New challenges

New challenges facing the government in deepening trade system reform include both internal and external constraints.

Domestic constraints

In the 1980s and early 1990s, China experienced several periods of excess demand leading to domestic inflation that tended to undermine the opening of China to the world economy. Excess demand led to a deterioration of the trade account and to the imposition of more ad hoc controls on trade to prevent a depletion of China's foreign exchange reserves (Lardy 1992:139). However, since the end of 1997, China has faced a completely different but equally devastating situation, namely excess supply, which has been manifested by weak domestic demand.[14] Weak demand has been compounded by over-capacity in many industries, poor economic performance (particularly of SOEs), financial risks, increasing unemployment and a slowdown of economic growth.

Past experience shows that a smooth transformation of economic and trade system requires macroeconomic stability. It is also conditional on relatively high economic growth, though neither too high nor too low economic growth rates are the most ideal for reform programs. This implies that growth targets and reform objectives are not always compatible. For example, a rapid growth rate may sacrifice the progress of reform if it arises from low quality and inefficient growth. On the other hand, reform objectives have to be balanced with other broad objectives of a transitional economy such as social stability. There is also a time dimension to the balancing act between reform and growth, that is, achieving a balance between short, medium and long-term objectives. The current domestic constraints to reform reflect the fact that the Chinese economy has reached a stage where a more delicate balance between growth and reform targets needs to be sought and maintained (Song 1998c:7).

Figure 4.1   Contribution of exports to economic growth, 1990-98
(percentage points)

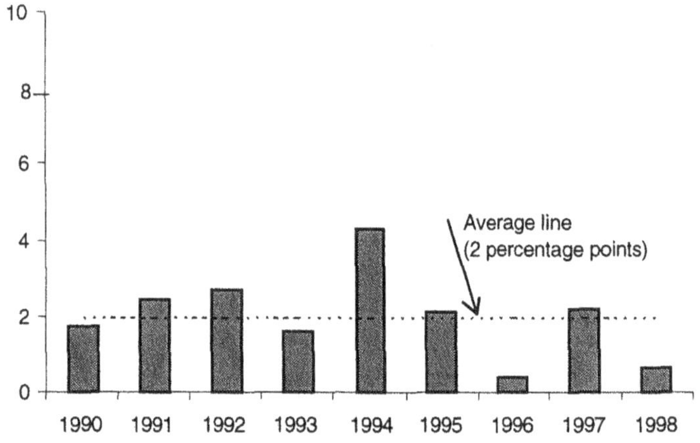

Source: Author's calculations based on United Nations Trade data at international Economic Databank, The Australian National University, Canberra; State Statistical Bureau, 1998. *Statistical Yearbook of China*, China Statistical Publishing House, Beijing.

External constraints

Weak domestic demand and a slowing of trade growth due to the financial crisis in East Asia have posed new challenges to the ongoing trade system reform and liberalisation program in China. Newly released figures show that China began to feel the impact of the financial crisis in 1998; in particular its export growth lost momentum throughout that year. China's overall foreign trade volume fell 0.4 per cent in 1998—the first decline in 15 years—to US$323.9 billion. Exports inched up 0.5 per cent from 1997 to US$183.8 billion, in the same year recording the lowest annual growth rate since 1983, while imports were down 1.5 per cent to US$140.2 billion (*China Daily*, 24 February 1999).

To combat weak domestic demand and the deterioration of external trade, the government has adopted more expansionary monetary and fiscal polices, but refrained from using exchange rate policy, which had been an effective means of adjusting the over-valued RMB exchange rate throughout the reform period before the Asian crisis.

Previous experience shows that exchange rate devaluation plays an important role in the process of trade liberalisation. This is because

a real devaluation is crucial for stimulating the growth of exports that, in turn, facilitates the liberalisation program. Particularly when the degree of protection of import competing industries is reduced as part of a trade liberalisation package, the expansion of exports is helpful in avoiding balance of payments pressures that would otherwise tend to undermine the liberalisation program (Lardy 1992:115).

A large trade surplus and capital inflows continued to produce a strong performance from China's balance of payments in 1998, but the ongoing slowdown of export growth is of concern.

It is important to note that trade reform and liberalisation have led to a rapid expansion of foreign trade in the past twenty years. But it is also important to recognise that sustained growth of trade will result from deepening trade system reform. From this perspective, maintaining the growth momentum of foreign trade in the next few years will be crucial to the success of the ongoing trade system reform at this stage of development.

China's export prospects will continue to rely on strong world demand and further improvements in productivity and competitiveness within the economy (Song 1998a:19). There will be increasing pressure for China to upgrade its industrial structure, produce high value-added and high quality products and further expand its trade destinations. China's imports will depend on the growth of national income and industrial outputs as well as the success of reform measures to further open up the domestic market.

Unfinished tasks

There are still some tasks to be completed before China can enjoy an open, transparent and efficient trade system. Some of the constraints outlined in the previous section make it even harder for the government to accomplish these tasks.

Accession to WTO

After twenty years of economic reform and nearly 13 years of endeavour, China is yet to be admitted to the WTO. There is general agreement that China needs the WTO in order to obtain more benefits from trade and carry out further its reform programs and the WTO needs China in order to strengthen the multilateral trade system. But substantial differences remain on the conditions under which China is to be admitted to the organisation.

It is true that China has made great achievements in developing its foreign trade over the past 20 years without being a member of GATT/WTO. But this fact does not and should not diminish the urgency of resolving the accession issue for China for two main reasons. First, China has come to a stage where more comprehensive reform programs are needed. China's accession to WTO would be conducive to enhancing such reform programs addressing the institutional, economic and legal frameworks underlying the Chinese system. Second, as a large trader and big emerging market, China's participation in the WTO before the new round of trade negotiations begins would help facilitate the trade organisation's ongoing and forthcoming negotiations on many trade and related issues such as anti-dumping, environmental protection, agricultural protection and service trade, and would therefore strengthen the effectiveness of the WTO.

A proper solution to resolving China's membership issue would be to 'allow relatively long phase-in periods for dismantling the barriers protecting China's most sensitive sectors, but to insist on more rapid reduction of trade barriers in less sensitive sectors and immediate reforms with respect to transparency, trading rights, and other systemic features of China's trading system' (Lardy 1996:180).

Liberalisation of the capital market

China has opened its current account but refrained from a quick opening of its capital account because the conditions for capital account liberalisation have not been in place (Song 1998b:115). This position has been further strengthened by the East Asian financial crisis in which the vulnerability of early capital market liberalisation has been shown. 'It is a lesson of the crisis that the strengthening of financial institutions should proceed on an early timetable, in advance of complete convertibility on capital account' (Garnaut 1998:357). This is particularly true for China, whose financial institutions are in need of an overhaul (see Hasenstab, Chapter 6).

Meanwhile, considering the need as well as benefits of opening its capital account, China continues to adhere to the principle of making the RMB fully convertible in the future. A practical solution is to treat capital account liberalisation not as instantaneous but as a gradual process, analogous to the methods used in the opening of the current account (Hanson 1995:401). By adopting this approach, China can mimimise some of the side effects of the mismatch between current and capital account liberalisation, such as adjustment costs.

For example, the liberalisation process could start by relaxing controls over long-term capital inflows ahead of short-term capital inflows. Similarly, the relaxation of controls over foreign direct investment should be preceded by relaxing controls over portfolio capital inflows; trade financing preceded by financial loans; stock transactions preceded by security transactions. Financial liberalisation, especially the opening of the capital market and the relaxation of short-term capital flows, should be implemented last in the whole process of realising full convertibility of the capital account (Chen 1998b:359).

The role of the private sector

Over the past 20 years, trade reform has focused more on shifts in trade policy and the behaviour of SOEs in production and trade. While increasing numbers of SOEs were granted direct trade rights, private enterprises continued to be denied these rights. Many of these private enterprises are export-oriented firms and they have had to export their products via enterprises with foreign trade rights.

Due to the restructuring of the economy, especially ownership reform, private enterprises in China are emerging as a new growth source in the economy. But their role in China's foreign trade is still hampered by slow progress in granting them much-needed foreign trade rights. Further difficulties faced by private firms include obtaining finance.

Things began to change in early 1999. As part of reform measures to change the way in which China manages its trade activities, and to encourage private enterprises to participate more actively in foreign trade, 20 private manufacturers were granted export and import rights in early January 1999. This was the first time since 1957 that non-public enterprises were entitled to conduct foreign trade independently, setting them on an equal footing with their state-owned and collectively owned counterparts. The much lower operation costs, more flexible trading methods and greater financial incentives of the private firms will put considerable pressure on SOEs (*China Daily*, 5 January 1999).

Just one month later, in February 1999, another 41 private enterprises were granted foreign trade rights (*China Daily*, 10 February 1999). The government's relaxation of control over trade rights for private firms at the beginning of 1999 represents a significant step in the reformation of the trade system. However, much more needs to be done to nourish this rapidly emerging and dynamic sector of the economy.

China's private sector emerged in the late 1970s and has grown quickly in the past 20 years. By the end of 1997, there were a total of 960,000 registered private firms in China, employing 13.49 million workers. The share of the non-state sector in total GDP increased from 0.9 per cent in 1978 to 24.2 per cent in 1997 (*People's Daily*, 23 January

1999). But, in a country where production and commercial activities have been dominated by SOEs for decades, there is still much discrimination against private enterprises in areas such as business registration and financing. It remains a big task to allow direct and wider participation by private firms in China's foreign trade.

Need for comprehensive reform

The ultimate goals of trade system reform cannot be achieved without the success of more comprehensive reform of many parts of the Chinese economy including the financial and banking systems, fiscal system, taxation system, price system, enterprise system and bureaucratic system. The experience of trade system reform over the past twenty years suggests that lack of reform in other areas could slow the progress of trade reform. For example, further reduction of government protection has been restrained by the lack of progress in reforming many inefficient SOEs. Another example is that the incompatibility of China's enterprise system, contract system, taxation system and personnel management system with standard international practice has hindered the implementation of some trade reform measures such as national treatment.

Equally important is to have in place a set of effective and efficient macroeconomic policy mechanisms aimed at managing an open economy in an indirect way. Such policies include monetary policy, fiscal policy, exchange policy and trade policy. With such mechanisms in place, China's economic activities in general and foreign trade in particular will eventually be free from direct administrative controls and interference. However, building these policy mechanisms hinges on a gradual but sustained development of markets (for goods as well as factors of production). At present, markets are expanding but not sufficiently for indirect policy mechanisms to be effective. There remains much room for government direct controls and interference over economic and trade activities.

Building a modern trade system also requires a transparent and effective legal framework under which new laws and regulations can be established and enforced. To become more integrated with the world economy and continue to benefit from such integration, China needs to address issues such as the protection of intellectual property rights (patents, trademarks, industrial designs and publications).

Progress has been made with regard to the establishment of regulations governing trade activities. For example, the Trademark Law came into force in March 1983, the first Patent Law became effective in April 1985, the Copyright Law came into force in June 1991 and the Law on Protection Against Unfair Competition became effective in December 1993. China also issued the legislation of border protection in September 1994. Under this legislation, goods that infringe on intellectual property rights are prohibited from being imported and exported (Huang 1996:223).

But problems remain. Huang (1996) summarises them as a lack of force behind law enforcement, local protection of copyright infringements, insufficient enterprise awareness of intellectual property rights and intellectual property rights protection, insufficient consumer awareness of intellectual property rights protection, lack of professional personnel, and incompleteness of legislation. Resolution of these issues is a necessary condition for China's trade system to effectively operate on a sound legal basis.

In summary, progress has been made on all fronts but China still faces formidable tasks in fully accomplishing reforms.

Conclusion

Deepened domestic reform and continued trade liberalisation will provide an institutional guarantee for accomplishing these unfinished tasks. In particular, further reforms are needed to carry out more extensive structural adjustments, enhance competition, reduce the protection of non-tariff barriers, further open up the service sector, including financial services, to foreign competition and increase the transparency of the trading system particularly the import system,[15] and build the rules-based trade system. APEC trade liberalisation and China's accession to the WTO offer two important vehicles for China to fulfil these tasks.

Notes

* Comments made by Ron Duncan are gratefully acknowledged.
[1] See the discussion in Shi (1998:158).
[2] Part of this section is taken from the section of trade system reform in China in Song (1996b) with updating.

[3] Processing trade continues to account for a large proportion of China's foreign trade.

[4] Some studies such as Shi (1998) and Li (1996) treat this period as part of stage one of the trade system reform.

[5] There are still debates about whether the contract system was a necessary step in reforming SOEs or whether it actually went astray and therefore delayed the reform of SOEs (see Renwei, Chapter 9).

[6] When China established an import licensing system in 1988, it covered 53 commodities accounting for about one-third of China's total imports. In 1992, the total number of commodities that were subject to import licensing was reduced by 16 (Shi 1998:166).

[7] By the end of 1993, China publicised 47 internal documents on imports and exports which were still in use, abandoned 122 such documents and promised to publicise all internal documents within one year (Shi 1998:166).

[8] This stage of reform will probably end with China's accession to WTO and China will enter a new phase of reform thereafter.

[9] In 1998, the government closed down the remaining foreign exchange swap markets.

[10] For example, by the end of 1997 the number of enterprises that had rights for conducting foreign trade reached 13,000 (Shi 1998:169).

[11] From January 1999, the government planned to extend the trade registration system to 6800 large industrial enterprises (*People's Daily*, 1 March 1999).

[12] Mandatory planning for exports was abolished in 1991; at the same time state budgetary subsidies to foreign trade corporations for exports were also eliminated. By 1992, planning for imports covered only 11 broad product groups, accounting for about 18 per cent of total imports. It was further reduced to about five broad product groups in 1993 (see Tseng *et al.* 1994:4).

[13] On average, exports contributed 2 percentage points to the average real GDP growth of 10 per cent for the period 1990–98.

[14] By January 1999, the benchmark retail price index was in negative territory for the 16th consecutive month. It sank by 2.8 per cent in that month, compared to a 2.6 per cent fall for 1998 as a whole (*China Daily*, 15 February 1999).

[15] After China's accession to the WTO, the coverage of non-tariff barriers would fall dramatically, according to the Chinese government. After full phase-in, the only significant remaining measure would be state trading, mainly in agriculture, which is covered by special provisions under the WTO (World Bank 1997e:15).

State-owned enterprise reform

Yiping Huang[*]

China's agricultural sector was the first to experience significant success from reform, but initial reform efforts in the late 1970s were directed at state-owned enterprises (SOEs). In 1978, when farmers started to experiment—secretly and illegally—with the now famous household responsibility system (HRS) in several villages in Anhui province, the government was already introducing the first set of policy experiments with SOEs in Sichuan province and then in other places in the following years. The government's rationale for focusing on reform was obvious—the state sector dominated the Chinese economy in terms of both production and urban employment, so it was logical to think that the success of reform would be based on the smooth transformation of SOEs.

The path of SOE reform in the following two decades, however, was far more complicated than that of agricultural reform. In many years during the reform period, especially in the early 1990s, SOE reform was assigned top policy priority but failed to achieve policy objectives fully. After twenty years, SOE reform is still one of the most difficult tasks facing the Chinese government.

The state sector experienced significant changes during the reform period. On the one hand, the state sector expanded significantly. Output of industrial SOEs grew at 6.5 per cent per annum between 1978 and

1997 which, though lower than gross domestic product (GDP) growth, was respectable by any standard. The net value of capital stock (at current prices) rose by 16 per cent per annum between 1985 and 1997, while total employment first increased steadily and then stagnated. The state sector remains the major contributor to government revenue. On the other hand, the relative importance of the state sector declined sharply. The share of SOEs in the country's industrial output dropped from 78 per cent in 1978 to 27 per cent in 1997. SOEs now only dominate in a handful of industries such as oil and gas mining and processing, transportation equipment manufacturing, and electricity and water. The share of all state-owned units in urban employment also declined, but at a much slower rate, from 78 per cent in 1978 to 63 per cent in 1997.

The reform tasks were (and remain) more complicated in the state sector. Old problems such as lack of incentive and production inefficiency remain, and new problems have arisen, such as forfeiture of state assets and a rise in loss-making. These become increasingly heavy burdens on the economy through their impact on the government budget, the financial sector and the efficiency of resource allocation. When Zhu Rongji announced his dramatic reform plans in early 1997, including completion of SOE reform within three years, even with the anticipation of possible 'landmines and abysses' ahead the Chinese government already had problems. The government realised that it could no longer nurture the inefficient SOEs without seriously compromising prospects for the Chinese economy.

A review of past reform experiences and their impact is no easy task since SOE reform in China has been such a controversial subject in the literature. Economists disagree on almost everything, ranging from the effectiveness of past policies to the direction of future reform (see Table 5.1). There are two opposing judgments about SOE productivity performance during the reform period. While some economists believe that productivity growth was significant, others present cases for stagnant or even negative productivity growth. There is no disagreement about the worsening financial performance of SOEs. Some economists attribute increased loss-making to increased market competition, others suggest that undisciplined spending behaviour of the enterprises is a more significant cause. China's gradual approach to reform has generally been approved of by academics given its favourable outcomes in comparison with the reforms in Eastern Europe and the former Soviet Union (EEFSU).

The exact contributions made by SOEs are, however, not clear. Some economists believe the importance of SOEs lay in their role as a safety net, and the role that the safety played in the smooth progress of other reforms; others point to the increasing burdens imposed by SOEs on the macroeconomy, including fiscal deficits, a weak financial sector and macroeconomic instability. Most economists believe that privatisation is a necessary step in the transformation of the state sector. But there are also strong arguments among Chinese economists that ownership is not a necessary condition for efficient firms and that SOEs can perform efficiently if they are provided with a fair and competitive market environment.

Table 5.1 Controversies about China's state sector reform

Issue 1: Productivity performance

Argument I	Total factor productivity growth was significant
Argument II	Productivity stagnated

Issue 2: Causes of rising loss-making

Argument I	Increased competition was the dominant factor
Argument II	Over-spending on wages was a more significant cause

Issue 3: Macroeconomic contribution

Argument I	The state sector served as a safety net for China's reform
Argument II	The state sector was an important macroeconomic destabiliser

Issue 4: Importance of privatisation

Argument I	SOEs can perform efficiently in a fair and competitive market
Argument II	Privatisation is an inevitable reform step

Reform experiences

A small group of outspoken Chinese economists began to voice ideas about reforming the SOE system from as early as the late 1950s. In a paper first published in 1957, Gu Zun pointed out that the root of the inefficiency problems of the SOE sector and the whole Chinese economy lay in the implementation of central planning and the government's direct intervention in enterprise management (Gu 1957). He recommended that compulsory production plans and state prices be abolished to leave prices freely floating; that returns to workers in an enterprise be linked with its profitability; and that SOEs make production decisions according to changes in prices. In 1961, Sun Yefang also suggested that enterprise operation should be left to managers, while the state plan should focus on new investment (Sun 1961). He further argued that profits should be taken as the core indicator of enterprises' performance.[1]

Reform of the SOE sector was seen as one of the most important challenges once reform had begun. The reformist economists reached a consensus that the SOEs must be transformed from administrative units to independent economic identities. Xue (1981) argued that SOE reform was the most important of the two problems urgently requiring solution in economic reform, and that the objective of reform was to transform SOEs into truly live economic management units. Dong (1985) proposed that one crucial task of economic reform was to make SOEs relatively independent commodity producers. Jiang (1980) argued for an 'enterprise-based economy' in which enterprises should have independent management and accounting under state leadership and monitoring. He even recommended that reform should grant SOE workers a corporate interest in their firms.

Detailed reform measures proposed at that stage focused almost exclusively on expanding enterprise autonomy and sharing profits between the state and enterprises. Reform programs drafted by 'think tank' groups were almost all related to enterprise autonomy, with complementary reforms in prices, taxation, and planning to follow later (Naughton 1995). Ideas of creating incentives for SOEs were reflected in proposals for both profit-retention at the enterprise level and floating wage rates at the employee level. As noted by Wu (1993b) and Naughton (1995), these early discussions and proposals were heavily influenced by the Yugoslav-style worker management model.

The responsibility system

China's SOE reform was started in Sichuan province where, in October 1978, a program of expanded enterprise autonomy was introduced to six factories. The experiment defined that, after fulfilling state plans, these SOEs would have certain flexibilities in deciding about production plans, product marketing, worker employment and technological innovation. They would also share the profits according to specified plan and above-plan profit retention rates. The number of SOEs experimenting with this new system increased to 100 in Sichuan province from the beginning of 1979. Because the above-plan profit retention rate was higher than the plan rate, this system also had the potential to punish previously more profitable firms. From 1980, the provincial government also started to adopt a unified profit retention rate. At the same time, there were also experiments with changing profit remittances to taxes in some SOEs.

Learning from the experiences in Sichuan province, the central government began its own program in eight firms in Beijing, Tianjin and Shanghai from May 1979. The content of this program was similar to that of Sichuan. In July that year, the central government announced a new responsibility system for profits and losses, the core of which was that SOEs would have the right to retain a share of profits, enjoy accelerated depreciation and have the right to sell above-plan output (Xu and Li 1996). By June 1980, the number of SOEs adopting this responsibility system had risen to 6,600, accounting for about 16 per cent of SOEs, 60 per cent of SOE output and 70 per cent of SOE profits. In early 1981, about 42,000 SOEs chose the system of 'responsibility for profits and losses'. By 1983, almost all SOEs had adopted this responsibility system. In May 1984, in an effort to consolidate and improve the responsibility system, the government further expanded SOEs' decision-making rights in nine areas including production planning, raw material purchasing, product marketing, allocation of retained funds, determination of wages and bonuses, cross-region and cross-industry cooperation, employee recruitment and appointment of middle level managers, disposition of redundant assets, and exporting (Xu and Li 1996). In September 1985, the state further announced that SOEs could determine their production structure according to market demand and enterprises' comparative advantages, conditional on fulfilment of state plans.

To complement the reforms, autonomy and incentive, two steps of 'tax for profit' reforms were carried out. In February 1983, a reform experiment was introduced in a number of SOEs, such that they would no longer pay fees for usage of fixed assets and working capital but would pay a 55 per cent tax on their total profits. The after-tax profits, however, were still shared by the state and the enterprises in certain proportions. The proportion of after-tax profit remittance was calculated from their 1982 performance. This was called the first step of 'tax for profit'. The second step of 'tax for profit' was introduced in September 1984, the main purpose of which was to replace the previous co-existence of tax and profit remittance with a simple tax system. Enterprises were to adopt 'four taxes and two fees': annual fees for fixed assets and working capital financed from budgetary grants, a 50 per cent income tax, taxes on real estate, vehicle tax and adjustment tax.

Meanwhile, the '(repayable) loan for (free) grants' reform was also initiated. A few experimental projects were set up in November 1979. At the end of 1984, a decision was made that all state investment would be on a repayable basis, allocated through the state banking system.

Implementation of the responsibility system and associated reforms was crucial to providing both autonomy and incentives to the enterprises, and achieved at least partial success. But there were a number of problems. First, at a time when the central plan still controlled a dominant proportion of SOEs' activities, enterprises could hardly exercise autonomy. The objectives of the state plan and the SOEs were often different; when they were in conflict the state would intervene in enterprise management (Wu 1993b). From the point of view of the government, if prices were seriously distorted, managers could not achieve optimal resource allocation even when they had the freedom to make production decisions. This provided further reasons for state intervention. SOEs, therefore, remained effectively subordinated to the bureaucratic apparatus and continued to be bound by the overlapping control mechanisms (Naughton 1995).

Second, the reforms actually provided little incentive to SOEs. The reform of 'bank loans for budgetary grants' did not succeed because state banks could not effectively force unprofitable SOEs to repay their loans. The system after the first step of 'tax for profit' was rather complicated and often left the SOEs with very little retained profit, while the second step of 'tax for profit' implied that profitable enterprises ended up with relatively low marginal retention rates because of the adjustment tax. Within SOEs, relaxation of state controls over wages and, especially, bonuses in the early 1980s helped to steadily raise workers' incomes and living standards. But in terms of reforming the incentive mechanism, the impact of these policy changes was very limited.

Third, the early reforms did not define clearly the responsibilities of SOEs after the autonomy was expanded, apart from 'responsibility for profits or losses' (which was again difficult to enforce under the circumstances). This became a concern because, if not properly disciplined, managers and employees would engage in opportunistic behaviour for short-term benefits and might act against the long-term interests of the enterprises. Overspending on wages and bonuses, for instance, was widely observed during the reform period (Lin *et al.* 1997; Sachs and Woo 1997).

The contract system

Policy discussions in the mid 1980s turned to enhancing the responsibility component of the responsibility system and a number of proposals were put forward including the contract system, the shareholding system, the asset responsibility system and others such as leasing and bankruptcy. At the time the debate was most intense between proponents of the contract system and the shareholding system. Supporters of the contract system argued that, while maintaining state ownership, SOEs would perform efficiently with clearly defined responsibilities, rights and benefits of both the state and the enterprises by contracts (Yang 1990). Proponents of the shareholding system argued that it was a matured enterprise institution after 200 years of development in market economies. The shareholding system could solve completely the problem of inseparability between government administration and enterprise business and promote optimal resource allocation (Li 1987). The 'asset responsibility system' recommended consisted of three important aspects: asset evaluation, return sharing and asset responsibility. This new system was intended to solve the problems of incomplete information and the 'soft-budget' constraint (Hua *et al.* 1986).

101

State-owned enterprise reform in the second half of the 1980s was dominated by the implementation of the contract system. A limited number of SOEs also experimented with the other proposals. The reason for the wide introduction of the contract system at that time was partly because it maintained state ownership, so politically it was more feasible, and partly due to the encouragement of the success in rural China. It was implemented against a background of industrial recession in 1986 (Dong and Tang 1992). The responsibility system and the contract system have some common elements, but the latter was an improvement on the basis of the former. The contract system emphasised the 'responsibilities' of the enterprises while retaining the rights and incentives of the responsibility system. The contract system was also more stable: contracts were often signed for three to five years.

In December 1986, the government announced a new policy encouraging adoption of the contract system (Xu and Li 1996). By the end of 1988, about 93 per cent of SOEs had adopted various forms of the contract system. There were five main types of contracts at that time. The first type specified that the contractors must guarantee profit remittances, technological transformation and, sometimes, compulsory plans, while the firms' total wage bills were linked to their profitability. It required the contractors to remit the quota profit regardless of the firms' financial performance.[2] The second type required that enterprises, after paying taxes, had to remit a fixed amount of profit, which increased over time according to an agreed growth rate. The difference between the third type and the second was that the base quotas for profit remittances were fixed over time, but the firms had to share the extra profits with the state based on a retention rate. The fourth type of contract was specifically for loss-making enterprises and set targets of fixed amounts of losses to be subsidised by the state each year. The fifth type of contract emphasised input-output relations and was applied completely to the industries of oil, coal, iron and steel, railway, post and communications, chemical and civil aviation.

At the same time, other forms of enterprise institutions were also under experimentation. In November 1984, one SOE in Shanghai issued shares to the public. In December 1986, seven SOEs in Shanghai formed a shareholding company that was dominated by the state. Other firms in Shanghai also made progress in this direction. Meanwhile, from the mid 1980s, a limited number of small SOEs were leased to collectives or individuals.[3] It was reported that by the end of 1987, about 46 per cent of the small SOEs had been contracted or leased (Xu and Li 1996).

These reforms had some positive impacts on SOEs' performance (Xu and Li 1996), but overall they still did not achieve the objective of turning SOEs into efficient enterprises. The contract system had a number of problems. First, it did not guarantee that SOEs became independent economic identities. Enterprise managers' decisions could be overturned by the state or their supervisory agents, especially with respect to investment and employment. The intervention was in some cases strengthened because the state had the final decision on who would get the contract (Wu 1993b). Second, negotiation of the contracts was extremely difficult. Not only were the two negotiating parties, the state and the contractors, in unequal positions, but also the state lacked necessary information about the operation of the enterprises. Contract terms thus depended significantly on the negotiation process itself. It was even suggested that the contracts were often the outcome of administrative arrangements (Zhou *et al.* 1994). Third, the contracts were often easy to realise when firms performed well, but very hard to implement when firms could not meet the quota for profit remittances. The contract was thus weak as a discipline for governing contractors.[4] Fourth, the contract did not solve the short-term behavioural problems of the managers and employees. Their behaviour was still driven by short-term motivations, impinging on the interests of the owner, the state, and damaging firms' long-term development (Huang *et al.* 1997a). Other explanations were also given for the lack of success of the contract system including lack of a monitoring mechanism, incompleteness in expanding enterprise autonomy, and lack of separation between government administration and enterprise management. In 1991 and 1992, many SOEs had difficulties in renewing or settling new contracts (Dong and Tang 1992).

Why then was the contract system so successful in the countryside but so problematic in the state sector? There are a number of differences between the rural and urban systems to account for the different performance. First, after the household responsibility system was implemented in the countryside, agricultural production was managed by individual households. Management among family members, often by the household head, is relatively easy; management of an SOE with hundreds and even thousands of employees is relatively more complicated. Second, the farm household receives the residual return from land after fulfilling agricultural taxes, state purchase quotas and collective levies. All these remittances are fixed in either quantities or in values and thus there is no need to monitor farm households' operations. Monitoring of SOEs is difficult but critical, considering the possibility of managers manipulating information for either reduced remittances or increased subsidies (Dong and Tang 1992). Third, while the revenue from SOEs has always been an important component of the government budget, the revenue from the agricultural sector was minimal. The probability of government intervention was thus much higher in the SOE sector than the agricultural sector. Finally, the length of contracts was different. In the agricultural sector, the contract term was for 15 years to begin with and later extended for a further 15 years; the initial length of contracts for SOEs was between three and five years. The short-term performance of the household responsibility system and the SOE contract system is very different. However, they share a common long-term problem: contractors' lack of interest in investment for long-term development.

The shareholding system and privatisation

In the early 1990s, the key words in China's discussion of SOE reform were autonomy and monitoring. Monitoring became a new focus because it was recognised that enterprises would hardly fulfil their full responsibilities if there was no effective monitoring (Lin *et al.* 1997; Zhang 1995). Economists focusing on autonomy argued that the lack of success in the SOE sector was mainly because the enterprises did not enjoy sufficient autonomy in decision-making. They sought to solve the issue of autonomy either through further expansion of enterprise autonomy or property rights reform. Economists focusing on monitoring argued that under the current regime SOEs would not perform efficiently without effective monitoring, even with sufficient decision autonomy. They sought to solve the monitoring problem through either property rights reform or the establishment of modern enterprise institutions. In short, economists could be divided into three groups according to their recommendation for further reforms—those supporting the expansion of enterprise autonomy, those supporting improvement of the internal corporate governance, and those supporting the establishment of a competitive environment.

The enterprise autonomy group pledged that full decision autonomy was a necessary and sufficient condition for SOEs to be efficient. It pointed particularly to the administrative intervention in enterprise decisions. Liu (1996) argued that the continued lack of autonomy in SOEs was largely associated with state intervention in enterprise affairs, even though separation of administrative functions from enterprise business had been a policy for at least a decade. He called for leaders to make a decisive move towards the removal of the administrative function from all SOEs.

The internal corporate governance group recommended either privatisation or divestiture. Many economists argued for modern enterprise institutions, with limited shareholding or limited responsibility corporations as the role models. Forming large company groups was also recommended as a way to increase international competitiveness (Macroeconomic Institution 1996). Wu (1993a) and Zhou et al. (1994) proposed to convert the state assets in SOEs to shares controlled by holding companies at various levels of government. The state would thus continue to dominate the former SOEs. Zhang (1995), on the other hand, recommended conversion of state assets into debts owed by SOEs (instead of shares). He suggested that this was not only cost-effective (saving monitoring costs) but also guaranteed stable value-adding in these assets. Zhang further argued that a crucial element of SOE reform was to form a mechanism for selecting the best entrepreneurs to run the firms.

The competitive environment group paid particular attention to the unequal burdens and economic environment for SOEs. Lin et al. (1997) argued against changing SOEs' ownership structure because private ownership is neither a sufficient nor a necessary condition for an enterprise to be efficient. The essential step in China's SOE reform, they suggested, was to create a market environment in which enterprises with all kinds of ownership arrangements could compete with each other in a fair environment in which 'the fittest survives'. Therefore, the main task of SOE reform was to eliminate the existing policy-determined burdens on SOEs so as to create a level-playing field.

From 1994, the government started to adopt a flexible reform approach toward SOEs which was popularly characterised as 'emphasizing the big and liberalizing the small'. This strategy was officially implemented after its confirmation at the 15th Party Congress in October 1997 and the 9th National People's Congress in March 1998. In essence, the policy attempts to maintain about 1,000 large SOEs through the introduction of the 'modern enterprise institution', dominated by the shareholding system, and to privatise the small and medium-sized SOEs through selling, auctioning, merging and bankrupting.

The concept of 'modern enterprise institution' was defined officially to include four important aspects: clearly defined property rights; clear division of autonomy and responsibility; separation of administrative function from enterprise decisions; and scientific management. The dominant form of the new institution was the shareholding system. The government also attempted to alleviate large SOEs' policy-induced burdens. This involved lessening the burden for SOEs disadvantaged by excessive capitalisation, such as converting military plants into civil factories, further liberalising (or adjusting) prices for state-controlled products, such as coal, reducing SOEs' pension burden by building a new pension system, such as one along the lines of the government-preferred Singapore model, which combines contributions from enterprises and individuals, reducing the number of redundant workers by granting enterprises autonomy in employing and dismissing workers, and introducing a new policy, 'state investment for bank loans', to reduce the pressure on SOEs of interest payments.

The policy toward the small and medium-sized SOEs was more liberal. Spontaneous privatisation was, in fact, already underway. The 'Zhucheng model' provides a good example. In 1993, the Zhucheng city government began to establish shareholding companies for all of its SOEs by selling shares to enterprise employees (Zhucheng Municipality Government 1996). Before reform, 60 per cent of the 150 enterprises were in debt to the value of 147 million yuan; 30 SOEs suffered a loss of state assets of 100 million yuan. In 1993, the municipality government sold all its SOEs to enterprise employees. Similarly, Shunde City of Guangdong province offered a very similar 'Shunde model' (Shunde City Government 1997). With the removal of the ideological constraint on ownership reform, it is expected that privatisation of SOEs will accelerate.

Assessment of enterprise performance

Total factor productivity

There are two important issues about SOE production efficiency that are under dispute in the literature. The first issue is the size of total factor productivity (TFP) growth, assuming that there was indeed positive

TFP growth. The second issue is whether this growth could be attributed to the specific reform measures that were implemented.

Researchers have found an amazingly wide range of TFP growth rates (see Table 5.2). The high TFP growth rate in Chen *et al.* (1988b) was based on downward adjustments of official data on labour and capital inputs.[5] From the debate between Woo *et al.* (1993, 1994a) and Jefferson *et al.* (1994), it appears that the high TFP growth rate in Jefferson *et al.* (1992) was the result of using input deflators that understated inputs. Groves *et al.* (1994) and Perkins and Raiser (1995), using input deflators constructed in the manner of Jefferson *et al.* (1992), also found high TFP growth rates.

There is now a growing body of literature reaching the opposite conclusion on productivity performance. Using data aggregated at the city level, Xiao (1991) found productivity in the state sector to be stagnant between 1985 and 1987. He also found a positive statistical relationship between the TFP growth of a city and its share of industrial output produced by non-state enterprises. Employing National Industrial Census data and applying various functional forms, McGuckin *et al.* (1992) uncovered significant negative TFP growth in China's state industry in the period 1980–84. Estimations by Woo *et al.* (1994b) on data from 300 SOEs established that TFP growth was zero at best during 1984–88. More recently, in a comparative analysis of Chinese industry using a survey data set of 967 SOEs, Huang and Meng (1997) found negative TFP growth for the SOEs during 1985–90.

It must be noted that some studies that found productivity improvement found that TFP growth declined over time. Wu and Wu (1994) found that TFP increased in the 1979–84 period but was stagnant in the 1985–92 period. Perkins *et al.* (1993) discovered that the TFP index for industrial SOEs rose from 100 in 1981 to 104 in 1985 and then declined steadily to 81 in 1989.

In a recent study, Huang *et al.* (1998b) attempted to decompose the productivity growth into technological progress and technical efficiency for six sampled industries between 1980 and 1994. It was found that while productivity growth in these industries was in general not very significant, it was mainly achieved through improvements in technical efficiency, and technology largely stagnated.

Besides the disagreement on the actual TFP performance in the SOE sector, there is also an equally contentious debate over the fundamental issue of the actual contribution of reform policies to SOEs' TFP performance. Groves *et al.* (1994) estimated direct links between productivity increases and a range of incentives offered to SOEs. It now appears, however, that these direct links were very tenuous ones. Lee (1990) focused on three SOE reform measures—the contract management system, the managerial responsibility system and the internal contract system. Using a sample of 75 large and medium-sized steel SOEs in 1986, he concluded that the impact on output from any single reform measure was not significant. While the effects of some combinations of reform measures were significant, the magnitudes of the impacts were very small.[6] Using data from 769 SOE surveys for 1980–89, Du and Guo (1995) looked at four particular indicators of reform—the proportion of raw materials purchased from the free market, the share of product marketed to the free market, the proportion of contracted workers in the total workforce, and the profit retention rate. They found that, while the coefficient estimate for the product marketing variable was statistically insignificant, the estimates for the other three policy variables were all significantly negative. Huang and Duncan (1997) identified a longer list of reform measures including market competition, and incentive and autonomy, and used data from 300 enterprises between 1980 and 1992. While they found that some measures contributed positively to SOEs' productive performance, the overall contribution of reform to TFP growth was negligible.[7]

Table 5.2 Selected studies on TFP growth in China's SOEs

Study	Period	Data set	TFP growth (%)
Chen *et al.* (1988c)	1978–85	National industry aggregate	4.0–5.0
Dollar (1990)	1979–82	20 SOEs survey data	1.2
Jefferson *et al.* (1992)	1984–87	City/county aggregate data	2.4
Perkins (1995)	1980–90	300 enterprises survey data	2.7
Li (1997)	1980–89	272 SOEs survey data	4.7
Xiao (1991)	1985–87	City aggregate data	-
McGuckin *et al.* (1992)	1980–84	National industrial census	<0
Woo *et al.* (1994a)	1984–88	300 SOEs survey data	≤0
Huang and Meng (1997)	1986–90	967 SOEs survey data	-2.2
Huang *et al.* (1998b)	1980–94	800 SOEs survey data	0.3

Profitability

The financial performance of the state sector worsened sharply during the reform period. The total losses of industrial SOEs rose from 4.2 billion yuan in 1978 to 34.9 billion yuan in 1990 and 72.7 billion yuan in 1996—an astonishing annual growth rate of 17 per cent between 1978 and 1996 (SSB 1996, 1997). It is widely estimated that in the 1990s, about one-third of SOEs made explicit losses and another one-third made implicit losses (Liu 1996). In 1996, about half of the SOEs became money losers and the state sector as a whole faced a net deficit of 38 billion yuan (SSB 1997).

The poor financial performance of SOEs is not a controversial issue among economists, but the cause of it certainly is. Based on the perception that SOEs experienced positive TFP growth but rising loss-making, Sicular (1995) suggested that SOE managers were hiding their profits. On the other hand, Naughton (1995) and Rawski (1995) have argued that the rising losses were a natural outcome of increased competition from the rising non-state sector, coupled with changes in government policies toward prices, taxation, depreciation and interest payments.

However, Fan and Woo (1996) have pointed out that the competition argument cannot explain why profitability fell across the board, even in heavy industry where there was negligible new entry, and in industries where prices had not fallen. Furthermore, if falling profitability in SOEs was the result of an increasingly competitive market, then similarly low profitability should have been observed in non-state sectors. The fact is that although collective and other (private and joint ventures) enterprises in 1996 had, on the average, assets about 67–70 per cent smaller than that of state enterprises, their profits were 18–23 per cent larger than those of state enterprises.[8] The profit-asset ratios in non-state enterprises (3.1–3.2 per cent) were about four times those of SOEs (0.8 per cent) (SSB 1997).

Huang and Duncan (1999) investigated the empirical relationship between competition and profitability using enterprise survey data. They found no evidence to support a negative correlation. In a later study, Huang (1998b) suggested that the relationship between competition and profitability during economic transition was not the same as that in a conventional market. Increased competition could cause enterprise

Table 5.3 State-owned enterprise profits and real wages,
1985–96

Year	SOE net profit (billion yuan)	Net value of capital	Profit-capital rate (%)	SOE/Collective (1978=100) Real wages	SOE/Collective (1978=100) Labour productivity
1985	70.6	399	17.7	100.0	100.0
1986	63.5	454	14.0	103.2	89.2
1987	72.6	525	13.8	102.1	79.5
1988	81.0	603	13.4	103.6	68.2
1989	56.3	701	8.0	105.3	62.9
1990	3.9	809	0.5	108.3	58.9
1991	3.5	958	0.4	105.9	53.6
1992	16.6	1092	1.5	108.7	44.1
1993	36.5	1340	2.7	108.6	32.3
1994	34.6	1564	2.2	117.8	26.0
1995	12.5	1752	0.7	114.0	23.3
1996	-30.9	2088	-1.5	120.7	19.8

Sources: State Statistical Bureau, 1996, 1997. *Statistical Yearbook of China*, China Statistical Publishing House, Beijing.

profitability to fall or rise depending on the magnitudes of changes in output prices, input prices and input-output coefficients following the introduction of a free market.

Likely, the two fundamental reasons for the worsening financial performance of SOEs were stagnant (or declining) productivity and over-spending on direct and indirect wages. This is partly indicated by the statistics in Table 5.3. Between 1985 and 1996, the relative wages of SOEs to collective enterprises increased by 21 per cent while their relative labour productivity declined by almost 80 per cent. This argument is also supported by a recent investigation of 2,000 loss-making SOEs by China's State Statistics Bureau, which showed that 9.1 per cent of SOEs made losses because of policy factors, 9.2 per cent made losses because of changes in the macroeconomic environment and 81.7 per cent made losses because of mismanagement and inefficiency (Tan 1996).

Macroeconomic implications

The transition of SOEs has obviously contributed to the success of the Chinese economy in its own way. In the early stages of reform, the growing SOEs provided a base for firms that were developing outside the plan. In fact, many successful township and village enterprises (TVEs) started their businesses through sub-contracting from urban SOEs (Perkins 1999). The rapidly increasing demand for inputs by SOEs and for consumption goods by their employees provided expanding purchasing power for goods produced by the non-state sectors. Some SOEs themselves also improved productive efficiency through policy reforms and increased competition with non-state firms (Jefferson *et al.* 1992, 1996; Jefferson and Rawski 1994; Rawski 1994). Another important contribution by SOEs was the provision of a safety net for China's economic reform by containing the redundant workers within the factories (McMillan and Naughton 1992; Naughton 1995). This helped to create a stable socio-political environment for growth elsewhere in the economy.

While the safety net was particularly important, it is debatable whether the Chinese approach followed the most efficient path. The main function of the SOE 'safety net' was to keep redundant workers on an enterprise payroll is order to ensure social stability. It is true that China has a big unemployment problem, especially after taking into account surplus agricultural labour. But China also has a very dynamic non-state sector which created about 210 million new jobs between 1978 and 1996, almost double that of the total SOE workforce in 1996 (SSB 1997:27).[9] In 1997, about 12 million workers were laid off by SOEs but these workers continued to receive a proportion of their wages and enjoy other welfare benefits. By the end of 1997, at least 6 million had found new jobs (Meng 1998). The re-employment problems in some regions in the short run cannot be denied, but a more efficient safety net would be provided by the pooling of enterprise welfare funds under the supervision of a social security system or the Ministry of Civil Affairs. Assuming the current average of 2,000 yuan per annum paid to each laid-off worker, the direct government subsidy to loss-making SOEs could easily support 16 million workers,[10] and would not waste resources on producing unsaleable products.

Examination of the cost of the SOE 'safety net' is more complicated. Some proponents of the cushioning effect provided by SOEs recognised that it meant forcing consumers to buy low quality products for a while (McMillan and Naughton 1992). However, the negative impact of the safety net extend far beyond this.

Woo (1994) argued that the financial weakness of SOEs destabilised the economy through two channels. The first was through the state budget and the second through the banking system. At the beginning of economic reform, SOEs accounted for well above 80 per cent of total budget revenue; this ratio fell to about 60 per cent in the mid 1990s. The budget deficit increased from 8 billion yuan in the Sixth Five-Year Plan period (1981–85) to 59 billion yuan in the Seventh Five-Year Plan period (1986–90), and 195 billion yuan in the Eighth Five-Year Plan period (1991–95) (SSB 1997). SOEs contributed to this rapidly rising budget deficit in two ways: one related to the slow growth of revenue from the SOE sector and the other related to the increasing budget subsidies to SOEs. Direct subsidies to loss-making SOEs rose from 18.2 billion yuan—1.2 per cent of gross national product (GNP)—in 1988, to 84.4 billion yuan—2.4 per cent of GNP—in 1993 (Table 5.4). The widening budget deficit had historically tended to lead to faster monetary growth.

Yin (1995) also noted that SOEs were a constant source of inflationary pressure. He observed that whenever SOEs faced increased competition, they would intensify their lobby for credit, and monetary expansion would result, such as in the mid 1980s and early 1990s. Perkins and Raiser (1995) argued that 'China's high growth rate is at least partly attributable to fortuitous exogenous factors, while its tendency to reproduce costly inflationary episodes may be related to remaining budget softness for industrial state-owned enterprises' (Perkins and Raiser 1995:12).

SOE loss-making had significant implications for the banking system. When SOEs' losses could no longer be fully covered by the budget, they turned to the state banks. Because of the soft-budget constraint, SOE managers were always hungry for investment, regardless of their enterprises' financial performance (Kornai 1980). Their demands on the state banks for financing were often quite persuasive because their demands were couched in terms of the 'safety net' function and the ideological importance of state ownership. The result was that the state banks largely ignored the financing needs of the new, dynamic non-state sector, and focused their lending on SOEs. In an empirical study using city data in the period 1989–91, Wei and Wang (1996) found that the higher a city's initial proportion of SOEs, the higher the growth rate of bank loans going to that city. In the industry as a whole, SOEs accounted for 74 per cent of investment, but produced only one-third of output in 1994 (World Bank 1996).

Perkins and Raiser (1995) estimated the amount of fiscal and banking system subsidies to SOEs between 1986 and 1992.[11] Their lowest estimates showed that total subsidies to industrial SOEs rose from 6 billion yuan in 1980 to 268 billion yuan in 1992. The latter amounted to approximately 10 per cent of GNP in 1992. To realise the enormity of the resource cost, one should note that the total value added by industrial SOEs was only about 14 per cent of GDP in 1996 (SSB 1997:42, 428).

Table 5.4 Losses and subsidies to SOEs in China (billion yuan)

	1980	1986	1988	1990	1991	1992	1993	1996
Losses of industrial SOEs[a]	3.4	5.5	8.2	34.9	36.7	36.9	45.3	72.7
Direct subsidies to deficit SOEs[b]	..	..	18.0	12.4	57.9	50.6	84.4	..
Ratio to GNP (%)[c]	..	..	1.2	0.7	2.7	1.9	2.4	..
Estimated subsidies to industrial SOEs[d]								
Fiscal subsidy	5.4	34.5	48.2	111.8	114.7	167.2	..	..
Monetary subsidy	0.9	28.7	42.3	51.8	85.9	100.5	..	..
Total subsidy	6.3	63.3	90.5	163.6	200.6	267.7	..	..
Ratio to GNP (%)	1.4	6.2	6.1	8.8	9.3	10.0	..	..
Budget deficit[a]	-6.9	-8.3	-13.4	-14.7	-23.7	-25.9	-29.3	-54.8
Ratio to GNP (%)	-1.5	-0.8	-0.9	-0.8	-1.1	-1.0	-0.8	..

Notes: [a]State Statistical Bureau official data; [b]World Bank data; [c]GNP data used in this table all from State Statistical Bureau; [d]Perkins and Raiser (1995) estimates at bond rate.
Sources: State Statistical Bureau, 1997. *Statistical Yearbook of China*, China Statistical Publishing House, Beijing; World Bank, 1995. *Reform and the Role of the Plan in the 1990s*, World Bank Country Study, Washington, DC; Perkins, F. and Raiser, M., 1995. *State Enterprise Reform and Macroeconomic Stability in Transitional Economies*, Economic Division Working Papers, Development Issues 95/1, Research School of Pacific and Asian Studies, The Australian National University, Canberra.

Concluding remarks

China's state sector is yet to achieve its full success, considering its productivity growth and financial performance. But the fact that SOEs did not collapse at the beginning of the reform period shows that they were an important facilitator of China's rapid growth in the following two decades, especially outside the plan system. This role of facilitation came at a cost in terms of fiscal burden, inefficiency in resource allocation, vulnerability of the financial sector and macroeconomic instability.

While the approach of reform without changing the ownership structure might have been favourable during the initial period, property rights reform is now long overdue. It is hard to determine the exact point in time when the Chinese government should have switched its SOE reform approach. But statistics suggest that the overall outcome would be much better if the switch had taken place in the late 1980s or early 1990s. It was after that time that enterprise performance worsened significantly both in terms of productivity and profitability. The reasons for the dramatic change were complicated and were probably a mixture of the following

- widespread excess capacity
- completion of the contract system reform
- development of the market system and intensified competition.

From the early 1990s, SOEs became more a burden than a positive contributor. Most SOEs had accomplished their historical responsibilities.

The cost of the inefficient SOE sector has now been fully recognised by the government, which announced a radical policy in 1998 to complete the reform of SOEs within three years following the principle of 'liberalising the small and emphasising the big'. The government intended to retain about 1,000 large SOEs in key industries and privatise more than 300,000 small and medium-size SOEs through leasing, shareholding, auctioning, merging and bankrupting. This means that both the ownership reform and non-ownership reform approaches, focusing on internal organisational structure and market environment, are adopted.

In 1998, affected by the East Asian financial crisis and weak domestic demand, the pace of SOE reforms slowed significantly. Rapid economic growth and thus fast new job creation, are a critical condition for SOE reform. Both external crises and deflationary effects bite hard on economic growth. In order to achieve its 8 per cent GDP growth target, the government introduced an expansionary fiscal policy to stimulate growth. While China failed only marginally to achieve the growth target, the jobs created by these new infrastructure projects did not help to ease urban unemployment pressure. The economic situation in 1999 and 2000 will probably be much the same. It is likely that China needs more than three years to complete its reform of SOEs.

Apart from the necessary conditions for SOE reform, such as new jobs and a social security system, the government also needs to think more carefully about the transformation of SOEs. While it is reasonable for the government to retain a number of large SOEs in the critical industries for the stability of the national economy, it must be recognised that monopolies do not usually deliver an efficient outcome. Alongside further changes to the management structure of these SOEs, introduction of market competition is the key to improving efficiency. Without transforming them into true market entities (with or without state ownership), including the complete elimination of the soft-budget constraint problem, SOEs can never perform efficiently. Lessons must be drawn from the Japanese *keiretsu* and the Korean *chaebol*, especially after the East Asian crisis.

Reform of the small and medium-size SOEs is easier and it can be expected that the pace of privatisation of these firms will be accelerated once China's macroeconomic situation improves. A more crucial issue, however, is how to ensure a favourable environment once they are privatised. The current resource allocation system which discriminates against non-state—especially private—firms must be corrected.

Zhu Rongji was right in coordinating the reform tasks in a single package, since the problems are closely related, especially fiscal, enterprise and financial problems. Some dramatic measures may also be needed, because Chinese reform proceeded in such a way as to tackle the easy tasks first and leave the difficult ones for later. But radical reform is neither in China's tradition, nor is it an easy task. Given the difficulties of the reform tasks and the structure of the political economy, it will probably take a few more years for China to accomplish SOE reform and reforms in other areas.

Notes

* This paper draws on earlier joint works with Ron Duncan, Fang Cai, Wing Thye Woo and K.P. Kalirajan. The author benefited from discussions with Weiying Zhang, Chunlin Zhang, Wenquan Yiin, Xuedong Ding, Justin Yifu Lin, Hongling Wang, Zuoyuan Zhang, Yongzheng Yang and Thomas Rawski. Funding for research was by the Australian Agency for International Aid (AusAID) and is gratefully acknowledged.

115

[1] Both Gu and Sun were later purged for their right-wing views.

[2] In reality, however, doing so was difficult as many contractors of poorly performing SOEs were not able to deliver the required amount of profits to the state.

[3] Small SOEs in this context were defined as firms with fixed assets of 5 million yuan and profits of 500 thousand yuan in Beijing, Tianjin and Shanghai; fixed assets of 4 million yuan and profits of 400 thousand yuan in fourteen independently planned cities; and fixed assets of 3 million yuan and profits of 300 thousand yuan in all other regions (Xu and Li 1996).

[4] On the other hand, the contractors also faced social pressures if they pocketed the large rewards defined in the contracts (Dong and Tang 1992).

[5] Lau and Brada (1990) also found high positive TFP growth, but this is to be expected because they used the reconstructed data of Chen *et al.* (1988c).

[6] All three studies by Lee (1990), Du and Guo (1995) and Huang and Duncan (1997) applied value-added/gross output production functions. Specific reform measures were then included as additional explanatory variables for examination of their contribution to output and productivity.

[7] There was substantial TFP growth in the Huang and Duncan (1997) study because they employed an input deflator constructed in the manner of Jefferson *et al.* (1992).

[8] These were based on the profits of each sector, ignoring losses by deficit firms. The net profits for state, collective and private sectors were, respectively, -31, 24 and 26 billion yuan in 1996 (SSB 1997).

[9] This has not taken into account a large number of labour migrants not registered with the government.

[10] According to Perkins (1999), direct government subsidies to SOEs was 32.2 billion yuan in 1995.

[11] In calculating the direct and indirect subsidies, they used both the government bond rate and international interest rate to capture the financial cost of capital to the Chinese government and the economic opportunity cost of capital to China respectively.

Financial system reform and implications

Michael Hasenstab

From 1978–98 China dramatically changed its mechanism for distributing capital within the economy from a strictly planned bureaucratic system to a hybrid of state and market allocation by dismantling the credit plan and promoting the development of new financial markets to service changes in the real sector. After creating a semi-commercial banking sector and private capital markets it became possible to begin securitising financial assets in the form of loans and securities and to increasingly do away with outright government transfers and subsidies. Although residual non-performing loans and an incomplete privatisation of the state-owned sector continue to limit the government's ability to liberalise the financial sector fully, and government intervention and market manipulation still occur, irreversible steps have been made towards a more comprehensive liberalisation in the future.

Reform of the financial sector has had several very important effects on the Chinese economy in the last twenty years. First, laying the foundations to create a real central bank, deepening government debt and money markets, and partially commercialising bank operations greatly improved the government's ability to direct monetary policy through open market operations. Second, market-driven securities markets provide essential information through real prices and capital to the real sector in a more efficient and profit maximising manner. Finally, government and private securities markets are essential for both the re-capitalisation and the privatisation of the state-owned sector.

Transition from planned to market allocated capital

As the credit and cash plans were dismantled, innovations in the banking, capital, and money markets quickly circumvented the remaining parts of the plan to develop a parallel—albeit slightly inefficient and small relative to the overall economy—market driven financial sector.

The credit plan

From the beginning of reform until recently, China operated under an increasingly broad credit plan—setting money supply as a function of planned growth, prices and trends in money velocity. Prior to 1978, enterprise profits were remitted to the government and then reallocated directly to priority firms through the credit plan aimed at banks and through the cash plan aimed at currency in circulation for household, enterprise and government cash needs.[1] The central and local branches of the People's Bank of China (PBC) executed this State Council plan, giving specialised and universal banks specific assets and liabilities, working capital, long-term loans, and technical renovation loan targets. The credit plan restricted specialised banks from freely lending funds and since deposits were often in excess of quota lending levels, banks were forced to hold costly excess reserves at the central bank.

Changes to the system of profit remittances, direct subsidies, and transfers to the real and banking sector were some of the first critically important modifications to the credit plan system. As firms were allowed to retain an increasingly large share of corporate earnings, financial deepening naturally resulted as firms began to increase their use of simple financial instruments (for example, holding cash outside the banking sector and taking on direct loans from banks and non-bank institutions) and decrease their reliance on government transfers. For example, by 1981 banks were allowed to retain 38 per cent of after-tax profits for lending and to pay employees' bonuses and provide welfare services.[2] Figure 6.1 provides an initial overview of financial deepening in China through such common measures as the ratio of M1 to GDP and M2 to GDP.

In addition to changes at the enterprise level, as the central banking system increasingly decentralised, the credit plan began to break down and credit was often extended in excess of the plan at the local level except during periods of strict monetary retrenchment. During the period 1986–90 the credit plan was usually exceeded by about 22 per cent according to Girardin's (1997) calculations, with the central bank ultimately filling this gap. Furthermore, although the government tried to bring new financial agents into the plan—non-bank financial institutions (NBFIs) were brought under the credit plan in 1988—unofficial and NBFI activity has been very difficult to regulate and they have tended to extend credit well in excess of planned credit limits especially during such periods as 1992–93. Finally, an increasingly dynamic inter-bank market made it nearly impossible to follow the credit plan.

Given the plan's outdated role, in 1998 the government abolished the credit quota system for state-owned banks—something already mandated for other commercial banks, cooperatives, and shareholding commercial banks—and thus moved closer to a market-driven banking system.

Figure 6.1   China's financial deepening, 1978–97

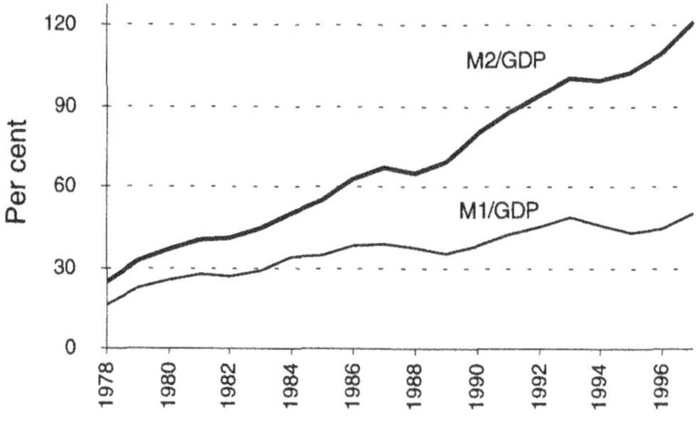

Notes: M1 = money held outside bank system + demand deposits, M2 = quasi money + M1
Source: International Monetary Fund (IMF), (various years). *International Financial Statistics*, IMF, Washington, DC, various issues.

Interest rates

In the early phases of reform the central bank maintained strict control over interest rates, setting preferential rates for priority sectors, regions, and types of loans. In the late 1980s and early 1990s the government increasingly liberalised lending rates, allowing banks to adjust rates plus or minus 10 to 35 per cent around the central bank set level. Furthermore, the development of a basic inter-bank market which eventually allowed lending between regions, and of non-bank financial institutions (NBFIs) which could offer higher deposit rates, began to circumvent the effectiveness of interest rate controls. However, the government continues to fix bank deposit rates at sub-market levels as a critical means of supporting the state-owned banking sector despite the distortions created throughout the economy.

Banking and financial services

Many researchers cite a fall in state appropriated investment in fixed assets as a measure of the declining role of the state. Such investment did fall from 16 per cent in 1985 to 3.2 per cent in 1994 (Girardin 1997). However, this does not necessarily imply a diminished role for state directed investment given that the state can still direct state bank lending. Examination of total assets in the banking sector given in Table 6.1, the emergence of multiple types of non-state bank financial institutions and the somewhat diminished role of state directed finance can better illustrate the changing role of the state. While this table illustrates some change, it also clearly shows that the least efficient state bank sector still has majority control over total assets and thus given the high levels of non-performing loans generated within this sector China continues to face the risk of a systemic bank sector crisis if reforms are not continued.

China's bank sector remains highly unprofitable and has some of the world's highest levels of non-performing loans in both absolute and relative terms, the result of heavy lending to the loss making state-owned sector, speculative investing, poor project risk evaluation, outdated accounting procedures, a lack of discounted cash flow analysis and the lack of a profit motive and an inefficient payment and settlement system forcing banks to hold excess cash for operational needs despite the high cost. Recently the People's Bank of China conservatively

120

Table 6.1   Breakdown of China's bank sector assets

Institution	Total assets as of 12/97 (billion yuan)	Percentage of total	Total assets as of 12/93 (billion yuan)	Percentage of total
State commercial banks[1]	7,213.45	67.9	3,319.45	78.0
Rural credit cooperatives	1,040.46	9.8	374.96	8.8
Other commercial banks[2]	778.11	7.3	196.57	4.6
Specific depositories[3]	681.27	6.4	232.81	5.5
Urban credit cooperatives	498.94	4.7	118.24	2.8
Foreign funded banks[4]	313.97	3.0	n.a.	n.a.
Finance companies	100.52	0.9	16.29	0.4
Total	10,626.72	100	4258.32	100

Notes: [1] State commercial banks include the Industrial and Commercial Bank of China, the Agricultural Bank of China (ABC), the Bank of China, and the People's Construction Bank of China. [2] Includes the Bank of Communications, China International Trust and Investment Corporation (CITIC), Everbright Bank, Hua Xia Bank, China Investment Bank, Guangdong Development Bank, Shenzhen Development Bank, Shenzhen Merchant Bank, Pudong Development Bank, Fujian Industrial Bank, Hainan Development Bank, Minsheng Bank, Yantai Housing and Savings Bank, Bengbu Housing and Savings Bank. [3] Specific depositories include Financial Trusts, Investment Companies and Policy Banks. [4] Converted into yuan at year end, rate of 8.2798 yuan/US$, data not available for 12/93.
Source: State Information Council (SIC). Website [online]. Available at <URL:http://www.chinaeco.com/emon.htm>. People's Bank of China, 1993–98. *People's Bank of China Statistical Bulletin*, various issues.

estimated that 20 per cent (approximately US$1 trillion) of the country's bank loans could be considered as non-performing (*Asian Wall Street Journal*, 4 January 1999), however market analysts estimate such loans to be greater than 30 per cent.

The Central Bank

The most fundamental changes in China's financial sector began in 1978 with the official separation of the People's Bank of China from the Ministry of Finance, although the People's Bank of China did not stop direct lending to the Ministry of Finance until 1994. The People's Bank of China was further developed in late 1983 with the transfer of its commercial banking operations to the Industrial and Commercial Bank of China—now one of China's four state-owned commercial banks. The People's Bank of China has maintained its supervisory role and its role as a lender of last resort. Recently, it has begun to assert its autonomy by attempting to effect monetary policy through open market operations.

Although the credit plan was still being used, by the mid 1990s the government began experimenting with open market operations through sales and purchases of short-term treasury bills on the Shanghai Exchange. However, while household deposits and non-state sectors are increasingly sensitive to rate changes, open market operations have been challenged by several key factors: a heterogeneous and underdeveloped treasury market inhibits the execution of open market operations; bank holdings of excess reserves with the central bank give these banks the freedom to draw on assets to counter tight monetary policy; the lack of market driven operations, ongoing subsidisation and guaranteed credit to many of the state banks and state-owned enterprises makes the economy largely insensitive to rate changes; and interest rate objectives of subsidising industry and banks limits attempts at contractionary open market operations.

Despite tremendous progress since 1978, the People's Bank of China still lacks full independence. Struggles over authority between the central and local People's Bank of China branches continue, with local branches maintaining a large degree of authority over lending and personnel despite a major recentralisation effort in 1993. As Ma (1997) observes, provincial endorsement for People's Bank of China provincial heads and provincial support for office logistics (including housing, childcare, education and general staff benefits) have greatly undermined the authority of the central bank.

In 1998 the central government addressed some of these shortcomings and restructured the People's Bank of China network to create a more efficient structure with nine regional centres that report to the central People's Bank of China and all other local People's Bank of China branches reporting to these nine regional centres. This new structure, modeled after the US Federal Reserve system, aims to increase the autonomy of the central bank, however until the People's Bank of China is no longer under the direct supervision of the State Council these recent reforms will be marginalised.

Recently, to strengthen its balance sheet and assume the role of a 'true' central bank, the People's Bank of China has also dramatically reduced its lending to the non-financial sector from 65.9 billion yuan at the end of 1996 to 10.5 billion yuan at the end of September 1998 (People's Bank of China and State Information Council publications and officials). However, interest bearing excess reserves of state banks held at the People's Bank of China do weaken the latter's balance sheet.

State-owned and policy banks

Although several of the major state-owned banks existed in name prior to 1979, their purposes changed dramatically during these initial years of reform from direct government distributors of capital to financial institutions issuing interest-bearing loans to their respective sectors. The Agricultural Bank of China was officially re-established in February 1979 to handle rural lending with the help of rural credit cooperatives that formed the grass roots base for this institution. The People's Construction Bank of China was first established in 1954 but not until 1979 did it begin to issue interest bearing bank loans for construction projects. In 1980 the Bank of China was placed in charge of imports and exports, foreign exchange, and international loan transactions. The bank maintained exclusive rights to handle foreign exchange until 1985 when the other specialised banks were granted these rights. At present, specialised banks are no longer restricted to their originally designated lines of business.

These state-owned banks helped to establish the ground work for China's transition to a lending-based distribution of capital, however these banks were still subject to the direction of the State Council and they never made the transition to lending on a commercial basis as lending still went to government priority, politically well connected, and high collateral projects. In an attempt to free the specialised banks of their burden of responsibility to the state-owned sector and partially due to the macroeconomic instability of 1993, three new policy banks were established by 1994 to further separate policy and commercial lending: the State Development Bank, the Agricultural Development Bank and the Export-Import Bank. However, the balance sheets of these banks are jeopardised by their attempts to compensate low yielding investments in government public works projects with speculative investments in such areas as real estate.

Seventy per cent of state bank lending still goes to the state-owned sector, saddling these banks with non-performing loans. Xu (1998)

123

reports that the central bank continues to fund the deposit-loan gaps created by such lending.[3] Furthermore, these banks have developed a major asset-liability mismatch. Seventy eight per cent of the national bank sector's[4] liabilities are in the form of deposits, where urban household deposits have reached a high of 57 per cent of total deposits while enterprise deposits have fallen to a low of 36 per cent. This accumulation of non-government controlled short-term urban deposits combined with government directed lending to the state sector (often long term) makes their balance sheets highly unstable. The decline of paid-in capital to the state-owned banks from 12.1 per cent in 1985 to a mere 2.2 per cent in 1996 is further evidence of their weakness (Lardy 1998).

Although the government has directed banks to reach the internationally accepted capital adequacy ratio of 8 per cent, this has only been achieved by accounting manoeuvres and little real capital has been injected. An example was the government's attempt to recapitalise the four state-owned commercial banks by issuing 270 billion yuan of 30-year special state treasury bonds with an annually paid coupon rate of 7.2 per cent. The banks list these bonds as assets on their balance sheets bringing their total capital adequacy ratios towards 8 per cent, however no new permanent capital has been created. According to Lardy (1998), by the time bad debts and subsidiary lending is accurately accounted for and the Basle standard risk weightings are applied, all four banks likely have negative capital adequacy ratios.

Non-bank financial institutions and non-state commercial banks

As a complement to changes in the state banking sector, the PBC allowed more flexible NBFIs to rapidly develop outside the rigidities of the formal banking system, to fund the development of non state-owned enterprises. The rapid growth of these institutions has also exerted competitive pressures on other parts of the financial sector, forcing the government to increasingly liberalise the state banking sector. Of all the NBFIs, trust and investment corporations (TICs) are by far the most significant in terms of assets and market influence, although the others (finance companies, financial leasing companies, securities companies and insurance companies) all play crucial roles in allocating capital to different parts of the real economy often not serviced by the state banks.

The first international TIC, China International Trust and Investment Corporation (CITIC) was established in 1979 to promote technology transfers and joint ventures. Its role has now expanded such that CITIC lends to most sectors of the economy. In the 1980s CITIC was clearly at the forefront of China's financial market innovation although other international TICs were soon to follow. For example, in 1982 CITIC issued China's first international corporate bonds in Tokyo for 10 billion yen, to fund the Yizheng Chemical Fibre plant. Most international TICs are funded by deposits from enterprises, different levels of government, and institutions. Most of their liabilities are in the form of deposits, while inner bank lending often constitutes the next largest part of their liabilities.

Because they do not face the regulations imposed on state banks, TICs can successfully attract enterprise and individual deposits by offering higher interest rates, participating in a wider range of business lending activities, and engaging in foreign exchange transactions. As outlined by Hong and Yan (1997), TICs act as commercial banks by treating deposits as fixed income instruments and reaping the spread earned above this deposit rate as retained profits—not as equity as in most industrial countries. Without interest controls or sector lending requirements the TICs have greater latitude than commercial banks but at the same time until recently they had an implicit guarantee of a government bail out in the event of their default with creditors. This type of unrestricted lending environment combined with moral hazard problems led trusts to over-expose their portfolios to speculative lending and investments in the equity markets.

NBFIs flourished and by the end of 1981 there were over 600 TICs. By late 1989 the total assets of TICs reached 6.3 per cent of total financial assets (Girardin 1997). NBFIs actually play an even greater role, as market participants indicate that a significant amount of activity occurs between NBFIs and state banks outside the credit plan and thus outside official statistics. While trusts provided a vehicle for banks to allocate excess capital to firms with an excess demand for credit, the People's Bank of China's inability to effectively regulate this sector led them to temporarily suspend their operations after periods of 'excessive' credit expansion. The number of international TICs peaked in mid 1988 at 745 but ended the year at only 300 after the People's Bank of China enforced closures. The People's Bank of China has continued to address abuses in the TIC sector through such landmark cases as its January

1997 takeover of the China Agribusiness Development Trust and Investment Corporation and the October 1998 takeover of Guangdong International Trust and Investment Corp (GITIC).[5] As one of the largest and most trusted international TICs, GITIC's assets and liabilities of US$2.7 billion and US$4.3 billion, respectively, as of the end of January 1999 indicate the tenuous nature of this sector.

Other NBFIs include the over 55,000 rural credit cooperatives that operated under the guidance of the Agricultural Bank of China until 1996 when they became independent. Prior to separation rural credit cooperatives not only implemented Agricultural Bank of China lending programs, but also undertook their own deposit gathering and lending activities (to both the rural and urban sectors). Like the state banks rural credit cooperatives have significant numbers of non-performing loans accumulated from their Agricultural Bank of China directed policy lending, and their lending practices and performance are highly variable by region, but despite this they continue to be an incredibly effective vehicle for mobilising rural deposits.

Although not as numerous as rural credit cooperatives and only started in 1987, urban credit cooperatives aim to service urban individual and small business customers and have been an important vehicle for mobilising urban savings. Like the rural credit cooperatives, urban credit cooperatives are not totally independent. In 1989 urban credit cooperatives fell within the credit plan and different urban credit cooperatives were under the supervision of either the Industrial and Commercial Bank of China, Bank of China or People's Construction Bank of China.

The insurance sector began officially after the People's Insurance Company of China was set up subordinate to the People's Bank of China in 1980. However at present, regulations restricting the deposit base of insurance companies have created a seriously underfunded insurance sector and forced many insurance companies to set up securities companies illegally to supplement their low yielding assets base of financial and government bond holdings. As a result the insurance sector has become increasingly unstable in the late 1990s and will likely undergo a shakeout similar to the restructuring of the TICs in the near future.

Non-state commercial banks. The China Investment Bank, founded in 1981, was the first major non-state bank to be created, and was designed to attract medium and long-term capital from overseas and to facilitate lending with the World Bank. The more commercially oriented and comprehensive non-state banks didn't begin independent operations until the Bank of Communications was restructured in 1986 and the CITIC Industrial Bank (a subsidiary of CITIC) began operations in 1987. After 1987 similar types of banks were established in the Special Economic Zones. By the end of 1997 these banks controlled assets of 788 billion yuan and had sourced funds both domestically and internationally.

Foreign banks

Foreign institutional presence in the banking sector has been very limited due to strict government regulations. Despite this, by the end of 1997 142 foreign banks had branch offices in China and an estimated 450 representative offices had been set up (PBC 1998; SIC 1998; *China Daily*, December 1998). Although foreign banks were first allowed to open representative offices in 1981, it was not until 1996 that foreign banks were allowed to enter the renminbi business. In 1998 eight foreign banks[6] were given increasing access to local bond trading in Shanghai and several are pending approval in Shenzhen, however this trading is limited to the inter-bank market and excludes activities on either of China's stock exchanges. The government seems intent on expanding the number of banks, however even banks with access to renminbi business are still restricted from taking local deposits, thus relying mostly on deposits from joint ventures or foreign firms operating in China. This restriction on their liabilities marginalises their investment capacity. At the end of the first quarter of 1998 renminbi assets totalled a mere 916 million yuan, with loans of 591 million yuan and 566 million yuan in deposits (*China Daily*, 6 December 1998).

Inter-bank market

The inter-bank money market has provided a critical mechanism for borrowing and lending outside the credit plans as well as motivating deposit-seeking behaviour among banks that were previously limited in their lending and thus had no incentive to attract deposits. Due to the demand for liquidity borrowing created by a rigid credit plan, inter-bank activity boomed after its official introduction.

Formal inter-bank markets were developed in 1986 in the cities of Changzhou, Chongqing, Guangzhou, Shenyang, and Wuhan after experiments with an unofficial inter-bank market in the city of Wenzhou in 1983. Also in 1986 the Shanghai Money Market opened, headed by the Industrial and Commercial Bank of China which would come to dominate more than 50 per cent of inter-bank market activities by 1998. The market is facilitated by local financial institutions and sponsored by local branches of the People's Bank of China. It includes banks, NBFIs, and as of 1998, insurance companies. The dramatic increase in inter-bank lending over the years following the market's inception—to 200 billion and 524 billion yuan in 1987 and 1988 respectively—indicated the demand for more liquid money markets outside the state plan.[7] By 1987 over 360 money market centres had been developed across the country.

These markets were also motivated by the central government's transfer of its responsibility to finance firm's working capital to the banks despite the continuance of the credit quota system based on forecasted deposit levels. Specifically in October 1984, the People's Bank of China issued the 'Rules for the Management of Credit Funds' (linking lending to deposit levels, limiting direct overdrafts by the central bank, encouraging inter-bank lending and replacing direct transfers from the central bank with repayable credit). Additionally, motivating these markets were changes in the balance sheets of the national banking system (discussed earlier) creating a need for better access to liquid funds given the government's inability to guarantee the liabilities side of the balance sheet via administrative measures.

From the late 1980s though the mid 1990s, the inter-bank market remained poorly regulated and decentralised due to inefficient trading, settlement, and payment systems linking the different regional markets which operated at different times with different institutions dominating different markets.[8] The following characteristics were the result: interest rates differed significantly between regions; poor regulation led to a focus on loan creation not liquidity; local banks were forced by local governments to borrow excessively in the market to fund local SOEs; poor regulation and central bank support created moral hazard problems that directed inter-bank borrowing into speculative fixed asset investments; and a lack of banks operating under strict profit maximising functions limited the market's sensitivity to interest rate changes.

In 1989, in an attempt to regain control of this unauthorised lending, the government set up six regional inter-bank over-the-counter trading centres in Shanghai, Wuhan, Beijing/Tianjin, Shenyang, Xi'an, and

Chongqing. Additionally, the government stipulated that borrowing on the inter-bank market must not be used to finance fixed asset investments, as the market was designed to help banks meet short-term liquidity shortages and that banks were not permitted to borrow in excess of 5 per cent of the previous month's deposits. The PBC also set interest rate ceilings—at a premium to People's Bank of China daily lending rates to specialised banks.[9]

However this failed to stop unauthorised lending, and during the early 1990s banks would borrow from the inter-bank market to source lending to NBFIs that speculated on real estate. This speculation lead to a massive accumulation of non-performing loans that fed back into the inter-bank market and the central bank was forced to inject significant liquidity into the inter-bank market to prevent its collapse. Given that financial institutions currently in default or close to default—such as GITIC, GZITIC and Guangdong Development Enterprises (GDE), among others—have significant inter-bank liabilities, further defaults in the inter-bank market could be a trigger for a systemic bank sector crisis given that this market still appears underfunded. In fact, when netting out inter-bank activity for the balance sheets of the state commercial banks, the people's banks, other commercial banks and the postal savings network, there is a net liability of 198 billion yuan as of September 1998—a major reversal from net lending in the early to mid 1990s.[10] Even when factoring in other parts of the financial sector, additional credit has been created within the inter-bank market.[11] This could be explained by unofficial borrowing in this market or as a result of the massive non-performing loans accumulated during the real estate crash which was subsequently recapitalised by 200 billion yuan in People's Bank of China financing.

In April 1996 the People's Bank of China again attempted to reorganise the market, centralising it in Shanghai with links to 35 other inter-bank lending centres around the country and with the involvement of 17 banks. Whereas before, technical limitations and decentralised settlement and trading practices created a very inefficient market, now one rate (CHIBOR) is widely quoted for all inter-bank activity.

Despite changes, this market continues to remain relatively insensitive to interest rate changes and continues to provide the real sector with an important source of funding for fixed asset investment. As a result, recent inter-bank trading reflects the recent slowdown in non-government fixed asset investment as seen in Figure 6.2. The inverted yield curve for 1997 and 1998 inter-bank rates despite adequate liquidity also suggests market inefficiency and indicates the lack of arbitrage opportunities.[12]

Government debt and foreign exchange markets

Debt issuance and fiscal policy

Paying down the last of its domestic and foreign debts in 1974 and 1965 respectively, the central government first incurred new domestic and foreign debts in 1981 and 1978 respectively. With the central government cutting its traditional financing links to firms by phasing out full profit remittances in the beginning periods of reform while at the

Figure 6.2   China's inter-bank money market trading volume

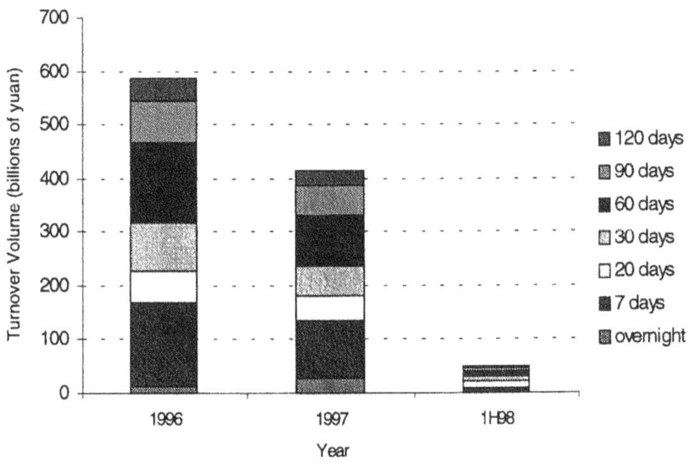

Sources: People's Bank of China, 1993–98. *People's Bank of China Quarterly Statistical Bulletin*, Beijing, various issues; State Information Council. Web site [online]. Available at <URL:http://www.chinaeco.com/emon.htm>.

same time having significant expenditure demands, the government has consistently maintained budget deficits since 1979 with the exception of 1985. These recurring budget deficits forced the government to develop their domestic and international bond issuance markets as an alternative source of finance. Figure 6.3 gives China's issuance and fiscal deficits trends to illustrate this point.

From the late 1970s to the mid 1980s both deficit and debt issuance values tended to move somewhat in tandem, with increased deficits forcing increased debt issuance (Figure 6.3). However, in the mid 1980s the government followed a steady trend of increased debt issuance while the government deficit, although deteriorating somewhat, remained relatively stable. This can best be explained by the fact that the official fiscal deficit does not capture the true extent of government spending. In fact, the government has large off balance sheet financing needs in the state-owned sector and banking sector that required large 'one-off' debt financing, and these costs do not appear as spending in the government budget. Additionally, the World Bank argues that if China were to calculate

Figure 6.3   China's fiscal deficit and debt issuance profile, 1978–98

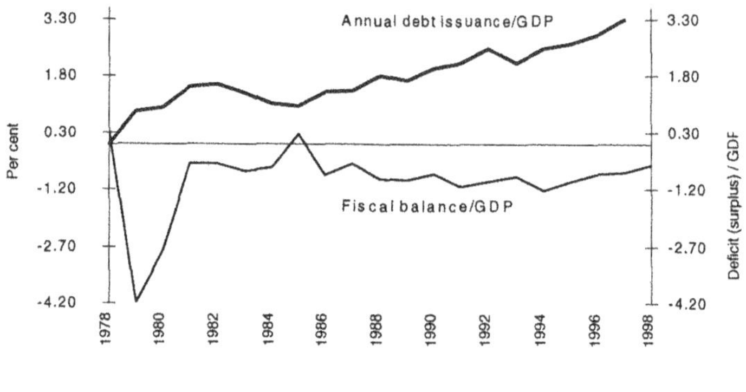

Per cent / Deficit (surplus) / GDP

Annual debt issuance/GDP

Fiscal balance/GDP

3.30 1.80 0.30 -1.20 -2.70 -4.20

1978 1980 1982 1984 1986 1988 1990 1992 1994 1996 1998

Sources: State Statistical Bureau, 1988–98. *Statistical Yearbook of China*, China Statistical Publishing House, Beijing, various issues; International Monetary Fund (IMF), (various years). *International Financial Statistics*, IMF, Washington, DC, various issues.

its government deficit on a consolidated basis to included People's Bank of China lending to the financial system, it would approach 5 to 6 per cent of GDP.[13] Furthermore, China's budget reporting lists proceeds from debt issuance as revenue. In the future, the massive debt recapitalisation needs of SOEs and the state bank sector will likely force this debt issuance as a percentage of GDP even higher. If formally incorporated in the budget, the fiscal deficit will likely exceed 5 per cent of GDP.

Domestic bonds

Placement. Since entering back into the debt markets the Ministry of Finance has issued multiple classes of bonds (treasury, fiscal, state construction, key constitution, special state, and inflation indexed) and has restricted the sale of these bonds to different holders (banks, enterprises, or individuals). The State Planning Commission also issues capital construction bonds and the various key ministries issue enterprise bonds. Bond sales in the early 1980s were forced onto investors as pay in-kind for wages and while this type of forced placement with workers no longer occurs the Ministry of Finance continues to force enterprises and state banks to buy fiscal bonds (late 1980s and early 1990s) and various other kinds of special state bonds (ongoing).

By offering investors 100–200 basis points above comparable bank deposit rates, the Ministry of Finance has been successful in placing the majority of new issues with retail investors and has thus become highly dependent on this class of investors and bank deposit rate controls. In 1997 China issued 241.2 billion yuan in T bonds, with 68 per cent in the form of certificate bonds and 16 per cent in unregistered bonds, both bought mostly by retail investors facing low deposit rates in the bank sector, a trend that continued into 1998.

The lack of a standardised debt market will likely hamper future issuance plans. Although yearly debt finance targets are currently given, no schedule of auction dates or sizes are provided. The government still relies on multiple classes of bonds issued by various government agencies, such as the 1.6 billion yuan 5-year Ministry of Railway bonds issued in late 1998. The lack of a smooth and liquid government yield curve from one to ten years greatly increases investor uncertainty, speculative behavior, secondary market volatility, and ultimately funding costs for the government. Additionally, while a distribution system for treasury bond auctions aimed at retail investors has been established via state bank branches, the government still relies on an *ad hoc* forced placement system for other investor classes, relying especially on the state banks to finance government spending. For example, in 1998 the central government placed 415 billion yuan in three separate bonds with state-owned commercial banks.[14]

Pricing. In addition to forced placement, bonds issued in the 1980s were not market priced. For example the 10 year bonds issued in the early 1980s paid an annual interest rate of 4 per cent payable at maturity despite 5 year bank certificate deposit rates of 6.8 per cent. After accounting for the time value of money and inflation, investors clearly lost money over this period and these bonds merely acted as a tax.

Bond issuance through the 1980s became very unpopular and to ensure the successful placement of bond targets, the government was first forced to shorten maturities while keeping coupon rates constant. Realising that current yields were well out of line with market pricing, the government increased household bond rates from 10 per cent to 14 per cent in 1989, and for the first time it issued construction bonds with floating rates. To issue this increasing volume of bonds successfully, by 1991 the Ministry of Finance was finally forced to use a public bidding to issue bonds at market determined rates. This has most recently extended to state affiliated issuers, where for the first time the State Development Bank and Export-Import Bank issued 5 and 3 billion yuan in bonds respectively through public bidding in the second half of 1998.[15]

Pricing of bonds in the secondary market also still follows outdated pricing mechanisms by using a variation of current yield versus standard yield to maturity calculations. This latter pricing mechanism fails to account for the time value of money and often underprices bonds in the primary market (World Bank 1995a).

Trading. After years of illegal black market trading in treasuries, the government officially sanctioned secondary trading in July 1988. Seven cities (Chongqing, Guangzhou, Harbin, Shanghai, Shenyang, Shenzhen and Wuhan) were established as trading centres, and securities companies and trusts began actively trading in the secondary market. However, a large supply of mispriced bonds already held by investors led to rapid selling pressure in the secondary markets in 1988 and the government was forced to use 1 billion yuan to prop up this market as individuals rushed to sell their bonds. In 1989 local governments were again forced to intervene in the secondary market—this time without central government financial support.

In 1990 the government coordinated a national satellite linked trading system to help unify pricing across regions and allowed futures contracts on bonds to help further advance the sophistication of this market. The 1993 introduction of repurchase (repo) trading further helped institutions manage risks and allowed market makers to hold larger inventories to promote better liquidity. By 1998 almost all secondary bond market trading was done on either the Shanghai or Shenzhen exchanges through the Securities Trading Automated Quotation System (STAQS) which involves 40 domestic securities and investment and trust companies and connects with over 70 cities (Figure 6.4).

Foreign bonds

While the government first returned to the debt markets via international issuance, the Ministry of Finance has increasingly taken a conservative approach towards foreign issuance. The changed bias towards domestic versus external issuance is best illustrated in Figure 6.5.

As a result of this conservative approach China only had US$131 billion in outstanding external State Administration of Foreign Exchange (SAFE) registered debt at the end of 1997, with a total debt service as a percentage of exports of goods, services and income of less than 10 per cent. By 1997, China had positioned its external debt portfolio inside a very safe range with US$45.3 billion in foreign direct investment for 1997, US$139.9 billion in foreign exchange reserves, a current account balance of US$29.7 billion, and a well managed maturity schedule and currency breakdown.[16] Figure 6.6 shows the stability of total external central government debt to GNP over time.

However, in addition to central government debt, numerous localities and domestic institutions have been accruing significant foreign liabilities and in the past few years numerous global high yield bonds have been issued by offshore companies written on Chinese project cash flows. Guarantees for many of these bonds are often unclear despite frequent claims during investor presentations by company officials of 'government support', and potential creditor disputes could create future disruptions to China's entrance into global capital markets.

China has recently begun to aggressively develop a global sovereign yield curve,[17] although there have been indications of Chinese government intervention marginalising its yields usefulness for international investors to price true China sovereign risk.[18] Figure 6.7

Figure 6.4   China's treasury bond trading

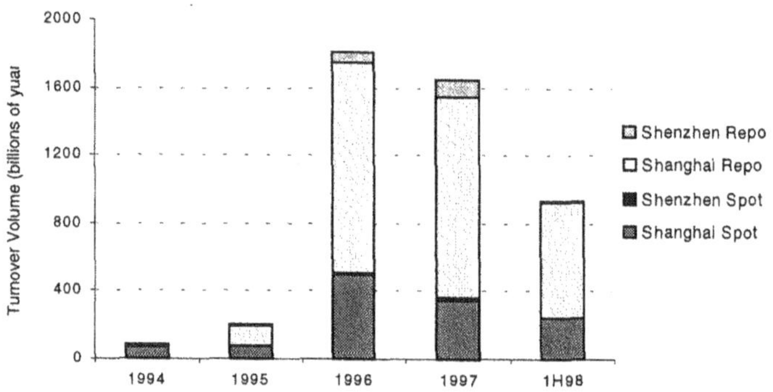

Sources: People's Bank of China, 1993–98. *People's Bank of China Quarterly Statistical Bulletin*, Beijing, various issues; State Information Council. Web site [online]. Available at <URL:http://www.chinaeco.com/emon.htm>.

Figure 6.5   China's annual domestic–external debt issuance mix, 1979–96

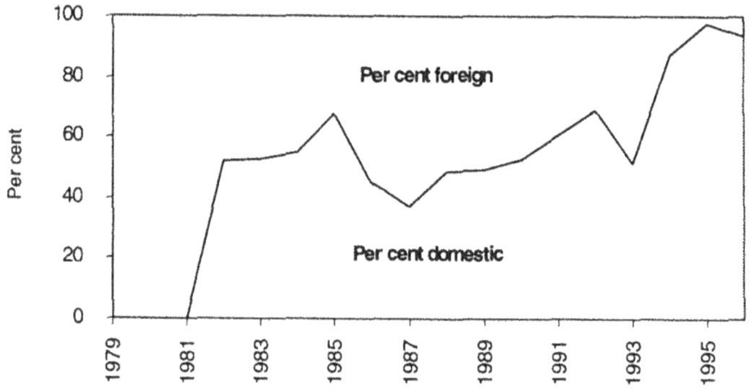

Source: State Statistical Bureau, 1988–98. *Statistical Yearbook of China*, China Statistical Publishing House, Beijing, various issues.

lists the major Chinese global bonds and their sensitivity to the East Asian crisis indicates some degree of real market pricing and liquidity. All bonds listed are non-call life global bonds for the People's Republic of China with the standard government repayment guarantees rated BBB- by Standard and Poor's, except the bond maturing on 2 January 2007 which is for the SDB and is considered a quasi-sovereign.

Foreign exchange. From 1980 to late 1993 China operated two separate foreign exchange markets, the Foreign Exchange Certificate (FEC) and the renminbi (local currency) markets. The FEC market was to service the currency needs of foreign companies and persons within China and it traded at a significantly higher value in US dollar terms than the renminbi market. Initially the government could effectively ensure the separation of these two markets, but as foreign participation in the Chinese economy grew significantly, grey markets developed extensively throughout China for the trading between FEC and renminbi and for direct trading of renminbi with foreign counter parties.

The FEC was eliminated at the beginning of 1994 and existing FEC holders were forced to exchange their currency into renminbi. The exchange rate moved from 5.81 to 8.69 yuan per US dollar for foreign holders. Although the renminbi market remains very controlled, foreign exchange daily trading turnover for 1994 reached US$200 million and involved 210 members, and currency swap centres (both informal and formal) have developed throughout the country. Officially, China has restricted currency transactions to the current account and the central bank has maintained a fixed and stable exchange rate under its closed capital account. This regime has provided stability, but it will stagnate China's attempts to develop off-shore bank markets and drive currency transactions into grey markets.

Illegal renminbi-Hong Kong dollar markets developed extensively in Shenzhen, although many of these were closed in 1998 as the government sought to enforce its strict currency regulations, limiting transaction to the trade sector only in an attempt to stabilise the yuan. Shanghai black market rates between the yuan and US dollar are also actively quoted and they have tended to put the yuan about 3 to 5 per cent lower than official rates (although they were as high as 9 per cent during periods of speculative pressure in 1998). The People's Bank of China has been seen trying to affect demand for US dollars by lowering US dollar deposit rates during 1998 in an attempt to stabilise the foreign exchange markets, however China's flat growth in reserves for the year

Figure 6.6   China: foreign debt expansion profile, 1981–97

Total Outstanding Foreign Debt —◆— Total Outstanding Foreign Debt / GNP

Source: State Administration of Foreign Exchange (SAFE), 1997. *Annual Report.*

Figure 6.7   China: sovereign bond performance, 8/97–10/98

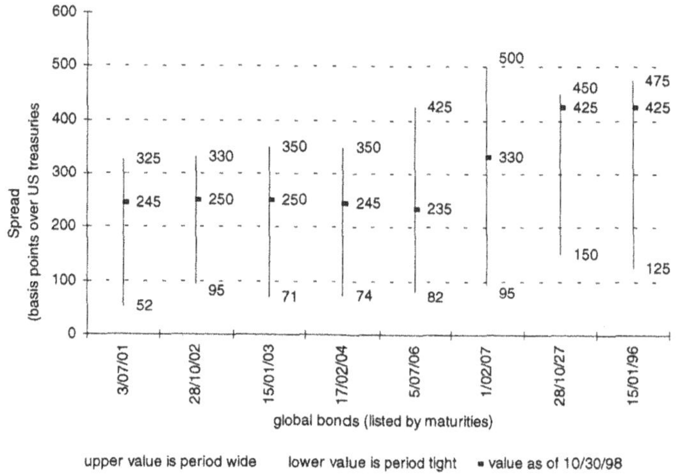

global bonds (listed by maturities)

upper value is period wide   lower value is period tight   ▪ value as of 10/30/98

Source: Merrill Lynch, 1998. *Asian Strategy Monthly*, Merrill Lynch and Company, various issues.

despite its significant trade surplus of US$45 billion indicates capital flight. Prior to this recent outflow, the central bank's accumulation of foreign exchange reserves from 0.16 billion yuan in 1978 to 139.89 billion in 1997 has dramatically effected domestic money growth. Although the PBC has recently allowed firms to retain increasing amounts of foreign exchange receipts and as a result has injected less renminbi into the system, the effect on the money supply remains significant.

When China moves towards opening its capital account, the current exchange rate regime will likely change significantly. Several possibilities exist, however pegging the currency against a basket of foreign currency (namely the US dollar, yen and euro) would best complement China's recent realignment of foreign exchange holdings. Another option would be to move toward a full floating exchange rate, however this idea has little support among central Chinese policymakers. With ongoing uncertainty in the Asian currency and capital markets an engineered devaluation for the sake of supporting the export sector appears very unlikely given the limited effect such a move would have on net export growth and the associated cost it would impose on China's infant capital markets.

Corporate securities markets: equities and bonds

China's tradable corporate securities markets developed on an informal basis in the mid 1980s and formally in the early 1990s. Of these markets, the equity markets have clearly been the main focal point and the most actively utilised for corporate finance and investment, leaving the corporate bond market comparatively undeveloped.

Equities

Primary issuance. Prior to the opening of the Shanghai and Shenzhen Stock Exchanges on December 1990 and April 1991 respectively, China began to issue non-tradable ownership shares as early as 1984 when it issued non-tradable employee shares for a Beijing state-owned department store. Over the next five years other SOEs issued shares after being incorporated, and joint stock companies began to emerge.

By the end of 1998 the total market capitalisation of over two trillion yuan for the 851 listed companies on the Shanghai and Shenzhen exchanges signified the importance of these markets as a source of capital.[19]

Once the exchanges were opened, domestic investors were restricted to the A share markets where multiple classes of shares are issued. 'Tradable A shares', which make up a minimum of 25 per cent of total shares at the time of the initial public offering but rarely make up a controlling stake, are the only class of shares that can be traded. The government often holds a controlling interest in listed firms through its direct ownership of non-tradable state shares, while the remaining shares are distributed between other non-tradable legal person shares—owned by domestic institutions—and employee shares. To tap foreign investment sources under a closed capital account regime, China also developed a B share market exclusively for foreigners. Foreigners can also invest in Chinese firms through H shares listed in Hong Kong, N shares listed on the New York Stock Exchange and Red Chip stocks listed in Hong Kong (these are Hong Kong firms with most of their cash flows derived from mainland Chinese operations and are essentially considered Chinese stocks by the market).[20]

The central government continues to set annual stock issuance and provincial quotas, and these quotas are often under pressure from banks and other government bodies who depend on public deposits and public debt issuance and are thus afraid of potential crowding out. In addition to several objective requirements necessary for a firm to issue stocks, many domestic market participants attach a great deal of importance to political decision-making in the selection process.[21] Access to initial public offerings also remains very restricted and has been a large factor in corruption scandals over the last few years.

Trading. All secondary market activity was pushed into the black market until the official exchanges were opened and even today cities such as Shenyang and Chengdu have informal stockmarkets. Cumulative trading volumes illustrate the level of activity in these markets and show their relatively high liquidity. Cumulative trading volume in A and B shares for the Shanghai and Shenzhen stock exchanges over the last 12 months ending 14 December 1998 reached US$301.5 billion (Figure 6.8).

The B share market is clearly of tertiary importance and Shanghai dominates Shenzhen; weekly trading volume for 1998 was 39 per cent higher in Shanghai.

In many aspects China's stockmarkets are remarkably well developed given their recent emergence. Trade settlements in the A share markets of one day (T+1) with a limited guarantee fund set up by trading members have helped prevent wide scale systemic shocks to this market thus far.[22] However, the settlement system effected by limited liability private sector corporations needs to be reformed as these corporations lack guaranteed funds in the case of wide scale defaults. Additionally, a simultaneous payment system (as opposed to an end of the day payment delivery system) would further limit default risk on both an individual and potentially systemic scale.

However, these markets have often been described by financial market observers as chaotic and speculative in their price movements. Figure 6.9 illustrates total returns in the respective markets. Some observers claim this is due to the speculative and untrained nature of local retail investors, however market manipulation, incomplete disclosure of financial statements, the regulatory structure of these markets, and government interference appear to be more significant causes of this behaviour. Moral hazard problems due to numerous government capital injections to troubled state firms listed on both exchanges have further distorted market trading behaviour.

Regulation of these markets has been incredibly difficult since their inception and massive price spikes with frequent cases of insider trading have characterised much of the domestic market's trading activity. Incorrect pricing of initial public offerings and suspect distribution have often resulted in price movements of over 100 per cent within the first two weeks of trading after issue. While the World Bank (1995a) found that A shares tended to be systematically underpriced, since 1994 empirical observations of the post initial public offering trading indicates that both under and overpricing does occur. Additionally, while Chinese authorities have prevented equity short selling in an attempt to stabilise the market, the lack of an equity repo market greatly limits the abilities of domestic institutions to manage portfolio risk and hinders the development of risk managed underwriting activities. Over the years the government has also imposed *ad hoc* restrictions on new share listings and daily price volatility bands—occasionally limiting daily prices changes to between 5 and 10 per cent of their opening value.

If properly enforced by the Securities Regulatory Commission, December 1998's landmark securities law—Article 214—to take effect from 1 July 1999, provides the first standardised country-wide

---

Figure 6.8   Total weekly trading volume for Shanghai and
              Shenzhen exchanges

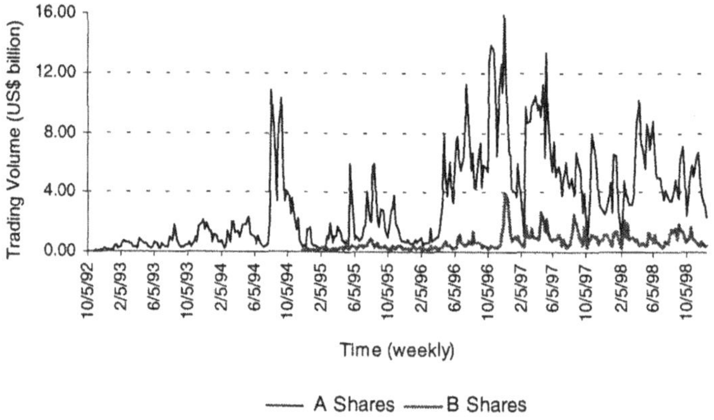

Time (weekly)

——— A Shares ——— B Shares

Source: DataStream.

---

regulations to help correct these problems by imposing stricter financial
reporting guidelines, insider trading regulations, the separation of
underwriting and trading activities, and the separation of client and
proprietary accounts.

Bonds. Despite China's rapid development of equity markets in recent
years, corporate bond markets have remained in their infant stages
and have thus played only a minor role in corporate finance. Although
China first started issuing corporate bonds in 1986, excessive
administrative controls over issuance and ad hoc secondary trading
mechanisms have burdened this market's development. At the end of
1997 the total volume of corporate bonds was 100 billion yuan with
only seven corporate bonds listed on the market. Additionally, many
corporate bonds are issued by the state banks or state-owned
enterprises and placed in the accounts of a few state banks or other
major financial institutions and little secondary trading ever occurs. Many
of these bonds are simply a continuation of triangle-debt and represent
refinancing loans from state banks to SOEs, and non-state firms have
been a relatively small part of this market. Trading that does occur mostly

takes place directly between two interested parties in the over-the-counter market as the major investment houses don't regularly make markets for such securities. Market participants have indicated that the approval process for corporate bond issuance is even more subjective and politicised than equity issuance and only politically well-connected companies can receive approval.

Like the equity issuance market, the government has also set an annual quota for the bond market, however the quota of a mere 20 billion yuan per year guarantees this market will remain underdeveloped. Additionally, different forms of corporate bonds are also limited, with non-straight debt such as convertible bonds making up a very small part of the overall debt market.

The lack of a liquid government yield curve also inhibits the development of a corporate bond market. Since corporate bond risk is priced in terms of bond spreads over comparable duration government bonds, then without a reliable government yield curve investors have great difficulty systemically and uniformly pricing new corporate debt. This only increases uncertainty and thus increases the cost of funding for firms forced to pay higher yields. Furthermore, China will need to establish a nationwide trading and settlement system and an active corporate bond repo market to allow underwriters to hedge their exposure when holding an inventory of their underwritten bond.[23]

Conclusion and future policy direction

Decentralisation and insufficient regulation have fostered overlending, brought non-performing loans to critical levels, and resulted in numerous and growing cases of institutional insolvency. However, if in the short term the People's Bank of China can successfully close, liquidate, and recapitalise the necessary institutions—primarily located in Guangdong Province—and in the long term continue to press hard for better supervision and upgrade financial reporting requirements, the benefits of allowing a vibrant private capital market to develop will greatly outweigh the costs of these problem institutions. Additionally, by actively promoting the development of the non-state banking institutions and forcing direct competition, the non-state sector will increasingly dwarf the size and influence of the less efficient state banking system.

China's future economic stability will rest largely on the ability of the PBC and Ministry of Finance to continue their proactive reforms and

Figure 6.9   Chinese share market returns, 1/93–12/98

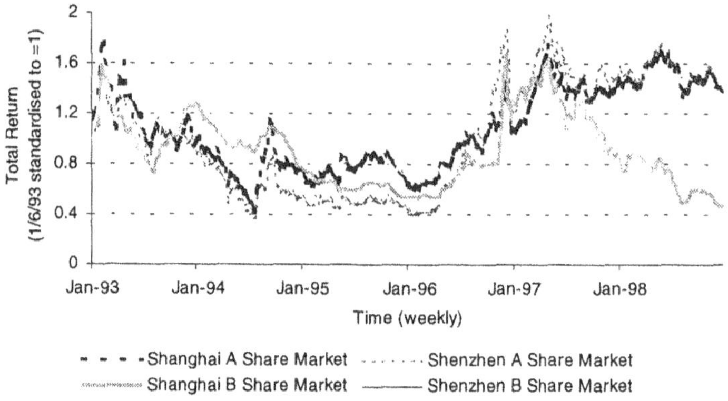

Time (weekly)

- - - -Shanghai A Share Market · · · · · · ·Shenzhen A Share Market
        Shanghai B Share Market ————— Shenzhen B Share Market

Source: DataStream.

better mobilise capital through a private market driven financial sector to fund the real sector. The state-owned sector will also increasingly rely on private capital markets to fund its recapitalisation efforts. The following are possible policy directions that could help achieve this goal.

• Regularised and standardised government debt issuance. Forced debt issuance only perpetuates circular debt (or triangle debt) and marginalises the legitimacy of the government bond markets as real institutions for long-term fund raising. Developing a regular auction timetable, pre-announcing volumes, issuing standardised treasuries available to multiple classes of investor, and pricing these instruments via public bidding would allow China to develop a deep and liquid yield curve while minimising speculative behavior. This developed government bond market would give real prices to government debt serving as an important feedback mechanism for government policy, provide a real benchmark for pricing other fixed income instruments, allow for better risk management through standard risk management hedging techniques, help end the ongoing cycle of non-transparent circular debt finance between the government, state banks and the state-owned sector, and ultimately lower government debt financing costs by lowering market uncertainty.

- Increase stock and bond issuance to effect changes in corporate governance. While continued stock issuance and thus the transfer of ownership rights could dramatically change corporate governance in both state-owned and non state-owned companies, the state's dominance in both tradable and non-tradable shares has largely prevented the development of a new political economy in corporate ownership. On the one hand, ongoing issuance of cash dividends to state holders and share dividends or rights offerings to non-state equity holders as described by Xu and Wang (1997) has helped decrease the state's once unequivocal majority ownership stake in listed firms. On the other hand, even new stock issuance does not necessarily change corporate governance, as Xu and Wang (1997) found official managers and party officials hold key board and supervisory positions in many SOE incorporated firms. Therefore, the ongoing securitisation of firms, the issuance of shares to non-state investors, and the de-emphasis of government appointed managers will increasingly empower shareholders to effectively pressure firms to maximise corporate profits.

  However, the influence of non-state shareholders is also critical to maximising these positive changes. Importantly, Xu and Wang's (1997) empirical modelling found that in China large institutional holders exert profit-maximising behaviour on firms while individual investors have little effect on Chinese listed companies. From these conclusions, it will be critical for China to continue developing the mutual fund industry and to promote other forms of institutional stock and bond portfolio management.[24]

  Finally, overall corporate bond issuance needs to catch up with total equity issuance to prevent an unbalanced capital market and provide firms with longer term debt finance options. Secondary markets need to be promoted in corporate bonds to allow the market to find real prices and limit the liquidity premium required by voluntary investors to hold such corporate securities. Furthermore, both issuance markets—but especially the corporate debt issuance market—need to be based more on objective financial criteria and be less politicised.

- Invest heavily in technical trading systems and vigilantly continue to upgrade financial reporting standards and legal rights of share and bond holders. Learning from the experience of countries like Japan, a lack of simulations payments, the lack of a corporate bond repo market, inefficient settlement systems, and the lack of unified real time price sources will dramatically hinder the development of both corporate and government securities markets. To date China has rapidly been upgrading its trading systems but additional investments are needed to keep pace with the increasing volume of total debt and equity issuance as well as to expand the scope of distribution. Without full financial disclosure, proper enforcement market regulations, and an extension of Article 214 to the bond and derivatives markets, the mechanism for shareholders to exert positive changes on corporate governance will be marginalised, poor firm investment decisions will go unchecked, and insider trading will dominate the exchanges. Finally, although hopefully assisted by the September 1998 formation of the China Chengxin Credit Rating Company—a joint venture including Fitich IBCA—accurate company risk ratings are still lacking.

- Actively open the domestic market to foreign banking and securities firms. Foreign firms will bring competitive bidding and risk valuations to the domestic market to determine real prices—real prices are a critical information component missing from the Chinese market at present and the longer prices remain distorted the greater the potential for asset bubbles. They will also facilitate financial services technology and skill transfer, and create future distribution links to foreign client markets for future placement of Chinese securities.

Fears that allowing domestic banks to compete directly in deposit-taking activity will lead to the immediate collapse of Chinese firms should not materialise given empirical historical examples in Japan and Latin America. The development of an advanced domestic capital market necessary to finance future government spending and assist in the recapitalisation of the state sector will take considerably longer in isolation.

Notes

[1] Prior to the reforms of the late 1970s and early 1980s the cash plan was set independently of the credit plan, thus creating monetary segmentation. However, by the late 1980s the cash plan was more indicative and of secondary importance.

[2] However, as reported by Wu (1995), until a profitable commercial based lending market was developed, it would remain in a bank manager's best interest to pay employees.

[3] Merrill Lynch (1998) lending estimates.

[4] In addition to the state-owned banks, the consolidated balance sheets for the national banking sector also includes the People's Bank of China, the Bank of Communications, CITIC Industrial Bank, and postal savings deposit institutions. However, this consolidated balance sheet provides the best available proxy for pure state banking behaviour.

[5] Other major PBC-forced closures include the closure of China Venturetech Investment Corp and Hainan Development Bank.

[6] The Industrial Bank of Japan, Dai Ichi Kangyo Bank, Citibank, Standard Charter Bank, the Hong Kong and Shanghai Banking Corp, Bankque Indosuez, Sanwa Bank, and Tokyo-Mitsubishi Bank.

[7] For 1988, inter-bank lending amounted to 345 per cent of total incremental bank lending for that year (Xia 1995).

[8] For example, Girardin (1997) founds that banks were dominant in Shanghai while financial institutions were dominate in Wuhan.

[9] See Girardin (1997) for full details of these new stipulations.

[10] Although consolidated inter-bank liabilities and assets should net to zero, Girardin (1997) has also found significant discrepancies in this market.

[11] Despite the lack of current inter-bank lending data for the entire inter-bank market, a net liability is clear since: RCC's and UCC's total inter-bank activity is on average less than 10 per cent of that for state bank activity; foreign banks have only recently begun to participate in the inter-bank market on a limited basis; TICs are net borrowers in this market; and total assets of the remaining categories are relatively insignificant. Clearly total assets and liabilities should net to zero if properly accounted for.

[12] In 1997 the weighted average interest rates were 10.4 per cent, 11.13 per cent, 10.64 per cent, 11.09 per cent, 11 per cent, 11.01 per

cent, and 10.6 per cent for overnight, 7 days, 20 days, 30 days, 60 days, 90 days, and 120 days respectively.

[13] As reported by the Economic Intelligence Unit (1998).

[14] 270 billion yuan of special treasury bonds were issued to recapitalise state-owned commercial banks in September 1998, 100 billion yuan of special treasury bonds were placed with state banks to fund the central government's fiscal expansion, and in April 1998 the Ministry of Finance auctioned 45 billion yuan in T bonds designated for the four sole state-owned banks. However the latter will be tradeable on the inter-bank bond market.

[15] Prior to this type of auction, the banks' sources of fund—of which 90 per cent came from bond issuance to commercial banks and savings deposit affiliates of the State Postal Bureau—were forced upon buyers through a mandatory quota system under government set interest rates. Equally importantly, greater freedom is being given to issuers to determine the terms of their debt issuance, coupon rate and maturity schedule.

[16] Figures taken from SAFE, Merrill Lynch (1998) and Reuters.

[17] For example China was the first country to issue global bonds after the Russian debt crisis in summer 1998 with its US$1 billion 10 year global bond that was sold at a yield to maturity of 7.346 per cent in autumn 1998.

[18] For example the US$100 million global bond issued in October 1997 and maturing in 2006 was widely believed to be largely bought by major Chinese state-controlled banks. Marginal spreads between various duration assets also create suspicion of both illiquid assets and intervention.

[19] Figures taken from *Financial Times*, London, 30 December 1998 and State Information Council.

[20] The East Asian crisis decreased activity on the H share market; in 1998 there were only two new H shares (Huaneng Power and Yanzhou) and one Red Chip (Zhu Kuan development), down from 1997 where there were 16 H share listings raising HK$32.04 billion and ten red chips raising HK39 billion. And while the Red Chip and to a lesser extent the H share market will likely stagnate in 1999 due both to the effect of GITIC's collapse on investor confidence in China and overall stagnation of the Hong Kong and Chinese economies, a recovery of China's economy will likely bring about a heavy calendar of new issues in both these markets in the coming years.

[21] Objective requirements are the following: a minimum capitalisation of over five million yuan; 25 per cent sale to the public; over 500 shareholders, with any shareholder holding over five per cent being registered and approved; and the company must have shown a profit for the last two years.

[22] The B share market's settlement period of T+3 is largely a function of exchange rate non-convertibility and an underdeveloped custodian system in this market.

[23] The lack of these two factors are just some of the major reasons behind the underdevelopment of similar markets in Japan.

[24] China only has closed-end mutual funds trading on the various exchanges. The Wuhan Securities Investment Fund was China's first, launched in 1991 and as of 1993 there were 73 listed mutual funds. However, since 1993 the PBC has increasingly regulated the issuance of new funds and only recently have officially registered funds begun to increase, although in 1995 there were 51 informally registered funds trading on China's various exchanges. The most recent new investment funds issued in 1998 were the Kaiyuan fund managed by the China Southern Securities company listed on the Shenzhen exchange, and the Jintai fund managed by Guotai Securities Company listed on the Shanghai exchange.

Labour market reform

Xin Meng

Over the last twenty years China has undergone transition from a planned to a market-oriented economy. Reforms have brought about remarkable economic growth, through transformations in the agricultural sector and rapid export growth. However growth until 1997 has not been accompanied by significant state-owned enterprise reform or labour market reforms in the urban sector. During the initial stages of economic growth such lack of structural change is not so serious, but as incomes rise further reform is essential. Due to the current East Asian financial crisis it seems unlikely that exports will make a large contribution to growth in the near future. Whether China can sustain its rapid growth rate will depend heavily on the government's willingness to pursue further internal structural reforms including the necessity for further labour market reform.

Problems with the pre-reform labour situation

For nearly half a century labour markets in China were not of a conventional nature. Traditional markets only started to emerge following the economic reforms that began in 1978. The main characteristics of the country's labour situation before reform were segregation of the rural and urban economies which meant that economic gains that arise from the efficient allocation of labour were forgone, extreme immobility of labour, which created serious problems of hidden unemployment and low productivity, and the disincentives prevalent in the income distribution system.

In the countryside income distribution was based on a work point system, where an individual's work points were evaluated on each day of work among the members of the team. At the end of each year the net distributable income of the production team was divided by the total work points earned by all members. This system separated individual effort and the distribution of benefits—an individual's earnings were not only determined by his/her own efforts but also by the efforts of other members of the team. The nature of agricultural production makes monitoring work effort very difficult so this system encouraged individuals to shirk in the hope that they could take advantage of other people's efforts, and created the belief that no matter how hard one worked, the results of the extra effort would be shared by all members of the team. Furthermore the more one attended the team production, regardless of whether effective effort was put in, the more work points one would receive. Subsequently individuals tended to supply more labour hours than were required. Additionally, the value of the work point had no impact on individuals' effective labour supply because it was not known until the end of each year (Burkett and Putterman 1993).

In the urban economy wages were determined by the central government on the basis of an individual's education, experience, occupation, and location of work unit. Although human capital was the basis for wage differentials the rates of return to schooling and work experience were extremely low. However, an individual's human capital stock is only an indicator of potential productivity. Without a mechanism to encourage individuals to work efficiently large human capital stock will not yield high productivity. In a market economy this mechanism exists in the form of the threat of employment termination. However in pre-reform urban China labour mobility was restricted because firms did not have the power to employ and fire workers, and workers were unable to choose suitable jobs. Thus it was not easy for firms to punish workers who provide inadequate effort levels, and workers were not in a position to choose jobs which best suited their interests or abilities. Often poor worker-firm relationships existed, and lack of interest in one's job reinforced shirking behaviour.

Impact of rural economic reform on the rural labour market

The years 1977 and 1978 marked a turning point in China. After 40 years under a centrally controlled economy, Chinese farmers for the first time reacted to their extremely poor living conditions by deciding to work on a family basis, ignoring the possible political and economic pressures from government. The success of their initiative—a dramatic increase in agricultural production—enlightened the Chinese government. In 1978 a new system called the household responsibility system (HRS)—began to be implemented throughout the country.

Impact on rural agricultural sector

Once agricultural production and income distribution were based around the family unit, labour allocation and income determination became family decisions. This provided the basis for a better incentive system as the returns to farm household production were directly linked to family effort.

Now household income variation was determined primarily by productivity-related variables. Table 7.1 presents an empirical estimation of the determination of rural household income.[1] It is shown that most of the productivity-related variables such as average household education level, average work experience, and labour and capital inputs are positive and significant determinants of household income.

Economic reform also changed rural household labour supply. Post-reform rural labour appeared to respond to wages in a normal way. Increases in the wage rate had a positive and significant impact on household labour supply up to a point, beyond which further increases in wages gradually reduced labour supply (see Figure 7.1).

Impact on rural non-agricultural sector

A similar, though more gradual change also occurred in the rural non-agricultural sector following the introduction of the HRS. With its introduction came an increase in grain prices in 1979 and a sharp rise in labour productivity, which generated two important changes: an increase in the agricultural surplus and an increase in surplus agricultural labour. These changes, combined with the fact that rural surplus labourers were not allowed to move to the cities to find jobs forced Chinese peasants to find other ways to increase their income—surplus agricultural output and labour were invested in already existing rural non-agricultural enterprises. Hundreds of thousands of new rural non-agricultural enterprises were soon established. These enterprises were originally entirely owned by the collective authorities—townships and villages—but later privately-owned enterprises were also encouraged.

After the introduction of the HRS the communes, brigades, and production teams lost much of their administrative and economic functions. When production and income distribution decisions in the agricultural sector were made within the household, it was impossible and meaningless for those who worked in the non-agricultural sector to

---

Table 7.1 Ordinary least squares estimation of household net income equation (1994–95 rural household survey)

	Log (NHI/Labour)	
	Coeff.	T-Ratio
Constant	6.402	21.83
Log total household workdays	0.230	4.83
Log land (MU)	0.474	14.27
Log animal ploughing and sowing (hrs)	-0.011	-1.55
Log plastic film (kg)	0.026	1.87
Log farm manure (kg)	-0.007	-1.60
Log pesticides input (jin)	0.036	2.35
Log seeds input (jin)	0.002	0.12
Log tractor ploughing and sowing (hrs)	0.036	3.06
Average years of schooling per labourer	0.045	5.50
Average potential work experience	0.007	3.16
Agricultural workdays/total workdays	-0.338	-5.70
Total female labourers/total labourers	0.070	0.68
Dummy variable for 1995	0.316	12.28
Jiangxi	-0.795	-17.06
Jilin	-1.017	-14.59
Sichuan	-0.855	-16.98
Shandong	-0.575	-11.80
Adjusted R^2	0.49	
Number of observations	1,863	

Source: Author's estimations.

have their income transferred back to their production teams. The income distribution system needed to be changed to a within-enterprise distribution system. Nevertheless, for quite a long time employment in rural non-agricultural enterprises remained under the control of the authorities. Township and village enterprises were granted wage determination, but not the right to employ and fire workers. This situation did not change until the mid to late 1980s.

Despite the inflexible employment system in the township, village and privately-owned enterprises (TVP) sector, enterprises paid workers according to their labour productivity. This is illustrated by the similarity of wage determination patterns of those paid by piece rates and those paid by time rates (Meng 1998). If piece rate payments reflect labour productivity, the consistent wage determination structures for the two groups suggest that workers in TVPs were paid according to their productivity.

Figure 7.1   Impact of daily wage change on annual labour supply (workdays)

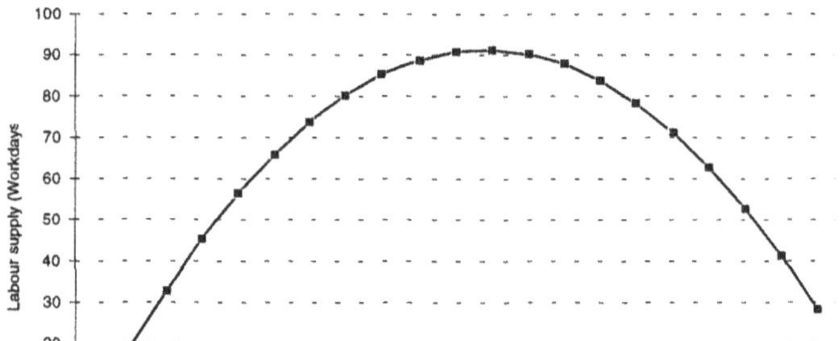

Source: Meng, X., 1998. Labour market reform in China, The Australian National University, Canberra (unpublished).

Inability to hire and fire workers did not stop the wage determination system in the TVP sector from evolving into a structure similar to that found in market economies. There are two possible explanations for this. First, TVPs operated in a very competitive market and under fairly hard budget constraints. To be successful, firms had to operate efficiently, which made it necessary to set up good incentive systems for workers. Alternatively, the only other employment opportunity for TVP workers was agricultural employment, which paid much less. Hence employees would not leave their jobs. Although managers were not allowed to fire workers, the right to determine wage levels and bonuses enabled them to punish shirking.

Since the mid 1980s the flexibility of employment in the TVP sector has increased rapidly. One survey of 300 township and village enterprises (TVEs) indicated that by 1991, 96 per cent of firms were allowed to make recruitment decisions and 95 per cent could dismiss workers (Xu *et al.* 1993). More importantly, privately-owned enterprises in the rural non-agricultural sector have grown rapidly. By 1995 about 53 per cent of total TVP employment was in the private sector (SSB 1996).

Urban labour market reform

Economic reform in the urban sector began in the early 1980s following the success of the agricultural reforms. This reform, however, was much tougher as socialist ideology clashed with market-based institutions. Conflict was two-sided from a labour market perspective.

On the one hand socialist ideology implies public ownership, which in turn suggests that workers are the owners of state property, should have the right to full employment and no one should be allowed to dismiss them. Thus labour market reform was—and still is—politically sensitive. This was one of the most significant reasons why urban economic reform bypassed factor markets and concentrated on goods markets for a long period of time. Labour market reform did not start until as late as the mid 1980s. Even then, reforms were implemented with great caution. On the other hand, public ownership and its associated soft budget constraints prevented enterprises from operating efficiently. There were insufficient incentives for efficient labour allocation and labour cost minimisation. This further weakened the effects of the already limited reforms.

The labour contract system was formally introduced between 1984 and 1986, and by 1995 involved about 39 per cent of the state sector workforce. It was a relatively flexible labour allocation mechanism in comparison to the rigid pre-reform system. The contract system allowed firms to select and hire suitable individuals. However, as managers in state-owned enterprises were not responsible for the state's assets but rather for their employees' wellbeing, this system did not produce the desired flexible hiring and firing outcome. Workers under contracts were guaranteed to have their contracts extended at the end of the period. Although managers were given the right to dismiss workers, they generally chose not to even when overstaffing became a serious problem. Furthermore, rather than minimising labour costs, managers would try to maximise employees' benefits to maintain their own popularity in the hope of keeping their job. As a result, a rapid and unchecked rise in labour compensation unrelated to gains in productivity was widely observed (Walder 1989). Because of these difficulties, labour market reform in urban China has not been very successful.

Change in individual wage determination patterns in the state-owned sector

Although economic reforms brought about structural change in the individual wage determination system, the rate of return to human capital related variables only changed slightly and wages still appeared to be seniority, rather than productivity, based. Most of the changes in wage structure were induced by changes in industrial wage differentials, which may have been due to the introduction of enterprise profit retention.

Table 7.2 provides a comparison of the rates of return to education and experience in China's state sector and a number of other industrialised economies. There are a number of important differences between wage determination in China's state sector and a market economy. First, although the signs and statistical significance of the human capital variables education and experience for China are similar to those for most industrial economies, the magnitudes differ significantly. An additional year of education increased individual earnings by 2.5 and 2.7 per cent in China in 1981 and 1987 respectively.[2] The US and UK studies report an increase in earnings of 5 and 7 per cent respectively. Psacharopoulos (1994) also reported a much higher return to education in developing countries. For low income countries, an additional year of schooling increased earnings by 11.2 per cent, while for Asian countries (excluding Japan) the figure was 9.6 per cent.

Figure 7.2 provides a comparison of experience-earning profiles for China's state-sector, Australia, the United States and the United Kingdom in 1980, 1987 and 1990. It indicates that the relationship between experience and wage levels for the market economies is of the traditional concave shape, whereas the profile is upward-sloping for the entire working life in China's state sector. In market economies a peak in earnings is reached when an individual is in his 30s to mid 40s (assuming that working life starts between the ages of 16 and 21), suggesting that the experience profile exhibits a relationship between productivity and the wage level. For China the experience profile rises continuously until retirement, suggesting that the profile is more likely to be related to seniority in China. Furthermore, the shape of the profile did not change over the period studied.

The most significant change in wage determination in the state sector during the 1980s was within industry. Meng and Kidd (1997a) found that in comparison to the wage determination pattern in 1981, of the 29 industry dummy variables included in the wage equation 25 played a significantly different role in wage determination in 1987.

Changes in individual wage determination were not towards a more productivity-based system over the period 1981–87. Rather, the evidence suggests that the majority of changes in the wage determination system came from industries, and may be traced to the introduction of profit-related bonus schemes. These may have arisen due to deeper problems with the current ownership structure within the state sector.

State ownership and its impact on SOE wage and employment determination

To determine whether the failure of labour market reform in the urban state sector was due to the ownership structure, a test was conducted using enterprise level data.

The data set comprises the state, collective, and private sectors with the private sector being used as a benchmark for market behaviour. To test how state and collective enterprises behaved differently to the private sector, wage and labour demand equations were estimated.

Table 7.2   Comparison of return to human capital between
China and some industrial countries

| | China | | | Australia | United States | United Kingdom |
	1981	1987	1990	1990	1989	1980
Experience	0.0273	0.0283	0.0213	0.039	0.037	0.028
Experience[2]	-0.0001	-0.0002	-0.0001	-0.001	-0.0006	-0.0005
Years of schooling[a]	0.0246	0.0266	0.0042	n.a.	0.05[b]	0.071

Note: [a] To make the results comparable with other studies, the author estimated two wage equations, one with years of schooling, the other with educational dummy variables. [b] The results are from Mincer and Higuchi (1988). The figure reported in Psacharopoulos' (1985) study is around 7 to 10 per cent.
Sources: Author's estimations for China (1981 and 1987); China (1990) from Shao, L., 1992. 'Income differentials within the state enterprises', in H. Du (ed.), *The Foundation for Efficient Management: employees' feelings and behaviour*, People's Publishing House of Shanghai, Shanghai:156–72; Kidd, M. and Meng, X., 1997. 'Trends in the Australian gender wage differential over the 1980's: some evidence on the effectiveness of legislative reform', *Australian Economic Review*, 30(1):31–44; Borland, J., Vella, F. and Woodbridge, G., 1995. Inter- and intra-industry earnings variation in Australia and the United States: what explains the difference?, (unpublished manuscript); Miller, P.W., 1987. 'The wage effect of the occupational segregation of women in Britain', *The Economic Journal*, 97:885–96.

Figure 7.2   Comparison of experience-earning profiles

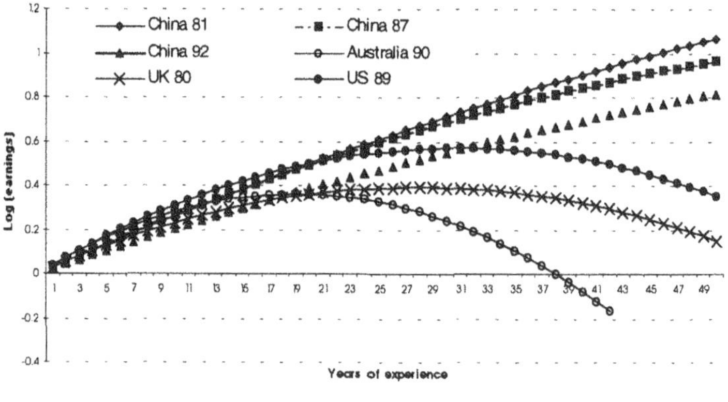

Source: Author's estimations.

The empirical results obtained indicated that state ownership prevented profit maximising behaviour by enterprises and in the public sector (both state and collective enterprises), labour compensation was related to a firm's retained profits rather than to productivity. Labour compensation in private enterprises, however, was solely determined by labour productivity.

Furthermore, although both state and collective firms were publicly owned, the degree of separation between risk bearing and decision-making was much greater in the state sector than in the collective sector. This implied that the former had softer budget constraints. As a result, the productivity incentives induced by profit sharing were much stronger in the collective sector than in the state sector. It was also found that overstaffing was more of a problem for the state and collective sectors than for the private sector.

Social security reform—a constraint for urban labour market reform

All results indicated that labour market reform in urban China has proceeded slowly. To achieve greater success in labour market reform requires deep-rooted changes in ownership structure. Ownership reform is not a simple task. One of the major difficulties is how to transform the current social security system without causing significant social and political instability. In the pre-reform era the state provided a lifelong enterprise-based social security system in the cities. The system included free child-care, free education, lifetime employment, free medical care, subsidised housing, and a full pension. This internal social security system had two major flaws. First, it put considerable financial pressure on state enterprises when they tried to become efficient and financially independent. Some enterprises had to pay pensions equivalent to their wage bills. Additionally it prevented efficient labour allocation by reducing labour mobility. Enterprises were afraid to sack workers for fear of social instability, and individual employees were unwilling to move for fear of losing their benefits.

Reform is inevitable; the question is how to reform. Two models could be followed—the western social welfare model and the East Asian private welfare model. A review of the two models revealed that most OECD countries that followed the welfare state model experienced high unemployment and rapid growth of government expenditure, while the countries that followed the private welfare system tended to have low unemployment rates, low government expenditure and high economic growth rates (Meng forthcoming). Importantly, simple predictions of the necessary expenditures on unemployment benefits and pensions indicated that it is beyond the Chinese government's financial ability to implement the welfare state model. China can only afford a welfare system which encourages individuals to take care of themselves. Such a system would induce more private saving, reduce labour costs, reduce unemployment and encourage economic growth.

Rural–urban migration

After more than 40 years of separation, the rural and urban economies were finally linked by rural–urban migration in the late 1980s and early 1990s. Like rural economic reform, rural–urban migration was not initiated by the government, but was rather the result of rural surplus labour and excess labour demand in the urban sector. The government reacted passively to this movement and controls on migration were gradually loosened. In 1996 about 80 million rural migrants were working in urban areas—about 18 per cent of the total rural labour force or one third of the total urban labour force.

China's rural–urban migration has two unusual features. The first is the labour market segregation of rural migrants and urban residents. Urban residents receive enormous subsidies and benefits not available to rural residents—even those rural residents who have moved to cities and taken up urban jobs. The jobs that rural migrants take pay less and have no job tenure or other benefits. More importantly rural migrants are not entitled to jobs in the formal sector. Other features are the ongoing institutional constraints on rural–urban migration. These include the Household Registration System, the compulsory agricultural production quota, and the fact that rural residents are not entitled to social welfare in urban areas.

Impact of rural-urban migration on economic growth

The features of rural–urban migration in China make the impact of such migration on economic growth somewhat different from that in other developing countries. The most important difference is that rural–urban migration is not the cause of urban unemployment. A simple theoretical model may be used to analyse the impact of migration on economic growth in China. Assume there are three sectors: rural, urban informal and urban formal, and that there are barriers to entry from rural to urban informal, and from urban informal to urban formal sectors. Thus, there are three different wage levels as shown in Figure 7.3, W_u, W_m, and W_o.

In the case where rural–urban migration is restricted and the urban wage level is set at W_u, the average urban wage level will be W_u and the average rural wage level will be $W_o{}'$. When migration is allowed but an institutional barrier for migrants working in the formal sector exists, the average urban wage level will be $\alpha W_u + (1 - \alpha)W_m$, where α is the fraction of urban residents in the total urban labour force. Clearly $W_u > \alpha W_u + (1 - \alpha)W_m$, which implies that migration will reduce average urban labour costs. Furthermore, the average rural wage level will increase from $W_o{}'$ to W_o.

Because of the segmentation in urban labour markets between urban residents and rural migrants, rural–urban migration has little impact on urban hidden unemployment. The level of hidden unemployment $L_{ub}L_{ub}{}'$, is the result of institutional wage setting and the inflexibility of the employment system, and is not directly related to rural–urban migration. Furthermore, as rural migrants cannot obtain jobs held by urban residents (beyond the point of $L_{ub}{}'$), the wage level paid to urban residents has no impact on rural migrants' expected urban wage. Rather, their expected wage is a function of the value of the marginal product of labour in the urban informal sector and the probability of obtaining a job in that sector. Given that about 80 per cent of migrants obtained a job before migration and the rest can normally find a job within a month after migration, the probability of getting a job is approximately equal to one. Thus the equilibrium condition of rural–urban migration is

$$W_r = \frac{W_m}{1 + t}$$

Figure 7.3   The three-sector model and rural–urban migration

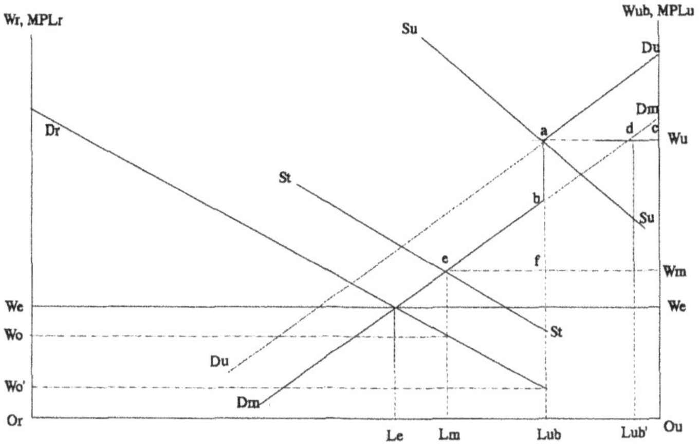

Source: Meng, X., (forthcoming). *Labour Market Reform in China*, Cambridge University Press, Cambridge.

where *t* represents the institutional barrier to entering the urban informal sector. The larger the barrier to entry, the greater the wage gap between the rural and urban informal sectors.

Thus the main impacts of rural-urban migration on economic growth were the reduction of labour costs in the urban sector and the increase in income in the rural sector. These outcomes are supported by empirical findings.

Economic gains from liberalisation of the two-tier labour market

Institutional constraints and other restrictions have created three different wage levels in the economy, and urban hidden unemployment. The existence of a two-tier labour market in urban China—segregation in the urban labour market between urban residents and rural migrants—is one of the most significant constraints to efficient allocation of labour within the urban economy. Eliminating these distortions should bring about further economic gains to the Chinese economy.

Table 7.3 presents the difference in occupational distribution and earnings between rural migrants and urban residents. Rural migrants were almost exclusively employed as trade, service and manual workers while more than 30 per cent of urban employees were professional, managerial and office workers. The wage gap between rural migrants and urban employees was significant. On average, the former earned 50 per cent of urban employees' hourly wage. Further decomposition of this earnings gap suggested that about 40 per cent of this wage differential could not be explained by labour productivity or other personal endowment differentials between the two groups, indicating the cause may be discrimination in favour of urban residents due to non-market institutional wage settings in the urban formal sector.

The removal of this distortion will bring about economic gains. Consider the three-sector model presented in Figure 7.3. The changes associated with the liberalisation of urban labour markets are presented in Figure 7.4. The removal of institutional wage setting between the urban informal and urban formal sectors implies that the labour demand curve in the urban sector will merge into one curve, $D_m D_m$.

Now consider two possible situations. First, assume the government intervenes in such a way that jobs are provided to urban residents first, and then to rural migrants.[3] Under this situation, the above changes will initially reduce the wage levels of urban residents to W_u', employment to OL_{ub}', and hidden unemployment in the formal sector to zero, and surplus workers in the state sector will be laid off. Thus the labour supply curve will move from $S_t S_t$ to $S_t' S_t'$, and wages in the informal sector will fall from W_m to W_m'. Thus, the removal of institutional wage setting in the urban informal sector will reduce total urban labour costs from $OL_{ub} a W_u + L_{ub} L_m ef$ to $OL_{ub}' g W_u' + L_{ub}' L_m' ih$.

Table 7.3 Occupational distribution, hours worked and earnings
of rural migrants and urban residents in Shanghai, 1995

| | Occupational distribution | | | | Hours worked by occupation | | | |
| | Migrants | | Urban residents | | Migrants | | Urban residents | |
	Freq	%	Freq	%	Mean	SD	Mean	SD
Professionals and technicians	34	0.70	355	17.05	47.15	15.56	41.21	5.52
Managerial staff	89	1.84	150	7.20	53.93	14.76	40.79	8.47
Clerical	29	0.60	234	11.24	53.86	14.65	39.53	6.42
Wholesale and retail trade	1264	26.07	149	7.16	61.03	23.42	47.11	16.27
Service workers	754	15.55	192	9.22	58.26	16.18	44.16	11.56
Production workers	2510	51.76	826	39.67	52.66	13.24	41.04	6.96
Other	169	3.49	176	8.45	54.06	16.81	42.78	13.40
Total	4849	100.00	2082	100.00	55.73	17.43	41.75	9.16

| | Monthly earnings | | | | Hourly earnings | | | |
| | Migrants | | Urban residents | | Migrants | | Urban residents | |
	Mean	SD	Mean	SD	Mean	SD	Mean	SD
Professionals and technicians	792.42	530.64	989.69	435.53	4.18	2.55	5.67	2.71
Managerial staff	1144.62	842.53	1147.28	618.52	5.46	3.63	6.98	4.33
Clerical	723.21	362.22	916.02	490.35	3.41	2.24	5.40	2.66
Wholesale and retail trade	560.54	660.97	904.26	484.34	2.68	4.34	5.06	2.74
Service workers	478.13	426.53	823.01	541.79	2.07	1.99	4.70	4.05
Production workers	558.03	243.28	889.62	507.81	2.58	1.29	5.31	5.90
Other	566.91	358.73	728.50	549.80	3.33	7.12	4.42	3.61
Total	558.98	409.38	911.86	515.82	2.60	2.59	5.37	4.57

Source: Author's calculations.

Instead assume that the government does not intervene in terms of job provision and both urban residents and rural migrants have equal job rights. This implies that the division of the urban formal and informal sectors will be eliminated. There will be no special labour supply curve for urban residents but a total labour supply curve for urban sector $(S_t'S_t')$ and wage levels in the urban formal sector will further fall to W_m'. Thus total labour costs will be further reduced from the area of $OL_{ub}'gW_u'+L_{ub}'L_m'ih$ to $OL_m'iW_m'$.

Thus theory suggests that the removal of non-market wage settings in the urban formal sector would reduce hidden unemployment as long as a flexible wage setting system was in place. Furthermore, if this condition held, the fall in hidden unemployment would not conflict with rural–urban migration. In reality, though further freeing up of the urban labour market is inevitable, it is not an easy task.

Figure 7.4   Impact of elimination of labour market distortions on urban employment and wages

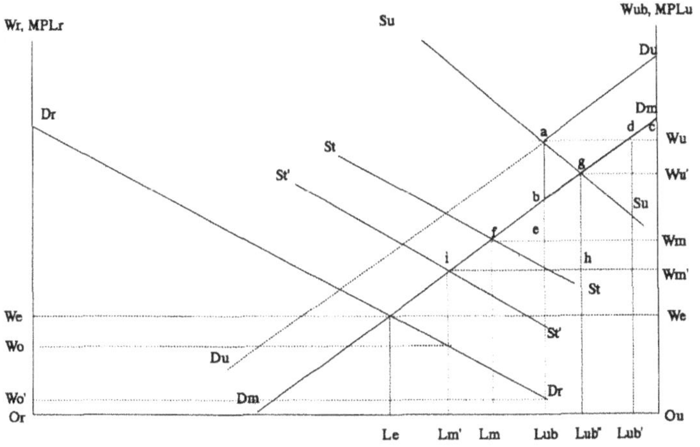

Source: Meng, X. (forthcoming). *Labour Market Reform in China*, Cambridge University Press, Cambridge.

Current issues

Problems with the ownership structure of SOEs have caused overstaffing. Additionally the competitiveness of state enterprises has been very low and is declining. In 1996 the total losses of SOEs exceeded profits (see Figure 7.5). A worse situation prevailed in 1997. Drastic reform of state enterprises was needed. A policy of 'grasping the big, let go the small' was introduced.[4]

In 1997, about 12 million urban SOE employees were laid off under this new reform initiate—roughly 10 per cent of SOE employees and 7 per cent of total urban employment. By the end of 1997 more than six million of these redundant workers were re-employed. In 1998, up until June, another three million were laid off. Informal estimates suggest there may be nine million redundant workers who have not yet been re-

Figure 7.5   Industrial SOE profits and losses

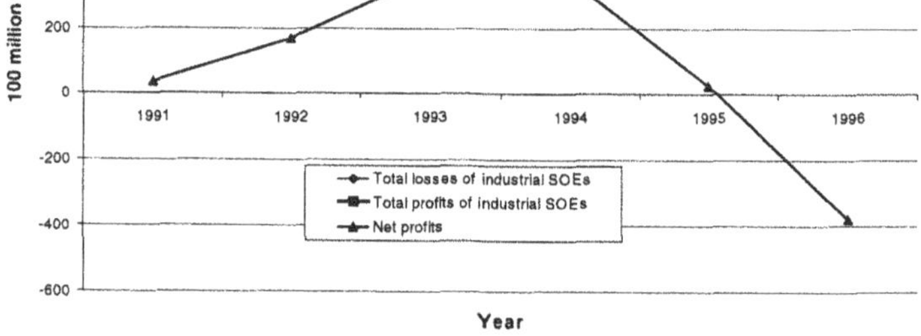

Source: State Statistical Bureau, various years. *Statistical Yearbook of China*, China Statistical Publishing House, Beijing.

employed. Although the rate of lay off has been reduced the need for further adjustment remains critical. In addition, the large number of redundancies has created unrest among urban residents, causing deep concern among policymakers and academics within and outside China. The government announced its policy towards redundant workers in June 1998, the basic theme being that reform of state enterprises is an inevitable process and is consistent with the long-run objective of economic growth. During this process laid-off workers may suffer temporarily and the government is committed to supporting them. Such assistance includes giving them priority over rural migrants for any available urban job, providing a living allowance while they are awaiting re-employment and providing them with the same pension benefits and housing arrangements regardless of whether they are re-employed or not.

The problem of unemployment due to state sector redundancies is not drastic. As indicated by national level data, of the 12 million redundancies in 1997, 50 per cent were re-employed within that year. A survey conducted in 55 cities also suggests some 62 per cent of laid-off workers were re-employed (Wang 1998).

The question is why the remaining redundant workers have not been re-employed. The most significant reason may be their unwillingness to take up 'low status' and 'low paid' jobs. Even though current government policy forbids employers from hiring rural migrants if there are redundant workers willing to take the jobs, there are still between 60 and 80 million rural migrants who are working in urban areas. These migrants came to urban areas with no government support or subsidy. If they were able to get jobs, the less than 10 million redundant workers should have had no difficulties had they been flexible.

The main issue is how to help urban residents adjust to the new flexible labour market environment. After 50 years of separation of the rural and urban economies and discriminatory treatment in favour of urban residents, some urban residents believe themselves to be superior to rural migrants. A recent study of urban redundant workers found that one of the most significant reasons laid-off workers had difficulty finding jobs was that they were unwilling to take what they believe to be 'low status' jobs. Some said they would rather voluntarily quit the labour market than accept the kind of jobs rural migrants take (Wang 1998). It will take time for redundant workers to accept that now in the market place everybody is equal.

Establishing a flexible labour market in China

Many of the deficiencies of the pre-reform labour arrangements will impede China's economic growth unless there is a complete restructure of the country's labour markets. The keys to freeing up China's labour markets include

- eliminating existing restrictions on rural–urban migration
- changing the labour market system within the urban sector. The majority of SOEs are being privatised. This will enable managers of enterprises to become more responsible for long-run growth and profits rather than the short-run benefits of employees. Labour market segregation between urban residents and rural migrants should be eliminated so that everybody has equal rights to compete in the labour market. All these changes will facilitate a flexible labour market, which will assist economic growth, generate jobs, and create higher income.
- designing a new welfare system, whereby individual employees play a more important role in the provision of their own safety nets.

Notes

[1] The data used for the empirical test are from a sample survey of about 1,000 rural households across five of China's provinces: Guangdong, Jilin, Jiangxi, Sichuan and Shandong. The survey was conducted in 1994 and 1995.

[2] To put this figure in the context of existing empirical literature, Byron and Manaloto (1990) report a 4 per cent rate of return to education in urban Nanjing, and Gregory and Meng (1995) report a 1 per cent increase in earnings for each additional year of schooling in China's rural industrial sector. Shao (1992) reported a less than 1 per cent rate of return to education. These studies confirm the low return to education in China relative to other market economies.

[3] This kind of intervention is common in urban China.

[4] Under this policy only 1000 large SOEs, which hold more than 70 per cent of SOE fixed assets and generate about 80 per cent of profit and tax, will remain under government control. The rest—more than 100,000 medium and small enterprises—will be freed by selling and leasing assets to workers, merging them with non-state enterprises, forming joint ventures with foreign enterprises, or auctioning them to individuals (EAAU 1997).

Changing income distribution in China

Li Shi *

Since the late 1970s, China has undergone transition towards a market economy. In terms of economic growth, China has achieved an impressive record. The average annual growth of GDP per capita was as high as 8.4 per cent during the period 1978 to 1997. The human development index also indicates an improvement in well-being on the average for the Chinese population (UNDP 1998). During this time, China has become strongly integrated into the world economy. China's exports grew an average of 16.7 per cent per annum over the last two decades. China absorbed US$205 billion as foreign direct investment during the period 1990–97.

Transition towards a market economy and openness has not been without its problems. An examination of the distribution of wealth in a fast growing economy such as China's provides us with an alternative criterion to evaluate its performance. This examination is primarily based on two similarly constructed household income surveys for 1988 and 1995, respectively. Both surveys have a large sample size drawn from rural and urban China.

Economic transition and income inequality in China

Since the late 1980s there have been big changes in sector composition. According to the national accounts, agricultural production grew by 57.6 per cent between 1988 and 1995, while services increased by 73.3 per cent. The manufacturing sector grew by 138.5 per cent. In rural China, industry also has grown remarkably, with annual average growth of 24.1 per cent during the period 1985 to 1995. Rural industry employed 28.6 per cent of the total labour force in rural China in 1995. Results from earlier studies indicate that China is shifting away from subsistence farming (Khan et al. 1992; Zhu 1994).

It is not surprising that the economic reforms have led to a significant change in the ownership structure of Chinese industry. The share of gross output value of industry by state-owned enterprises has been declining, from 57 per cent in 1988 to 26 per cent in 1997, while that of non-public owned enterprises has been increasing, from 7 per cent in 1988 to 36 per cent in 1997 (Table 8.1).

In urban China, employment in the publicly-owned sector increased by only 3.1 per cent from 1988 to 1997, while employment in the non-public sector—private, self-employed, joint-venture, foreign enterprises and so on—increased by an incredible 730.7 per cent and in 1997 accounted for 31.1 per cent of total employment in urban China.

China has been slow to develop labour markets, and labour mobility remained restricted in the mid 1990s. The economic sector is therefore an important institutional variable in determining workers' wages. Workers in a sector with a monopolistic position can share in the rents of their enterprise. Changes in the structure of employment are small but relative wages have undergone greater change (Gustafsson and Li 1998a). The wage ratio between the sector with the highest, and the sector with the lowest, average income increased from 1.58 in 1988 to 2.26 in 1997 (SSB 1989, 1998).

Another explanation for increased urban income inequality is the ongoing reform of state-owned enterprises. This had two effects. First, state-owned enterprises have been given a greater role in wage determination, creating a tendency for wages to be set higher for better skilled workers. Second, the enterprises have been permitted to lay off redundant workers more freely. Consequently, the number of unemployed workers has increased greatly since 1994. Official statistics show that there was a total of 15 million unemployed by the end of 1998; most of them have not been re-employed.

Economic transition in China has followed a clear regional pattern. Reforms were first institutionalised in the coastal areas. Such areas have since attracted a disproportionately large percentage of foreign investment and economic growth has been most rapid in those parts.

Table 8.1 Gross output value of industry by ownership in China
(billion yuan)

	1988	1991	1993	1995	1997
Gross value	1822.5	2662.5	4840.2	9189.4	11373.39
	(100)	(100)	(100)	(100)	(100)
State-owned enterprises	10.5.1	1495.5	2272.5	3122.0	2902.7
Collective-owned enterprises	658.8	878.3	1646.4	3362.3	4334.7
	(36.2)	(33.0)	(34.0)	(36.6)	(38.1)
Township enterprises	184.7	240.1	537.4	1193.2	n.a.
	(10.1)	(9.0)	(11.1)	(13.0)	n.a.
Village enterprises	170.4	234.7	516.3	1184.7	1794.0
	(9.4)	(8.8)	(10.7)	(12.9)	(15.8)
Joint enterprises	43.9	56.9	132.2	213.4	466.9
	(2.4)	(2.1)	(2.7)	(2.3)	(4.1)
Individual and private-owned enterprises	79.1	128.7	386.1	1182.1	2037.6
	(4.3)	(4.8)	(8.0)	(12.9)	(17.9)
Other ownership	49.5	163.1	517.4	1523.1	2098.2
	(2.7)	(6.1)	(10.7)	(16.6)	(18.4)
Shareholding			146.1	318.3	497.6
			(3.0)	(3.5)	(4.4)
Foreign-owned			185.3	540.8	827.2
			(3.8)	(5.9)	(7.3)
Overseas Chinese from Hong Kong, Macao, Taiwan			176.1	556.4	612.7
			(3.6)	(6.1)	(5.4)

Notes: 1 Gross output values are in current prices; 2 Shares of components are in parentheses (author's calculations).
Sources: State Statistical Bureau, 1994, 1996, 1998. *Statistical Yearbook of China*, China Statistical Publishing House, Beijing.

The other extreme is the less populated western areas. Inequality in (unweighted) average provincial per capita income has developed with a narrowing of provincial income inequality during the 1980s, but increasing thereafter (Table 8.2).[1]

Reasons for increased income inequality in China can also be attributed to the tax and social security systems. One of the taxes implemented in rural China is the agricultural tax, levied on the number of household members rather than on income. Subsequently, poor households pay no less tax than rich households. While urban Chinese have much higher incomes on average, only a small proportion of urban workers pay income taxes. Chinese social security is only available to urban workers, and the rural population must support themselves. Results indicate that the tax system has caused inequality not only in rural areas, but throughout China (Gustafsson and Li 1998b; Khan and Riskin 1998).

Economic reforms and subsequent changes in lifestyle have had a significant impact on equality of income distribution in China. As a result, income inequality has worsened within rural China and urban China, and between rural and urban areas. Tables 8.3 and Table 8.4 present the results estimated by the State Statistical Bureau (SSB), which indicate the changes in income growth and income inequality in rural and urban China from 1978 to 1997 in terms of the Gini coefficient. The coefficient increased by 55 per cent in rural areas during this period, from 0.212 to 0.329, while the increase was 82 per cent in urban areas during the same period, from 0.16 to 0.296. The growth of inequality in rural areas has been different from that in urban areas. There was an augmentation in inequality in rural areas in the early 1980s, triggered by the redistribution of land to individual households. Since then, rural inequality has risen gradually. In contrast, the growth of inequality in urban China is striking, rising in particular years, such as 1984, 1988 and 1994. These increases are related to the implementation of economic reforms (Li et al. 1998).

Meanwhile the income gap between the urban and rural sectors of China has been large. Official statistics indicated an increasing rural-

Table 8.2   Spatial inequality in China: provincial gross national product (GNP) per capita

Inequality index	1980	1984	1988	1995	1997
Coefficient of variance	0.951	0.753	0.675	0.665	0.686
Gini coefficient	0.350	0.304	0.298	0.312	0.316
Quintile					
1	0.1024	0.1097	0.1061	0.0964	0.0976
2	0.2225	0.2371	0.2341	0.220	0.2198
3	0.3608	0.3851	0.3877	0.3707	0.3696
4	0.5228	0.5737	0.5889	0.5892	0.5840
5	1.0000	1.0000	1.0000	1.0000	1.0000
Number of provinces	30	30	30	30	30

Source: State Statistical Bureau, various years. *Statistical Yearbook of China*, China Statistical Publishing House, Beijing.

urban gap for cash income between 1985 and 1997. Table 8.5 shows the trend of income inequality since the mid 1980s.

Due to increasing inequality of income distribution both within and between rural and urban China, it is not surprising that income inequality in China has been rising since the late 1970s. Results from the two surveys indicated that the Gini coefficient for the whole country increased from 0.382 in 1988 to 0.452 in 1995 (Khan and Riskin 1998).

Data and assumptions

The data analysed come from two surveys conducted by the project team on China Income Distribution, affiliated with the Institute of Economics, Chinese Academy of Social Sciences (with assistance from the State Statistical Bureau). The first survey of household income in 1988 was conducted in the spring of 1989 and has been analysed by the project team led by Griffin and Zhao (1993) and in some extended studies (Gustafsson and Li 1997, 1998a, 1998b). More detailed descriptions of the survey can be found in Eichen and Zhang (1993) and Khan *et al.* (1992).

The household income survey for 1995 was conducted during the period January to March 1996. Like the first survey the second had different sample procedures for households in rural and urban areas. Both surveys used large samples from the State Statistical Bureau. Due to budget constraints the sample size for the second survey was reduced by 5000 to 15000 households (with 8000 in the rural and 7000 in the urban sample). The 1995 rural sample covered 109 counties located in 19 provinces while the urban sample covered 11 provinces.[2] The provinces were chosen with China's geographic differences in mind.[3] A more detailed discussion of the 1995 survey can be found in Khan and Riskin (1998) and Gustafsson and Li (1998b).

The questionnaires were designed by members of the project team. Most questions in the first survey reappeared in the second. The second also contained some new questions. Income-related questions in the urban surveys were posed with the objective of determining household disposable income; households were required to answer questions regarding income-in-kind and the market value of housing subsidies as well as imputed rent of privately-owned houses. In the rural questionnaires, the present value of private houses was asked in order to derive their imputed values by adopting a discount rate. Both the

Table 8.3   Income growth and income inequality in rural
China, 1978–97

Year	Gini coefficient		Real income per capita	
	Level	Change (%)	Level (yuan)	Change (%)
1978	0.212	-	134	-
1979	0.237	11.8	140*	4.5
1980	0.238*	0.4	146	4.3
1981	0.239	0.4	161	10.3
1982	0.232	-2.9	191	18.6
1983	0.246	6.0	210	10.0
1984	0.258	4.9	231	10.0
Annual growth rate 1978–84 (%)	3.33	n.a.	9.50	n.a.
1985	0.264	2.3	238	3.0
1986	0.288	9.1	240	0.8
1987	0.292	1.4	246	2.5
1988	0.301	3.1	247	0.4
1989	0.300	0.3	228	-7.7
1990	0.310	3.3	249	9.2
Annual growth rate 1985–90 (%)	3.11	n.a.	1.26	n.a.
1991	0.307	1.0	252	1.2
1992	0.314	2.2	266	5.6
1993	0.320	1.9	275	3.4
Annual growth rate 1991–93 (%)	1.06	n.a.	3.37	n.a.
1994	0.321	0.3	295	7.3
1995	0.341	6.3	325	10.2
1996	0.323	-5.3	368	13.1
1997	0.329	1.9	397	7.9
Annual growth rate 1994–97 (%)	0.7	n.a.	9.61	n.a.

Notes: *Estimated as the mean of figures from the previous year and next year due to omitted value for this year.
Sources: Ping, T., 1995. 'Analysis on income level and inequality of rural households in China', *Management World*, 2. State Statistical Bureau, various years. *Statistical Yearbook of China*, China Statistical Publishing House, Beijing. Gini coefficients for years 1994–97 provided by General Team of Rural Household Survey, State Statistical Bureau.

Table 8.4   Income growth and income inequality in urban China, 1978–97

Year	Gini coefficient Level	Change (%)	Real income per capita Level (yuan)	Change (%)
1978	0.16	-	316	-
1979	0.16	-	359*	13.6
1980	0.16	-	401	11.7
1981	0.15	-6.3	408	1.8
1982	0.15	-	433	6.1
1983	0.15	-	451	4.2
Annual growth rate 1978–83 (%)	-1.3	n.a.	7.4	n.a.
1984	0.16	6.7	5.07	12.4
1985	0.19	18.8	510	0.6
1986	0.19	-	577	13.1
1987	0.20	5.3	586	1.6
1988	0.23	15.0	594	1.4
1989	0.23	15.0	594	1.4
Annual growth rate 1984–89 (%)	7.4	n.a.	2.1	n.a.
1990	0.23	0.0	625	8.7
1991	0.24	4.4	662	5.9
1992	0.25	4.2	721	8.9
1993	0.27	8.0	794	10.1
1994	0.30	11.1	864	8.8
Annual growth rate 1990–94 (%)	5.5	n.a.	10.9	n.a.
1995	0.282	-6.0	906	4.9
1996	0.284	0.7	940	3.8
1997	0.292	2.8	972	3.4
Annual growth rate 1995–97 (%)	-0.9	n.a.	4.0	n.a.

Sources: Ren, F. and Cheng, X., 1996. 'To investigate income differential from income of urban households', *Reference of Economic Research*, 157 (in Chinese). State Statistical Bureau, various years. *Statistical Yearbook of China*, China Statistical Publishing House, Beijing. Gini coefficients for years 1994–97 provided by General Team of Urban Household Survey, State Statistical Bureau.

rural and the urban questionnaires had comprehensive questions regarding household consumption as well as household assets, both financial and physical.

Household disposable income is defined as individual income and household income not attributed to individuals. The former includes earnings, pensions, monetary and in-kind subsidies; the latter, household income from farming, family enterprise and property. Seventy per cent of urban households were still living in public apartments in 1995, paying rents much lower than the market price. Subsequently, housing subsidies for those households were a crucial part of their income. This was calculated as a differential between the respondents' estimate of the market rent and the rents actually paid.[4] It was also considered important to include imputed rent of privately-owned houses and apartments. For rural China this was done by applying a discount rate of 8 per cent to the present value of the house (as estimated by the respondent).

Table 8.5   Changes in income inequality between rural and urban China, 1985–97

Year	Ratio of urban to rural (real) income	Change (%)	Ratio of urban to rural (nominal) income	Change (%)
1985	1.72	-	1.72	-
1986	1.94	22	1.95	13
1987	1.91	-3	1.98	3
1988	1.94	3	2.05	7
1989	2.03	9	2.10	5
1990	2.02	-1	2.02	-8
1991	2.11	9	2.18	16
1992	2.19	8	2.33	15
1993	2.32	13	2.54	21
1994	2.36	4	2.60	6
1995	2.25	-11	2.47	-13
1996	2.05	-20	2.27	-20
1997	2.00	-5	2.23	-4

Source: State Statistical Bureau, various years. *Statistical Yearbook of China*, China Statistical Publishing House, Beijing.

In all tables, reported disposable income for 1995 has been expressed in 1988 prices. This has been done using price indices specific to the rural and urban parts of each province as published by the State Statistical Bureau (1996).

Decomposition analysis of income components

Changes in inequality as measured by the Gini coefficient can be traced to changes in the size and share of the different income types. The Gini coefficient of individual disposable income is decomposed using

$$G = \Sigma \, \mu_i c_i$$

where μ_i is the mean value of an income type Y_j as a proportion of individual disposable income, and C_{is} is the concentration ratio of income type i. The concentration ratio is based on the concentration curve which shows cumulated proportions of income type ranked according to disposable income. It is defined as the area between the concentration curve and the diagonal. Unlike the Gini coefficient, which ranges from zero to one, the concentration ratio can take values ranging from -1 to 1.

Assume first an income type taking positive values. A positive value for the concentration ratio means that the income type contributes positively to total inequality. For taxes, taking negative values, the reverse holds. Each type of income contributes to the Gini coefficient of disposable income by the product of its concentration ratio and its average share of income types.

Many studies argue that non-farming income of rural households has played an important role in increasing the inequality of income distribution in rural China (Khan et al. 1993; Zhu 1994; Khan and Riskin 1998; Li et al. 1998). Using the above approach decomposition analysis of income components was conducted to determine whether non-farming income has increased income inequality in rural China. Rural individual disposable income was decomposed into three components: household production income, individual wage income, and other income including household property income, imputed rental value of privately-owned housing, transfer income and so on (Table 8.6).

Rural inequality in terms of the Gini coefficient increased by nearly 27 per cent between 1988 and 1995, from 0.338 to 0.429 (Table 8.6).

The concentration ratios of the three income components increased by 1.4 per cent, 4.9 per cent and 24.9 per cent respectively. It is obvious that the increase in inequality of the three income components can only explain a small part of the overall increase in inequality. For the most part it is explained by changes in the share of the three income components. To illustrate this point, we can do two exercises. In one exercise we assume that 1995 disposable income has the same income shares as 1988 disposable income and calculate a simulated Gini coefficient of 0.360, which is 6.8 per cent higher than the actual coefficient. The difference between the simulated and actual Gini coefficients is due to changes in the distribution of income components. In the other exercise, we assume that each income component in 1995 had the same distribution as that of 1988, and compute a different simulated Gini for rural China, being 0.402. This simulated Gini is 18.9 per cent higher than the actual one. The increase is explained by changes in the share of income components alone. We can conclude that increased inequality in rural China is predominantly due to changes in the share of income components of household income, which reflect rapid but unbalanced growth of industry in rural China.

Table 8.6   Decomposition analysis of income inequality in rural China, 1988 and 1995

Income and its	1988			1995		
components	Ui(x100)	Ci or G	ei(x100)	ui(x100)	Ci or G	ei(x100)
Household production income	74.21	0.282	61.8	59.56	0.286	39.7
Individual wage income	8.73	0.710	19.3	23.62	0.745	41.0
Other income	17.06	0.394	19.9	16.82	0.492	19.3
Total income	100	0.338	100	100	0.429	100

Notes: Other income includes household property income, imputed rental value of privately-owned housing and transfer income, and so on. Concentration ratio of other income is calculated by the author. e_i is the contribution of ith income to total inequality. It can be formularised as $e_i = (U_i C_i)/G$, where G is Gini coefficient of total income.
Sources: Khan, A.R., Griffin, K., Riskin, C. and Zhao, R., 1993. 'Sources of income inequality in post-reform China', *China Economic Review*, 4:19–35. Li, S., Zhao, R. and Zhang, P., 1998. 'Economic transition and income distribution in China', *Economic Research*, April:42–51 (in Chinese).

The results from decomposition analysis indicate a different pattern of change in income inequality for urban China. The urban individual disposable income was decomposed into five components: workers' wage income, workers' non-wage income, income of retirees, income in-kind and other income. Our simulation analysis shows that over 95 per cent of the increase in inequality in urban China is due to changes in the distribution of income components, while a small part is due to changes in share of income components (Table 8.7).

Inequality and personal location

Many studies have shown that a large part of inequality of income distribution in China is created by regional disparities (Tsui 1993, 1996; Knight and Song 1993; World Bank 1997d; Gustafsson and Li 1998a and 1998b). In this section the population is decomposed into mutually exclusive subgroups according to their location variables. Using the additively decomposable inequality index—the Theil index—inequality in various location subgroups is investigated and their relative contribution to total inequality in China at two points in time is determined.

Table 8.7   Decomposition analysis of income inequality in urban China, 1988 and 1995

Income and its components	1988			1995		
	u_i(x100)	C_i or G	e_i(x100)	u_i(x100)	C_i or G	e_i(x100)
Worker wage income	32.57	0.130	18.2	32.83	0.169	19.4
Worker non-wage income	25.33	0.253	27.5	24.58	0.336	28.9
Incomes of retirees	6.83	0.335	9.8	10.96	0.324	12.4
Income in-kind	29.51	0.276	9.5	25.20	0.341	30.0
Other income	5.76	0.384	35.0	6.43	0.451	9.3
Total income	100	0.233	100	100	0.289	100

Notes: Income in-kind includes subsidies in-kind for public housing, in-kind income from work units, imputed rental value of privately-owned housing and so on. Other income covers property income, earnings of private owners and self-employees and private transfer income.
Sources: Khan, A.R., Griffin, K., Riskin, C. and Zhao, R., 1993. 'Sources of income inequality in post-reform China', *China Economic Review*, 4:19–35. Li, S., Zhao, R. and Zhang, P., 1998. 'Economic transition and income distribution in China', *Economic Research*, April:42–51 (in Chinese).

The Theil index is defined as

$$T(y, N) = \frac{\sum_i \left(\frac{y_i}{\mu} \right) \log \left(\frac{y_i}{\mu} \right)}{N}$$

and the mean logarithmic deviation (MLD) as

$$MLD(y, N) = \frac{\sum_i \log \left(\frac{\mu}{y_i} \right)}{N}$$

where μ is the mean equivalent income and N the total number of individuals.

Tables 8.8 and 8.9 show the results of decomposition analysis, obtained from work recently produced by Gustafsson and Li (1998b). The entire population was examined by location: rural-urban, east-central-west (also called the 'three belts'), and rural-urban and east-central-west integration. In analysing the rural-urban divide, Table 8.5 shows the income differential increased by 16 per cent in the period 1988 to 1995. It can be seen from the decomposition results presented in Table 8.8 that almost two-fifths of inequality in China in 1988 was attributed to differences in mean income between rural and urban China. As the inequality within each sector—especially rural China—has increased much faster, total inequality in 1995 is down to one-third, although the rural-urban income gap has widened.[5] Analysis by Gustafsson and Li (1998b) also illustrates that one-sixth of the increase in inequality in China is due to the increased income gap between rural and urban China.

Table 8.9 shows that within the 'three belts' region, inequality in western China was as significant as in the coastal areas in 1988 but became the worst affected area by 1995. Mean income in the western part increased at the slowest rate. Therefore the possibility that living standards in the west have deteriorated at the lowest income levels cannot be ruled out. Table 8.8 shows that 7.5 per cent of the inequality in China was attributed to the difference in mean income between the three regions in 1988. This figure rose to 9.3 per cent in 1995. Regional disparity worsened from 1988 to 1995.

Integrating the rural-urban and east-central-west regions yields six groups. Results of the investigations indicate that inequality within the rural-east sector was the greatest both in 1988 and 1995, and increased

Table 8.8   Decomposition of within-group and between-group
inequality in 1988 and 1995 by individual location

Sample partition	Year	Mean logarithmic deviation			Theil		
		Average inequality	Within -group inequality	Between -group inequality	Average inequality	Within -group inequality	Between -group inequality
Rural-urban							
	1988	258.31	159.6	98.7	253.3	145.6	107.7
	(%)	(100)	(61.8)	(38.2)	(100)	(57.5)	(42.5)
	1995	378.41	255.9	122.5	373.14	242.3	130.9
	(%)	(100)	(67.6)	(32.36)	(100)	(64.9)	(35.1)
'Three belts'							
	1988	258.31	238.8	19.5	253.3	233.6	19.7
	(%)	(100)	(92.5)	(7.5)	(100)	(92.2)	(7.8)
	1995	378.41	343.1	35.4	373.14	336.9	36.2
	(%)	(100)	(90.7)	(9.3)	(100)	(90.3)	(9.7)
Six regions							
	1988	258.31	138.4	119.9	253.3	125.8	127.5
	(%)	(100)	(53.6)	(46.4)	(100)	(49.7)	(50.3)
	1995	378.41	206.6	171.8	373.14	202.7	170.4
	(%)	(100)	(54.6)	(45.4)	(100)	(54.3)	(45.7)

Notes: [1]Income is individual equivalent disposable income. [2]Subgroups are defined as: rural-urban = rural, urban; 'Three belts' = east, middle, west; Six-regions = rural-east, rural-middle, rural-west, urban-east, urban-middle, urban-west.
Source: Gustafsson, B. and Li, S., 1998a. 'Inequality in China at the end of the 80s—location aspects and household characteristics', *Asian Economic Journal*, March:35–63.

significantly between those years, by 68.7 per cent. The rural-west sector experienced the most significant increase in inequality during this time period—73.9 per cent—much greater than that of the rural-central sector. Although the absolute inequality in the three urban sectors was relatively low, the increase was nonetheless remarkable. For instance, inequality increased by 53 per cent in the urban-east sector and by 55 per cent in the urban-central sector. Nearly half of China's inequality can be explained by the difference in mean income between the six sectors.

Table 8.9 Inequality of sub-group population in 1988 and 1995
by location

	1988				1995			
	Mean income (yuan)	% of sample	MLD (x1000)	Contribution to total inequality (%)	Mean income (yuan)	% of sample	MLD (x1000)	Contribution to total inequality (%)
Rural	822	74.1	184.4	52.9	1218	71.9	307.4	59.3
Urban	2131	25.9	88.7	8.9	3439	28.1	125.8	9.5
East	1449	38.9	251.9	37.9	2508	36.4	354.2	34.6
Middle	1011	38.4	217.2	32.3	1486	37.6	287.1	28.9
West	920	22.6	252.9	22.1	1423	26.0	408.4	28.5
Rural-east	1044	28.7	188.1	20.9	1786	26.0	317.4	22.1
Rural-middle	708	27.2	151.2	15.9	981	27.4	185.5	13.6
Rural-west	641	18.2	134.7	9.5	770	18.5	233.0	11.6
Urban-east	2587	10.2	89.8	3.5	4322	10.4	137.7	3.8
Urban-middle	1744	11.3	59.9	2.6	2841	10.2	92.9	2.5
Urban-west	2065	4.4	64.8	1.1	3032	7.5	84.1	1.7

Source: Gustafsson, B. and Li, S., 1998a. 'Inequality in China at the end of
the 80s—location aspects and household characteristics', *Asian Economic
Journal*, March:35–63.

Conclusions

The evidence indicates the rapid growth of household per capita
income over the past two decades has been matched by a significant
increase in income inequality. The results of our analysis, using both
the official and survey data, indicate that the growth of income
inequality has been quite general, and has taken place along a number
of different dimensions.

Decomposition analysis by income components shows that a large
part of the increased inequality in rural China can be explained by
changes in the share of income components, resulting from rapid
but uneven growth of industry in rural areas. Increased inequality in
urban China can be explained by changes in the distribution of
income components.

Location is a significant cause of income inequality. The urban-rural income gap was large by international standards in the 1980s and has continued to widen in the 1990s. However, inequality within urban China and particularly within rural China grew even more rapidly and therefore in the mid 1990s a smaller proportion of total inequality in China was attributed to the rural-urban gap.

The growth of household income differed across regions. Households in the already better-off eastern part of China experienced much larger income growth on average than households living elsewhere, and only a modest increase in inequality among them. In contrast, the mean income in the western part of China has increased at the lowest rate, while inequality there has increased most significantly. Results suggest that low-income groups in the west might even have experienced a decline in income. A larger proportion of Chinese inequality in 1995 can be attributed to the difference of mean income between eastern, central and western China. Combining the rural-urban gap and the eastern-central-western gap accounts for nearly half the total inequality in China.

Increased inequality between rural and urban China and among different regions has resulted from the slow development of the labour market and various restrictions on mobility and employment, particularly of rural workers. Some restrictions result from the policies of various Chinese governments. Therefore, some changes in present policies are needed to narrow rural-urban and regional disparities by allowing the labour force, especially rural workers, to have more freedom to migrate and experience less discrimination in employment.

Notes

* The author is grateful for the useful comments from Professor Bob Gregory. The draft chapter was also discussed at the Conference of Openness and Disparities in China, organised by CERDI-IDREC on 22–23 October 1998 in Clermont-Ferrand, France. This work has been financially supported by the Asian Development Bank and Ford Foundation.

[1] The figures may overestimate the real development due to migration. In the Chinese statistics, migrants are usually included in the population of the provinces of origin, not in the province of destination. Moreover migrant remittances are included in GDP for the province of destination, not in the province of origin. However, it is difficult to determine the extent of the inaccuracy.

[2] The provinces in the rural sample were Beijing, Hebei, Shanxi, Liaoning, Jilin, Jiangsu, Zhejiang, Anhui, Jiangxi, Shandong, Henan, Hubei, Hunan, Guangdong, Sichuan, Guizhou, Yunnan, Shaanxi and Gansu. The provinces in the urban sample were Beijing, Shanxi, Liaoning, Jiangsu, Anhui, Henan, Hubei, Guangdong, Sichuan, Yunnan and Gansu.

[3] A striking difference in household income was found between eastern coastal areas and western areas. Liaoning, Jiangsu, Zhejiang, Shandong and Guangdong represent the eastern coastal area; Hebei, Shanxi, Jilin, Anhui, Jiangxi, Henan, Hubei and Hunan the interior areas; and Sichuan, Guizhou, Yunnan, Shanxi and Gansu the western areas. Beijing is a member of the three large province-level municipalities.

[4] The question in the urban questionnaire was phrased: 'If you could rent out your house or apartment estimate the monthly rent.'

[5] The rural-urban income gap measured by MLD increased from 0.0987 in 1988 to 0.1225 in 1995, a rise of 24 per cent.

Review of economic reform in China: features, experiences and challenges

Zhao Renwei

In comparison to Eastern Europe and the former Soviet Union, economic reforms in China have some distinct characteristics. As noted by Harvard Professor Dwight H. Perkins, there is a particularly Asian pattern of reform of socialist economic systems. According to this view, the reforming Asian economies have three characteristics: economic reform precedes political reform, the socialist countries in Asia are much poorer than their counterparts in Eastern Europe and the former Soviet Union, and the majority of people in Asian socialist countries are employed in the agricultural sector. Small and medium-sized enterprises account for the lion's share of industry output. Professor Perkins also points out that these three characteristics are closely related.

If China's particular social and economic environment is taken into account, economic reforms in China possess another three related characteristics. These can be summarised as follows. First, the degree to which the economic system derived from the former Soviet Union exerted influence on the Chinese economy varied from sector to sector. The sector that was most influenced was the backbone of the national economy, that is, those sectors that have been industrialised. The influence on the disaggregated agricultural sector and small industries was significantly less. Although the previous economic system in China could broadly be defined as a 'centrally planned (material) resource allocation system', its influence on the economy was confined to certain parts because of the influence of other factors such as low income. Some sectors of the economy were actually market oriented before reform (Ishikawa 1986). Some economists therefore use the term 'low coverage rate of the planned economy system' to describe this characteristic. This characteristic provided some support for the economic reforms in China.

Second, the economic reforms in China started from a highly centralised economy, differing from the reforms in Eastern Europe and the former Soviet Union. During the twenty years after the establishment of the centrally planned system (1956–78), there were some important changes. The economic system in 1978 (before reform) was more monotypic in ownership structure, more centralised in terms of decision-making and resource allocation, more demonetised in economic activities (more emphasis was placed on using material planning rather than the market mechanism to allocate resources) and more equal in income distribution. It was a closed economy and featured more flexibility in organising the economy than it had in the beginning of the centrally planned system. Although we may characterise the economic system before the reform as a conventional centralised economic system, it actually differed from a conventional one because it featured a supply system more in the style of militaristic communism. If the economic system in Eastern Europe and the former Soviet Union before reform was a typically centrally planned economy (Stalinist model), then the economic system in pre-reform China can be regarded as a model of quasi-militaristic communism. Figure 9.1 illustrates that reforms in China began at an earlier stage than reforms in the former Soviet Union and Eastern Europe.

So far we have only looked at the starting point of the reform by examining the economic system. If other factors outside the economic system are taken into consideration, such as the lack of theoretical guidance for reform and the lower level of economic development, the starting point of China's reform could have been much lower than that of the former Soviet Union and Eastern European countries.

Third, economic reform in China was more closely related to economic development than was the case in the former Soviet Union and Eastern Europe. The former countries had been industrialised and were regarded as developed countries before their reform, while China was still a developing country. China not only experienced a transition from a

Figure 9.1   The starting point of economic reform in China

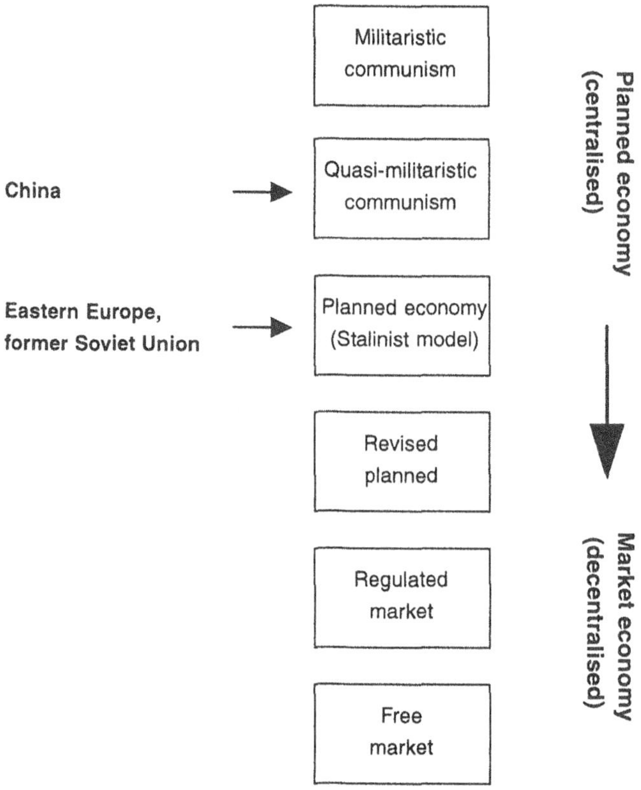

centrally planned to a market oriented economy, it also underwent a transformation in economic development from autarky economy to market economy. China underwent transformation from a dual economy to a modern economy (Figure 9.2).

In comparison to development transformation, the transition of an economic system is generally a more difficult process. This is because development transformation is a kind of natural evolution while the transition of an economic system depends on the instigation of reforms.

Figure 9.2 China's transition of economic system and
transformation of economic development

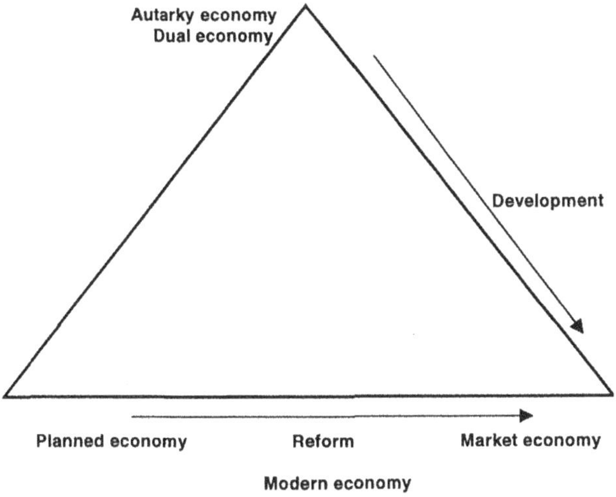

Autarky economy
Dual economy

Development

Planned economy   Reform   Market economy

Modern economy

Further, the process of reform tends to encounter many man-made obstacles, mainly resulting from ideological problems and interest groups. Of course, people's cognitive process is not a straight line. This is another underlying reason that the reform process of the last twenty years has been complicated; the goal of economic reform is a typical example.

The reform process has experienced success and setbacks since the Third Plenum of the 11th Central Planning Committee was held in December 1978. At the beginning of economic reform, the widely accepted view was that there was a need to introduce the market mechanism into the economic system, but there was no consensus on how far China should move along the path of marketisation. 'Market-oriented economists' did not totally abandon the idea of a centrally planned framework; advocates of a planned economy supported the proposed changes, but differed in their views on the extent of the role the market mechanism should play.

However, as the reforms progressed, differences in the views of market and planned system economists widened. During 1981 and 1983, those who proposed to reduce the extent of central planning were criticised while those who argued that the market mechanism should play only a small role were very popular and their view was regarded as the goal of economic reform by the 12th Central Planning Committee meeting. In retrospect, this was understandable. In the early 1980s, people strongly appealed against the chaos experienced during the 'Cultural Revolution'. However, the theoretical preparation for reform was insufficient and China began by simply introducing reform theories from Eastern Europe. China had only recorded good economic growth figures in 1956 and 1965. The logical extension, therefore, was to continue to rely on the central plan but permit a limited role for the market mechanism. Although this mainstream thinking was challenged and would eventually be discarded, it remained influential in the formation of goals of economic reform for quite some time.

The Third Plenum of the 12th Central Planning Committee, held in 1984, formally put forward as the goal of economic reform a 'centrally planned commodity economy'. The main aim was to reduce the extent of compulsory planning. In 1987, the Central Planning Committee opted for indirect macroeconomic controls that 'government adjust and control the market, and the market guides the firm'. This approach represented quite a shock to the traditional centrally planned economic system and was an important step towards achieving the goal of market-oriented economic reform. This period (1984–88) can be regarded as the one in which the reform process advanced significantly.

Due to the failure of price reform in 1988 and the Tiananmen Square incident of 1989, reforms came to a standstill. The aforementioned indirect macroeconomic control disappeared in Party documents. It was replaced by the views that had prevailed ten years before: central planning should be the focus, and the market take on a subordinate role.

This retreat from market reform did not last long and its effects were minimal. It was halted by the ideas put forward by Deng Xiaoping when he travelled to southern China in 1992. Based on his ideas, the 14th Central Planning Committee meeting in October 1992 made a socialist market economy the goal of reform.

Although China's economic reforms were market oriented from the beginning, it took about 14 years for the objective of the reforms to be clearly stated as 'market economy'. This does not imply that the debate about the goal of reform was finished after 1992. The argument remained in all debates that the essence of a socialist economy is a planned economy and central planning is the model of macroeconomic control. However, these arguments were not mainstream and in fact became labelled as unofficial because 'socialist market economy' had been officially accepted as the goal of reform.

Experience and lessons

Economic reform in China has had remarkable results. It is not possible to list in detail every achievement, but they can be summarised. First, the pure public ownership structure has been replaced by a multi-ownership structure with different economic elements. Second, the market mechanism has played a critical role in certain important areas and the construction of a competitive market structure has advanced dramatically. Third, the use of indirect control has been the core of macroeconomic management; economic rather than administrative measures are now used due to various reforms in public finance, taxation, banking and investment. There have been significant substantial changes in the labour market and with respect to income distribution. Essentially, a multi-dimensional framework has been put in place.

Economic reform and economic development go hand in hand; they can mutually advance each other. Prezeworski (1991) argues that at the beginning of reform, whether it is gradual or radical, the decline in the level of output and consumption is inevitable and therefore, output growth has to be sacrificed. He states that the only difference is that it declines and picks up more quickly under radical reform than under gradual reform. This is illustrated in Figure 9.3. S denotes the start of reform, R and G represent radical and gradual reform, respectively.

The experience in China was totally different to that described by Prezeworski. Economic reform and development occurred simultaneously (Figure 9.4). China experienced a long period of rapid economic growth. The average growth of GDP in China between 1978–96 was 9.8 per cent; in the period 1991–96, average growth was 11.8 per cent. Although the two years that followed 1996 had lower growth rates, the annual average for the past twenty years is still above 9 per cent. Every single economic reform in China, whether in the rural or urban sector, has aimed to achieve economic growth through improvement in incentives. New reforms were only introduced when the success of former ones become apparent. This

Figure 9.3 The tradeoff between economic reform and economic development

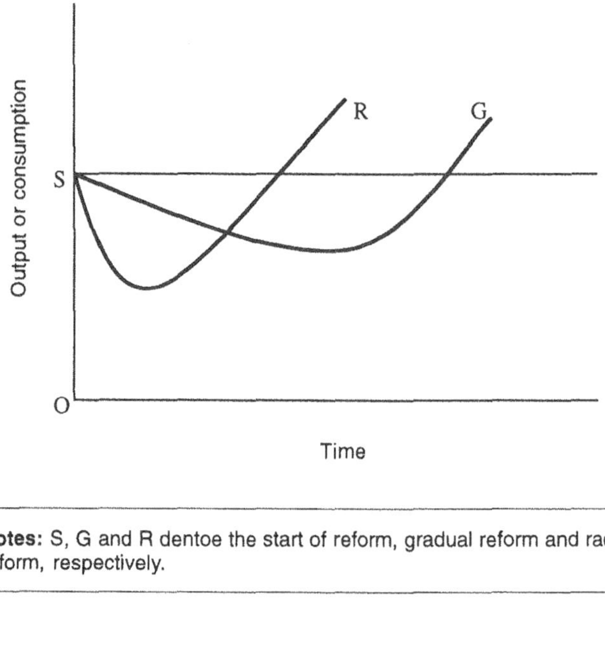

Notes: S, G and R dentoe the start of reform, gradual reform and radical reform, respectively.

approach applied to the implementation of the rural household production responsibility system, price reform for agricultural products, policies that encouraged the development of township and village enterprises (TVE) and non state-owned sectors, state-owned enterprise (SOE) reform in the urban sector, reform in retaining of foreign exchange earnings, and the establishment and development of special economic zones (Lin *et al.* 1994).

Without rapid economic growth, it would be impossible to make the rich richer and bring 0.2 billion people out of poverty; that is, raise the overall standard of living (World Bank 1997d). It was officially estimated that the population below the poverty line had dropped substantially from 0.25 billion in 1978 to 6 million in 1996 (Li and Zhao 1997). An important feature of economic reform in China to date has been that economic growth and reform have gone hand in hand, forming a 'virtuous cycle'. This should be regarded as an important success of the reforms in China thus far.

Figure 9.4   Economic reform and economic development: a 'virtuous cycle'

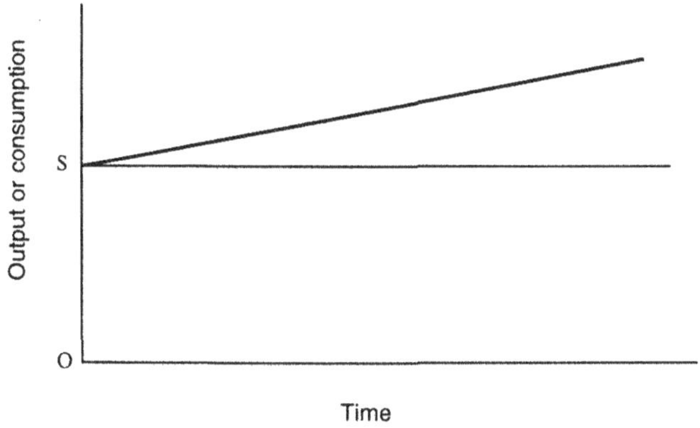

Another important lesson from China's economic reform is that gradualism has reduced the costs and risks associated with reform. There is heated debate on the pros and cons of gradualist versus radical reform (Wu 1996). However, with the exception in the early 1980s of rural sector reform, which had some elements of radicalism, China's reform can be broadly regarded as gradualist. In the rural sector, it took only two years—from September 1980 when the Central Planning Committee announced its desire to further strengthen the rural household production responsibility system, to autumn 1982—for the three-tier ownership structure under the commune system to be replaced by the rural household production responsibility system. This can be regarded as radical reform. But this was only part of the whole package of rural reform. Other aspects, including price reform and reform of the urban sector, can be regarded as gradual reform. Taking into account China's particular social and economic environment, this gradual reform can be regarded as successful. Harvard Professor J. Sachs, the proponent of radical reform in Eastern Europe and the former Soviet Union, agreed that gradual reform in China had been successful when he came to China in the early 1990s. Professor W. Brus, of Cambridge

University, who had suggested a so-called 'package' reform (radical reform) in his visit to China in the early 1980s to avoid the friction resulting from the two-tier price system, agreed with Sachs when he also visited China in the early 1990s.

There are two main areas in which gradual reforms have been successful. The first is in price reform, due to the introduction of the two-tier price system. This system allows the prices of those goods and services under planned control to be adjusted gradually to match the market price. Although friction costs have resulted from this transitional reform, it has been less risky than radical price reform, in which market prices are applied to all goods and services prices at once.

The other particular success has been the gradual reform in ownership structure. Non state-owned enterprises were allowed to be established first. This increased the size of the non-SOE sector, and had a very positive impact on economic growth. So-called 'incremental' reforms were consistent with reducing the extent of central planning and with the transition from dual to modern economy (Fan 1996). They also demonstrate that reform and growth go hand in hand.

Price reform in the rural sector was a micro version of price reform in China. In the rural sector, collective ownership of land has been retained, but farmer's rights and responsibilities are now clear since the leasing period is long (15 years initially with an extension of a further 30 years). Figure 9.5 provides a broad picture of the benefits to farmers of price and ownership reform in the rural sector. Farmers had to sell to the government all the remaining grains and other important agricultural products at a very low price before the reform. The benefit is the area ACDF. After reform, the additional benefit to farmers is the area HJAC. This area can be decomposed into two parts: one that arises from 'price adjustment' within the planned price framework, area HIAB; the other that from 'price release', area IJBC. 'Price adjustment' entailed the government gradually increasing the planned purchase price and changing the relative price of agricultural goods to manufactured goods (depicted by the three little arrows in Figure 9.5); while 'price release' involved the gradual reduction of the quota that farmers were required to sell to the government. The reduction of the quota enabled farmers to sell part of their produce in the market at market prices (as shown by arrow 1 in Figure 9.5). 'Price release' in fact implies alteration of the price mechanism, from planned pricing to market pricing. The policies behind rural price reform were thereafter introduced as part of many urban sector reforms.

Figure 9.5   Price and ownership reform in the rural sector

Output

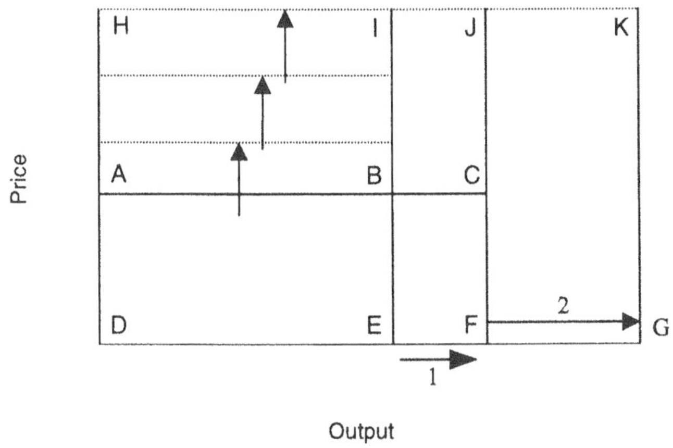

Source: Author's calculations.

Ownership reform in the rural sector had significant effects. For example, total agricultural production increased by 42.2 per cent during the period from 1978 to 1984 (as shown by arrow 2 in Figure 9.5), of which 46.9 per cent is from the increase in productivity due to the introduction of the rural household production responsibility system. The success of economic reform in the rural sector not only increased total output but also benefited farmers greatly as they were able to sell their produce at a higher price than in the planned economy. This is shown as area JFKG in Figure 9.5. The success of the development of the non state-owned urban sector and rural TVEs can be attributed to the gradual 'incremental' nature of reform.

There are several lessons to be learned from economic reform in China in the past 20 years. The economist Xue Muqiao points out that the shock therapy of price reform in 1988 and the contract system introduced to SOEs in the second half of 1980s to early 1990s were two policies from which lessons have been learned. He regarded these two policies as 'going astray' (Xue 1998).

Price reform was introduced suddenly in June 1988 (hence the label 'shock therapy'). The justification for such price reform at the time was that 'long pain is no better than short pain', and that market prices should be put in place at once. The macroeconomic environment was very unfavourable for such policies: inflation was very high (18.5 per cent) and friction from dual pricing was at its worst (for example, the planned price for steel was 700 yuan per tonne while the market price was 1800 yuan per tonne). Implementing price reform in these circumstances was impractical. When the news of discussions about radical price reform was released to the media in August 1988, there was a nationwide run on the banks and panic-buying by consumers. The incident ended ideas of further speeding up the pace of price reform, and lent support to gradual price reform. Of course, the difficulties in putting market prices in place at once did not cast doubts on the necessity of price reform. The ultimate objective of the two-tier price system was to achieve a unified market price. However, there were lessons to be learned about the conditions under which a dual price system could be merged into a market price system. The first is that the difference between the planned and market price should not be too large. The planned price should gradually approach the market equilibrium price through adjustment. This ensures that the friction of price reform is minimised. Second, the goods and services whose prices are determined by the market should account for a large proportion of total goods in the economy. Finally, the macroeconomic environment should be favourable, for example there should be an appropriate money supply and low inflation.

The second important lesson from China's economic reforms was the reform of the contract system for SOEs. The contract system was only trialled in certain areas and certain enterprises before 1986. In December 1986, the State Council announced 'certain regulations with regard to deepening enterprise reform and strengthening efforts to revitalise enterprises' momentum'. The contract system was then introduced nationwide. The basic ideas were fixing the bases, fulfilling planned quantities, retaining surpluses and earning additional income, and covering their own losses. Up until 1992 they had been contracted for two periods (three years for each contract period). In July 1992, the State Council announced regulations for reforming SOE's operating system and exposing SOEs to the market. It was after November 1993 when the Third Plenum of the 14th Central Planning Committee meeting proposed to establish the so-called modern enterprise system that the contract system became history.

There are three different views about the contract system within SOE. The first views the system highly and regards it as the strategic direction of economic reform. The second views the contract system as a transitional phase. The last view does not give much credit to the system and even regards it as 'going astray'. Xue is of this view. Two things give weight to it. First, the operating mechanism of the contract system strengthened the vertical one-to-one bargaining relationship between government and firm. It did not strengthen the competitive horizontal relationship between firms and in fact retained the bargaining relationship of the centrally planned system, and therefore was not consistent with market-oriented reform. In the centrally planned economic system SOEs bargained with the government over input and output quotas while under the contract system they bargained over the base for which the firm should deliver profits to the government. Second, under the contract system the government was able to maintain constant revenue in the short run. However, in the long run this was not guaranteed because there was no comparable, unified regulatory framework. In the bargaining process, the firm had incentives to bargain while the government officials did not. It became popular belief that the firm was responsible for profits but not losses. This is the key to understanding the loss of state capital. The contract system in name separated ownership from operation and appeared to be able to protect state capital. In fact, it reduced state capital. This was labelled by some as 'silent privatisation'. It appeared to be inconsistent with the original idea of protecting the state's ownership. As the loss of state capital and the extent of losses by SOEs became widespread, the contracts could no longer be maintained. This was pointed out by Xue: 'The direction and emphasis of SOE reform should gradually change to separation of government and enterprises and system innovation. The SOEs should become commodity producers and operators who have independent accounting, autonomy for operating, responsibilities for profits and losses, equal opportunity to compete and to be the winner through excellence or the loser by being inferior'. The contract system could not resolve these problems and therefore stunted the reform of SOEs (Xue 1998).

The challenges ahead

Although the economic reforms in China have been very successful since their beginnings twenty years ago, there are still considerable challenges ahead.

The pace of reform represents a significant challenge. The distinction between gradual and radical reform is not clear-cut. There is no consensus about which approach is best. Previous reforms have had success through gradual reform where lower risk and costs were ensured. However, this approach solved issues that were relatively easy to deal with anyway, but left difficult issues unresolved. The most difficult reforms are still incomplete. Examples include reform of SOEs, financial and banking system reform, housing system reform and social security system reform. Perhaps gradual reform is not the optimal way to alter these systems; a more radical approach may be the answer. The economic recoveries of those economies that underwent the 'big bang' approach would support this view.

A challenge of further reform is to ensure balance is maintained. It becomes increasingly important to maintain a balance between three aspects: economic reform, economic development and social stability. Some economists emphasise the importance of social stability and propose that economic reform should only go ahead if it will not jeopardise social stability. Controlling inflation is the first priority of economic policy. Other economists emphasise economic reform and development and argue that social stability can only be achieved through economic development. Growth and employment are their first concerns in economic management. The way to achieve the right balance is by understanding the short and long-term goals and China's current economic and social environment. The relationship between SOE reform and social security system reform is typical of where it is important to distinguish short and long-term interests. In the early 1990s, 'breaking three irons (iron chair, iron bowl and iron wage)' was the target of SOE reform. Due to the lack of an adequate social security system at that time, reform measures had to be halted in order to avoid massive unemployment. Several years after that reform, the problems that had led to the policy of 'breaking three irons' appeared again. The issues remain, to some extent, unresolved. Reform of the social security system is an important issue and necessary in tackling urban unemployment. SOE reform and social security reform need to be coordinated. Only in this way can economic reform proceed while maintaining social and economic stability in both the short and long run. Recently, the concept of sustainable development has been widely accepted. It is important to ensure that economic reform and development go hand in hand in a sustainable way.

It is also important to maintain a well balanced relationship between different reform programs. This issue was first raised at the beginning of reform but is more important at this stage. Maintaining a balance does not mean that all the reforms should be implemented simultaneously. In fact, previous reform programs have been carried out sequentially. For example, rural sector reform preceded urban sector reform and price reform preceded ownership reform.

However, the order of the reforms should be such that they can effectively help each other. This applies to economic reform in every aspect. With respect to current reforms, ownership reform is lagging behind market reform while factor market reform is lagging behind product market reform. These problems will be solved gradually. The degree of marketisation that has been achieved in China is very impressive. For example, 60 to 70 per cent of goods and services currently have their price determined by the market. The degree of marketisation of social retail sales of goods and services has reached 92.5 per cent (Wen 1998). Due to the lag of ownership reform, many SOEs are facing difficulties and this in turn has become the stumbling block of finance and banking reform. It is estimated that China's SOEs have more than 1,000 billion yuan in bad debts, about 600 to 800 billion yuan worth of non-performing loans in bank accounts. Some economists therefore argue that without 'real enterprises' there will be no 'real banks' (Yang 1998).

There is a similar relationship between housing marketisation and labour marketisation. On the one hand, employees cannot afford expensive housing. On the other hand, those houses sold to employees at relatively low prices are not allowed to enter the market. The immobility of residential housing restrains the mobility of labour. This has become another stumbling block for SOE reform. The various difficulties of reform are intertwined. To proceed, the knot must be disentangled.

There is also the relationship between economic reform, political reform and other non-economic factors. As economic reform deepens, the need for political, moral and cultural reforms arises. It has been one of the characteristics that economic reform precedes political reform in

China. This has its advantages. However, almost no one would argue that economic reform can proceed without political reform, or that political reform can be delayed indefinitely.

The relationship between the transformation of SOEs operational mechanism and that of government administrational functions is a typical example of the link between economic and political reform. One of the many important tasks of SOE reform is to separate SOEs from government organisation in order that SOEs become true market identities. It is obvious that it is impossible for SOEs to achieve this themselves. The transformation of SOEs' operational mechanism and shifts of government administrational functions are two sides of the same coin. When SOE reform deepens, shifting government administrational functions will be the key to further reform. Without the transformation of these functions, there is little hope for clear-cut intellectual property rights, separation of government from enterprises and independent operation.

Of course, the transformation of government administrational functions does not imply that there is no role for government. The World Bank 1997 report indicates that good government is not a luxury. Without an effective government, sustainable social and economic development is impossible. In the case of market failure, government intervention is necessary, but by no means guaranteed.

Where market failure occurs, social moral intervention is also necessary. The importance of morals in economic reform and development is well known. A classic problem that was raised in Adam Smith's lifetime was how to deal with the relationship between economic man and moral man. This issue has drawn the increasing attention of academics in China. The moral factor will become increasingly important as economic reform deepens.

In summary, the challenges facing continued economic reform in China are serious. World Bank economist Joseph Stiglitz praises the achievements of economic reform in China but also points out that the Chinese government is facing massive difficulties and challenges. It is often said that economic reform is a system. This is true in an economic sense. If one takes into account the non-economic factors involved with economic reform, it can be regarded as an even bigger system. It is essential that China is ready for the challenges ahead and finishes this great and unprecedented project.

Select bibliography

Anderson, K., 1997. 'On the complexities of China's WTO accession', *The World Economy*, 20(6):749–72.

Asia Pacific Economics Group, 1998. *Asia Pacific Profiles 1998*, FT (Asia Pacific), Singapore.

Bai, C., Li, D.D. and Wang, Y., 1997. 'Enterprise productivity and efficiency: when is up really down?', *Journal of Comparative Economics*, 24:265–80.

Borland, J., Vella, F. and Woodbridge, G., 1995. Inter and intra-industry earnings variation in Australia and the United States: what explains the difference?, Research School of Social Sciences, The Australian National University, Canberra (unpublished manuscript).

Bouin, O., 1998. 'Financial discipline and state enterprise reform in China in the 1990s', in O. Bouin, F. Coricelli and F. Lemoine (eds), *Different Approaches to Market Reform*, CEPII/CEPR/OECD Development Centre, Paris:115–52.

Burkett, J.P. and Putterman, L., 1993. 'The supply of labour by individuals to a Chinese collective farm: the case of Dahe Commune', *Economica*, 60:381–96.

Byrd, W. and Tidrick, G., 1987. 'Factor allocation and enterprise incentive', in G. Tidrick and K. Chen (eds), *China's Industrial Reform*, Oxford University Press, New York:237–75.

Byron, R.P. and Manaloto, E.Q., 1990. 'Return to education in China', *Economic Development and Cultural Change*, 38:783–96.

Chai, J.C.H. and Sun, H., 1993. *Liberalising Foreign Trade: experience of China*, Discussion Paper 135, Department of Economics, University of Queensland, Brisbane.

Chang, K., 1993. 'The peasant family in the transition from Maoist to Lewisian rural industrialisation', *The Journal of Development Studies*, 29(2):220–44.

Chen, K., Jefferson, G.H. and Rawski, T.G., 1992. 'Lessons from China's Economic Reform', *Journal of Comparative Economics*, 16:201–25.

——, Wang H. and Zheng Y., 1988a. 'Productivity change in Chinese industry: 1953–1985', *Journal of Comparative Economics*, 12:570–91.

Chen, J., 1998a. 'The reform of the rural economic system', in Z. Zhang, F. Huang and G. Li (eds), *Twenty Years of Economic Reform: looking back and forward*, China Planning Publishing House, Beijing:77–109.

——, Wang, H., Zheng, Y., Jefferson, G. and Rawski, T., 1988b. 'Productivity change in Chinese industry: 1953–1985', *Journal of Comparative Economics*, 12(4):570–91.

——, 1988c. 'New estimates of fixed investment and capital stock for Chinese state industry', *China Quarterly*, 114:243–66.

Chen, Q. (ed.), 1995. *Experiences of China's Enterprise Reform Experiments*, China Economy Press, Beijing (in Chinese).

——, 1998b. 'Reform of foreign exchange management system', in Z. Zhang, F. Huang and G. Li (eds), *20 Years' Economic Reform: review and prospects*, China Planning Publisher, Beijing:322–61.

Chen, S. and Ravallion, M., 1996. 'Data in transition: assessing rural living standards in Southern China', *China Economic Review*, 7:23–56.

China, various years. *China Monthly Statistics*, China Statistical Information and Consultancy Service Centre, Peiching.

Ding, L., 1999. 'Issues and challenges in agricultural reform', in Y. Yang and W.M. Tian (eds), *China's Agriculture at the Crossroads*, Macmillan, London.

Documents for Chinese Communist Party (CCP) 14th Conference, People's Publisher, Beijing, 1992.

Dollar, D., 1990. 'Economic reform and allocative efficiency in China's state-owned industry', *Economic Development and Cultural Change*, 39(1):89–105.

Dong, F., 1985. 'Nature and position of the state-owned enterprises', in F. Dong, *Selected Works of Dong Fureng*, Shanxi People's Press, Taiyuan (in Chinese).

——, 1988. 'Development theory and problems of socialist developing economies', in G. Ranis and T.P. Schultz (eds), *The State of Development Economics*, Basil Blackwell Ltd, United States:228–59.

—— and Tang, Z., 1992. *Reform of China's State-Owned Enterprises: institutions and efficiency*, China Planning Press, Beijing (in Chinese).

Dong, F. and Wang, H. (eds), 1995. *A Study on Institutional Innovation of China's State-owned Enterprises*, People's Press, Beijing (in Chinese).

Du, H. and Guo, J., 1995. 'The basic characteristics of expansion of SOEs' decision autonomy and its impact on efficiency', in F. Dong, Z. Tang and H. Wang (eds), *A Study on Institutional Innovation of China's State-owned Enterprises*, People's Press, Beijing (in Chinese).

East Asia Analytical Unit (EAAU), 1997. *China Embraces the Market*, EAAU, Department of Foreign Affairs and Trade, Canberra.

Economic Intelligence Unit (EIU), 1998. *EIU Country Profile 1998–99: China and Mongolia*, EIU, London.

Eichen, M. and Zhang, M., 1993. 'The 1988 household sample survey— data description and availability', in K. Griffin and R. Zhao, *The Distribution of Income in China*, Macmillan Press, London:331–46.

Enterprise Department, State Commission for Economy and Trade, 1995. *Policy and Practice of Experiments on Company Groups in China*, China Economy Press, Beijing (in Chinese).

Fan, G., 1996a. 'State-owned enterprises in the gradualist reform', in D. Xu and G. Wen (eds), *Reform of China's State-owned Enterprises*, China Economy Press, Beijing (in Chinese).

——, 1996b. 'The characters and trend of China's economic system reform' in Gradual or Radical: the choice of China's economic reform, *Economic Science Publisher*, 2:11–22.

—— and Woo, W.T., 1996. 'State enterprise reform as a source of macroeconomic instability', *Asian Economic Journal*, 10(3):207–24.

Fan, S.G., 1991. 'Effects of technological change and institutional reform on production growth in Chinese agriculture', *American Journal of Agricultural Economics*, 73(2):266–75.

Feder, G., 1983. 'On exports and economic growth', *Journal of Development Economics*, 12:27–9.

Findlay, C., Watson, A. and Wu, H.X., 1994. *Rural enterprises in China*, Macmillan Press, London.

Garnaut, R., 1998. 'Economic lessons', in R. McLeod and R. Garnaut (eds), *East Asia in Crisis: from being a miracle to needing one?*, London, Routledge:352–66.

—— and Ma, G., 1993a. 'Economic growth and stability in China', *Journal of Asian Economics*, 4(1):5–24.

——, 1993b. 'How rich is China: evidence from the food economy', *Australian Journal of Chinese Affairs*, 30:121–48.

——, 1994. *Grain in China*, East Asian Analytical Unit, Department of Foreign Affairs and Trade, Canberra.

——, 1996. 'The third revolution', in R. Garnaut, S. Guo and G. Ma (eds), *The Third Revolution in the Chinese Countryside*, Cambridge University Press, Cambridge.

Girardin, E., 1997. *Banking Sector Reform and Credit Control in China*, Development Centre of the Organisation for Economic Co-operation and Development, Paris.

Granick, D., 1990. *Chinese State Enterprises: a regional property rights analysis*, University of Chicago Press, Chicago.

Greenaway, D. and Sapsford, D., 1994. 'What does liberalisation do for exports and growth?', *Weltwirtschaftliches Archiv*, 130(1):152–74.

Gregory, R.G. and Meng, X., 1995. 'Wage determination and occupational attainment in the rural industrial sector of China', *Journal of Comparative Economics*, 21(3):353–74.

Griffin, K. and Zhao, R., 1993. *The Distribution of Income in China*, Macmillan Press, London:331–46.

Groves, T., Hong, Y., McMillan, J. and Naughton, B., 1994. 'Autonomy and incentives in Chinese state enterprises', *Quarterly Journal of Economics*, 109(1):183–209.

Gu, Z., 1957. 'On commodity production and value rule under the socialist system', in W. Zhang, Z. Zhang and J. Wu (eds), *Selection of Articles on Commodity Production and Value Rule under the Socialist System after 1949*, Volume 1, Shanghai People's Press, Shanghai (in Chinese).

Gustafsson, B. and Li, S., 1997. 'Types of income and inequality in China at the end of the 1980s', *Review of Income and Wealth*, 43:211–26.

——, 1998a. 'Inequality in China at the end of the 80s—location aspects and household characteristics', *Asian Economic Journal*, March:35–63.

——, 1998b. A more unequal China? Industrialisation, economic transformation and changes in the distribution of equivalent income processing, (in press).

Hanson, J., 1995. 'Opening the capital account: costs, benefits and sequencing', in S. Edwards (ed.), *Capital Controls, Exchange Rates* and *Monetary Policy in the World Economy*, Cambridge University Press, Cambridge and New York:383–430.

Harrigan, J. and Mosley, P., 1991. 'Evaluating the impact of World Bank structural adjustment lending', *Journal of Development Studies*, 27(3):63–74.

Hong, Z. and Yan, Y., 1997. *Trust and Investment Corporations in China*, working paper, Federal Reserve Bank of Cleveland, Cleveland.

Hsu, J.C., 1989. *China's Foreign Trade Reforms: impact on growth and stability*, Cambridge University Press, Cambridge.

Hua, S., Zhang, X. and Luo, X., 1986. 'Restructuring the microeconomic foundation: further on issues and thoughts of China's further reforms', *Economic Research Journal*, 3 (in Chinese).

——, 1988. 'Ten years of Chinese economic reform: review, reconsideration, and prospects', *Economic Research Journal*, 9:13–37 (in Chinese).

Huang, W., 1996. 'China's accession to the WTO and its intellectual property rights protection', in W. Cai, M.G. Smith and X. Xu (eds), *China and World Trade Organization: requirements, realities, and resolution*, Centre for Trade Policy and Law, Ontario:204–53.

Huang, Y., 1998a. *China's Agricultural Reform: get the institutions right*, Cambridge University Press, Cambridge.

——, 1998b. Market competition and enterprise performance in economic transition: the case of China's state industry, paper presented at the Trade and Development Seminar series, Research School of Pacific and Asian Studies, The Australian National University, Canberra, 11 August.

—— and Duncan, R., 1997a. 'How successful were China's state sector reforms?', *Journal of Comparative Economics*, 24:65–78.

——, 1997b. *State Enterprise Reforms in China: a critical review of policy*, Development Issues No.3., National Centre for Development Studies, The Australian National University, Canberra.

——, 1999. 'Did competition drive down the profitability in China's state industry?', *MOCT-MOST: Economic Policy in Transitional Economies*, Kluwer Academic Publishers, 9:49–60.

——, Duncan, R. and Cai, F., 1998a. Reform of state-owned enterprises in China: key measures and policy debate, paper presented at the international workshop 'Understanding the decline of China's state sector', The Australian National University, Canberra, 17–18 February.

Huang, Y. and Meng, X., 1997. 'China's industrial growth and efficiency: a comparison between the state and the TVE sectors', *Journal of the Asia Pacific Economy*, 2(1):101–21.

Huang, Y., Woo, W.T., Kalirajan, K.P. and Duncan, R., 1997. *Enterprise Reform, Technological Progress and Technical Efficiency in China's State Industry*', China Economy Working Paper 97/5, National Centre for Development Studies, The Australian National University, Canberra.

——, 1998b. Technological stagnation in the Chinese state industry, paper presented at the international workshop 'Understanding the decline of China's state sector', The Australian National University, Canberra, 17–18 February.

Hussain, A., 1990. *The Chinese Enterprise Reforms*, China Programme Paper No. 5, Development Economics Research Programme, London School of Economics, London.

Industrial and Commercial Bank of China (ICBC), 1998. Internet site. Available at <URL:http://www.icbc.com.ch>.

International Monetary Fund (IMF), 1994. *Economic Reform in China: A New Phase*, IMF Occasional Paper No. 114, IMF, Washington, DC.

——, 1997. *Direction of Trade*, IMF and International Bank for Reconstruction and Development, Washington, DC.

——, various years. *International Financial Statistics*, International Monetary Fund, Washington, DC.

——, various years. *World Economic Outlook*, International Monetary Fund, Washington, DC.

——, various years. *Balance of Payments Statistics*, IMF, Washington, DC.

Ishikawa, S., 1986. 'Socialist economy and China's experience: prospects for economic reform', *Science and Technology Herald*, 2:21–8.

Jefferson, G.H., 1989. 'Potential sources of productivity growth within Chinese industry', *World Development*, 17(1):44–57.

—— and Xu, W., 1991. 'The impact of reform on socialist enterprises in transition: structure, conduct, and performance in Chinese industry', *Journal of Comparative Economics*, 15(1):45–64.

Jefferson, G.H. and Rawski, T.G., 1994. 'Enterprise reform in Chinese industry', *Journal of Economic Perspective*, 8(2):47–70.

—— and Zheng, Y.X., 1992. 'Growth, efficiency and convergence in China's state and collective industry', *Economic Development and Cultural Change*, 40(2):239–66.

——, 1994. 'Productivity change in Chinese industry: a comment', *China Economic Review*, 5(2):235–41.

——, 1996. 'Chinese industrial productivity: trends, measurement issues, and recent developments', *Journal of Comparative Economics*, 23(2):146–80.

Jiang, Y., 1980. 'Enterprise identity', *China Social Sciences*, 1 (in Chinese).

Jingben, R. and Zhao, R., 1982. 'What economic model did we belong to?', *Economics Digest*, 2:27–30.

Kato, H., 1997. *China's Economic Reform and Marketisation*, Nagoya University Press, Nagoya.

Ke, B.S., 1999. 'On-farm grain stocks and their impact on market stability', in Y. Yang and W.M. Tian (eds), *China's Agriculture at the Crossroads*, Macmillan, London.

Khan, A.R. and Riskin, C., 1998. 'Income and inequality in China: composition, distribution and growth of household income, 1988 to 1995', *China Quarterly*, 154:221–53.

——, Griffin, K. and Zhao, R., 1992. 'Household income and its distribution in China', *China Quarterly*, 132:1029–61.

——, 1993. 'Sources of income inequality in post-reform China', *China Economic Review*, 4:19–35.

Kidd, M. and Meng, X., 1997a. 'Wage determination in China's state sector in the 1980s', *Journal of Comparative Economics*, 25(3):403–21.

——, 1997b. 'Trends in the Australian gender wage differential over the 1980's: some evidence on the effectiveness of legislative reform', *Australian Economic Review*, 30(1):31–44.

King, R. and Levine, R., 1993. 'Finance, entrepreneurship, and growth: theory and evidence', *Journal of Monetary Economics*, 32:513–42.

Knight, J. and Song, L., 1993. 'The spatial contribution to income inequality in rural China', *Cambridge Journal of Economics*, 17:195–213.

Kornai, J., 1980. *The Economics of Shortage*, North Holland, Amsterdam.

Krugman, P., 1994. 'The myth of Asia's miracle', *Foreign Affairs*, 73(6):62–78.

Kumar, A., Lardy, N., Albrecht, W., Chuppe, T., Selwyn, S., Perttunen, P. and Zhang, T., 1997. *China's Non-Bank Financial Institutions*, Discussion Paper No. 358, World Bank, New York.

Lardy, N.R., 1992. *Foreign Trade and Economic Reform in China, 1978–1990*, Cambridge University Press, Cambridge.

——, 1996. 'Comments on China's role and priorities in the WTO system by Zhao Gongda', in Joint US-Korea Academic Studies, Volume 7, *The Emerging WTO System and Perspectives from East Asia*, Ann Arbor, Michigan:179–80.

——, 1998. *China's Unfinished Economic Revolution*, Brookings Institution Press, Washington, DC.

Lau, K.T. and Brada, J.C., 1990. 'Technological progress and technical efficiency in Chinese industrial growth: a frontier function approach', *China Economic Review*, 1(2):113–24.

Lau, L. and Qian, Y., 1994. 'A proposal on restructuring China's banks and enterprise finance', *Reform*, 6 (in Chinese).

Legal Bureau of the State Council (LBSC), 1987. *ZHONG HUA REN MIN GONG HE GUO XIAN XING FA GUI HUI BIIAN -NONG LIN BIAN (A Collection of Effective Laws and Regulations of the People's Republic of China: Agriculture and Forest Edition)*, Law Press, Beijing (in Chinese).

Lee, K., 1990. 'The Chinese model of the socialist enterprise: an assessment of its organisation and performance', *Journal of Comparative Economics*, 14:384–400.

Li, J., 1995. 'An analysis of profitability of China's state enterprises', *Economic Research Journal*, 3 (in Chinese).

——, 1996. 'The reform of China's foreign trade regime', in W. Cai, M.G. Smith and X. Xu (eds), *China and World Trade Organization: requirements, realities, and resolution*, Centre for Trade Policy and Law, Ontario:79–106.

Li, K. and Ed, W., 1997. *Financing China Trade and Investment*, Praeger Publishers, Westport.

Li, S. and Zhao, R., 1997. 'The increasing income inequality and its causes in China', *Economic Research*, 9:19–28.

—— and Zhang, P., 1998. 'Economic transition and income distribution in China', *Economic Research*, April:42–51 (in Chinese).

Li, W., 1997. 'The impact of economic reform on the performance of Chinese state enterprises, 1980–89', *Journal of Political Economy*, 105(5):1080–113.

Li, Y., 1987. 'Exploration of economic system reform', *People's Daily Press*, Beijing.

Lin, J.Y., 1992. 'Rural reforms and agricultural growth in China', *American Economic Review*, 82(1):34–51.

——, 1997. State intervention, ownership and state enterprise reform in China, paper presented at a Trade and Development Seminar, Economics Division, Research School of Pacific and Asian Studies, The Australian National University, Canberra, January.

——, Cai, F. and Li, Z., 1996a. *The China Miracle: development strategy and economic reform*, Chinese University Press, Hong Kong.

——, 1996b. 'Creating an environment for fair competition is the core of enterprise reform', in D. Xu and G. Wen (eds), *Reform of China's State-owned Enterprises*, China Economy Press, Beijing (in Chinese).

——, 1997. *Perfect Information and State Enterprise Reform*, Shanghai Sanlian Bookstore and Shanghai People's Press, Shanghai (in Chinese).

Lin, Q., 1995. 'An analysis of efficiency variation and influencing factors in China's industrial sector since the reform', *Economic Research Journal*, 10:27–34 (in Chinese).

Lin, Y., Cai, F. and Li, Z., 1994. *China's Miracle: development strategy and economic reform*, Shanghai Sanlian Publisher.

Liu, J., 1996. 'Separation of government administration and enterprise management', in D. Xu and G. Wen (eds), *Reform of China's State-owned Enterprises*, China Economy Press, Beijing (in Chinese).

Lu, F., 1997. *The Adjustment of China's Agricultural Trade Policy and an Appraisal of the Risk of Grain Embargoes*, Working Paper Series C1997007, China Centre for Economic Research, Peking University, Beijing (in Chinese).

Lu, Y., 1996a. 'Flowing, splitting and value-adding of assets: the successful choice of SOEs walking out of the difficult situation', in T. Song and X. Wei (eds), *Multi-dimensional Thinking on Promoting State Enterprise Reform by 40 Economists*, Economics Science Press, Beijing (in Chinese).

Lu, Z., 1996b. 'Actively promoting reforms of small enterprises', *China Industrial Economics*, 4:30–2 (in Chinese).

Lucas, R.E., 1988. 'On the mechanics of economic development', *Journal of Monetary Economics*, 22:3–42.

Lyons, T., 1991. 'Interprovincial disparities in China: output and consumption, 1952–1987', *Economic Development and Cultural Change*, 39(3):471–506.

McGuckin, R.H., Nguyen, S.V., Taylor, J.R. and Waite, C.A., 1992. 'Post-reform productivity performance and sources of growth in Chinese industry: 1980–85', *Review of Income and Wealth*, 38(3):249–66.

McMillan, J., 1994. *China's Nonconformist Reforms*, Research Report 94-11, Graduate School of International Relations and Pacific Studies, University of California, San Diego.

——, Whalley, J. and Zhu, L., 1989. 'The impact of China's economic reforms on agricultural productivity growth', *Journal of Political Economy*, 97(4):781–807.

McMillan, J. and Naughton, B., 1992. 'How to reform a planned economy: lessons from China', *Oxford Review of Economic Policy*, 8(1):130–43.

Ma, H., Liu, Z. and Lu, B. (eds), 1998. *Report of China's Macroeconomic Policy*, China Finance and Economics Press, Beijing.

Ma, J., 1997. China's economic reform in the 1990s, manuscript, January. Available from internet at <URL:http://members.aol.com/junmanew/cover.htm>.

Macroeconomic Institution, State Planning Commission, 1996. *Research on Development Policies of Large Company Groups*, China Economy Press, Beijing (in Chinese).

Maddison, A., 1998. *Chinese Economic Performance in the Long Run*, OECD Development Centre, Paris.

Martellaro, J., 1996. 'China's economic miracle: myth or reality?', *Economia-Internazionale*, 49(3):417–37.

Martin, W., 1990. *Modelling the Post-reform Chinese Economy*, China Working Paper 90/1, National Centre for Development Studies, The Australian National University, Canberra.

Meng, X., 1998. Recent labour market development in China, paper prepared for the China Update 'China in the Middle of East Asian Financial Crisis', The Australian National University, Canberra, 5 August.

Meng, X., (forthcoming). *Labour Market Reform in China*, Cambridge University Press, Cambridge.

Merrill Lynch, 1998. *Asian Strategy Monthly*, Merrill Lynch and Company, various issues.

Miller, P.W., 1987. 'The wage effect of the occupational segregation of women in Britain', *The Economic Journal*, 97:885–96.

Mincer, J. and Higuchi, Y., 1988. 'Wage structures and labor turnover in the United States and Japan', *Journal of the Japanese and International Economies*, 2:97–133.

Ministry of Agriculture (MOA), 1989. *Statistics of China's Rural Economy (1949–1986)*, Agricultural Publishing House, Beijing.

Naughton, B., 1994. 'What is distinctive about China's economic transition? State enterprise reform and overall system transformation', *Journal of Comparative Economics*, 18:470–90.

——, 1995. *Growing Out of the Plan: Chinese economic reform 1978–1993*, Cambridge University Press, Cambridge.

Omiya, R., 1986. 'Competitive market mechanism and the role of enterprise', in J. Wu and H. Wang (eds), *Economic Theory and Economic Policy*, Economic Management Press, Beijing (in Chinese).

Papageorgiou, D., Michaely, M. and Choksi, A.M., 1991. *Liberalising Foreign Trade*, Blackwell, Cambridge, Massachusetts and Oxford.

People's Bank of China (PBC), 1993–98. *People's Bank of China Quarterly Statistical Bulletin*, Beijing, various issues.

——, 1995. *China Financial Outlook, 1995*, People's Bank of China, Beijing.

Perkins, D.H., 1993. 'Reforming the economic systems of Vietnam and Laos', in B. Ljunggren (ed.), *The Challenge of Reform in Indochina*, Harvard University Press, Cambridge:Chapter 1.

Perkins, F. and Raiser, M., 1994. 'State enterprise reform and macroeconomic stability in transitional economies', Kiel Working Paper No. 665, Kiel Institute of World Economics, Kiel University, Kiel.

——, 1995. *State Enterprise Reform and Macroeconomic Stability in Transition Economies*, Economics Division Working Papers, Development Issues 95/1, Research School of Pacific and Asian Studies, The Australian National University, Canberra.

Perkins, F., 1996. 'Productivity performance and priority for the reform of China's state-owned enterprises', *Journal of Development Studies*, 32(2):414–44.

——, 1997. 'Export performance and enterprise reform in China's coastal provinces', *Economic Development and Cultural Change*: 45(3):501–39.

——, 1999. 'The costs of China's state-owned enterprises', *MOCT-MOST: Economic Policy in Transitional Economies*, Kluwer Academic Publishers, 9:17–33.

——, Zheng, Y. and Cao, Y., 1993. 'The impact of economic reform on productivity growth in Chinese industry: a case study of Xiamen Special Economic Zone', *Asia Economic Journal*, 7(2):107–46.

Ping, T., 1995. 'Analysis on income level and inequality of rural households in China', *Management World*, 2 (in Chinese).

Prezeworski, A., 1991. *Democracy and the Market: political and economic reforms in Eastern Europe and Latin America*, Cambridge University Press, New York.

Psacharopoulos, G., 1985. 'Returns to education: a further international update and implications', *The Journal of Human Resources*, 20:583–604.

——, 1994. 'Returns to investment in education: a global update', *World Development*, 22(9):1325–43.

Qin, F. and Tian, W.M., 1999. 'Feeding the livestock: technological choice, trade policy and efficiency', in Y. Yang and W.M. Tian (eds), *China's Agriculture at the Crossroads*, Macmillan, UK.

Rawski, T., 1994. 'Chinese industrial reform: accomplishments, prospects, and implications', *American Economic Review*, 84(2):271–75.

——, 1995. 'Implications of China's reform experience', *China Quarterly*, (144):1150–73.

——, 1996. 'Implications of China's reform', in D. Xu and G. Wen (eds), *Reform of State-Owned Enterprises in China*, China Economic Press, Beijing (in Chinese).

Ren, F. and Cheng, X., 1996. 'To investigate income differential from income of urban households', *Reference of Economic Research*, 157 (in Chinese).

Romer, P.M., 1986. 'Increasing returns and long-run growth', *Journal of Political Economy*, 94:1002–37.

Rozelle, S., 1994. 'Rural industrialisation and increasing inequality: emerging patterns in China's reform economy', *Journal of Comparative Economics*, 19:362–91.

——, Park, A., Jin, H. and Huang, J., 1998. Market emergence and transition: arbitrage, transaction costs, and autarky in China's grain markets, paper presented at the Australian Agricultural Economics Society 43rd Annual Conference, Christchurch, 20–22 January.

Sachs, J. and Woo, W.T., 1994. 'Structural factors in the economic reforms of China, Eastern Europe and the former Soviet Union', *Economic Policy: A European Forum*, 9(18):101–45.

——, 1997. *Understanding China's Economic Performance*, National Bureau of Economic Research (NBER) Working Paper 5935, Cambridge.

Shao, L., 1992. 'Income differentials within the state enterprises' in H. Du (ed.), *The Foundation for Efficient Management: employees' feelings and behaviour*, People's Publishing House of Shanghai, Shanghai:156–72.

Shi, Y., 1998. 'Reform of foreign trade system', in Z. Zhang, F. Huang and G. Li (eds), *20 Years' Economic Reform: review and prospects*, China Planning Publisher, Beijing:156–76.

Shorrocks, A.F., 1983. 'Ranking income distributions', *Economica*, 50:3–17.

Shunde City Government, 1997. 'Shunde City's attempt in constructing the framework for socialist market economy', *China Rural Economy*, 8:8–13 (in Chinese).

Sicular, T., 1995. 'Why state-owned enterprises choose to make loss?', *Economic Research Journal*, 5 (in Chinese).

Solow, R.M., 1956. 'A contribution to the theory of economic growth', *Quarterly Journal of Economics*, 70:65–94.

Song, L., 1996a. *Changing Global Comparative Advantage: evidence from Asia and the Pacific*, Addison-Wesley, Melbourne.

——, 1996b. 'Institutional change, trade composition and export supply potential in China', in M. Guitian and R. Mundell (eds), *Inflation and Growth in China*, International Monetary Fund, Washington, DC:190–225.

——, 1998a. Understanding the rapid expansion of China's foreign trade, paper for the APEC and its Impact on the Chinese Economy conference, The Australian National University, Canberra, 16 February.

——, 1998b. 'China', in R. McLeod and R. Garnaut (eds), *East Asia in Crisis: from being a miracle to needing one?*, Routledge, London:105–19.

——, 1998c. New sources of China's economic growth, paper presented at the China Update, The Australian National University, Canberra, 5 August. Available online at <http://ncdsnet.anu.edu.au/online/workpaper.htm/update>.

Song, T. and Wei, X. (eds), 1996. *Multi-dimensional Thinking on Promoting State Enterprise Reform by 40 Economists*, Economics Science Press, Beijing (in Chinese).

State Administration of Foreign Exchange (SAFE), 1997. *Annual Report*, SAFE, Beijing.

State Information Council (SIC). Web site [online]. Available at <URL:http://www.chinaeco.com/emon.htm>.

State Statistical Bureau (SSB), 1988–98. *Statistical Yearbook of China*, China Statistical Publishing House, Beijing.

Sun, Y., 1961. 'Some issues regarding the internal financial system of the state-owned economy', in Sun, 1979, *Some Theoretical Issues of the Socialist Economy*, People's Press, Beijing (in Chinese).

Tan, C., 1996. 'Some issues of reform of the state-owned enterprises', in T. Song and X. Wei (eds), *Multi-dimensional Thinking on Promoting State Enterprise Reform by 40 Economists*, Economics Science Press, Beijing (in Chinese).

Tan, X.Y. and Xin, X., 1999. 'An analysis of China's corn market', in Y. Yang and W.M. Tian (eds), *China's Agriculture at the Crossroads*, Macmillan, London.

Tian, G., 1996. 'Approach and steps of China's state enterprise reform and economic system transition: on three stages of China's economic reform', in D. Xu and G. Wen (eds), *Reform of China's State-owned Enterprises*, China Economy Press, Beijing (in Chinese).

Tidrick, G., 1986. *Productivity Growth and Technological Change in Chinese Industry*, World Bank Working Papers No. 761, World Bank, Washington, DC.

Tseng, W., Khor, H.E., Kochhar, K., Mihaljek, D. and Burton, D., 1994. *Economic Reform in China: a new phase*, International Monetary Fund, Washington, DC.

Tsui, K.Y., 1993. 'Decomposing of Chinas regional inequalities', *Journal of Comparative Economics*, 17:600–27.

——, 1996. 'Economic reform and interprovincial inequality in China', *Journal of Development Economics*, 50:353–68.

United Nations Development Program (UNDP), 1996. Elimination of Poverty [online] [cited Oct. 1998], available at <URL:http://www.edu.cn/undp/shd/poverty.htm>.

——, 1998. *China Human Development Report 1997*, UNDP Beijing Office, Beijing:122–8.

Walder, A., 1989. 'Factory and manager in an era of reform', *China Quarterly*, 118:242–64.

Wan, G.H. and Cheng, E.J., 1999. 'A micro-empirical analysis of land fragmentation and scale economies in rural China', in Y. Yang and W.M. Tian (eds), *China's Agriculture at the Crossroads*, Macmillan, London.

Wang, H., 1993. *China's Exports since 1979*, Macmillan Press, London.

Wang, T., 1998. 'Difficulty and opportunity', *Xinhua Digest*, March (in Chinese).

Wang, X., 1997a. What contributed to China's rapid rural industrial growth during the reform period?, PhD dissertation, The Australian National University, Canberra.

Wang, X., (forthcoming). 'Rural development and population holding capacity', in *China's Sustainable Development Framework: Summary Report,* The United Nations University/Institute of Advanced Studies, Tokyo.

Wang, Z., 1996. 'Problems and solutions of the state economy', in T. Song and X. Wei (eds), *Multi-dimensional Thinking on Promoting State Enterprise Reform by 40 Economists,* Economics Science Press, Beijing (in Chinese).

Wei, S. and Wang, T., 1996. 'The twins: China's state-owned enterprises and state banks', in D. Xu and G. Wen (eds), *Reform of China's State-owned Enterprises,* China Economy Press, Beijing (in Chinese).

Wen, G., 1998. 'Price reform', in Z. Zhang, F. Huang and G. Li (eds), *Review and Prospects of 20 Years' Economic Reform,* China Planning Publisher, Beijing:118–30.

Woo, W.T., 1994. 'The art of reforming centrally planned economies: comparing China, Poland, and Russia', *Journal of Comparative Advantage,* 18:276–308.

——, 1998. 'Financial intermediation in China', in O. Bouin, F. Coricelli and F. Lemoine (eds), *Different Approaches to Market Reform,* CEPII/CEPR/OECD Development Centre, Paris:153–70.

——, Fan, G., Hai, W. and Jing, Y., 1993. 'The efficiency and macroeconomic consequences of Chinese enterprise reform', *China Economic Review,* 4(2):153–68.

——, 1994a. 'How successful has Chinese enterprise reform been? Pitfalls in opposite biases and focus', *Journal of Comparative Economics,* 18(3):410–37.

——, 1994b. 'Productivity change in Chinese industry: a reply to Jefferson, Rawski and Zheng', *China Economic Review,* 5(2):243–8.

World Bank, 1985. *China: long-term development issues and options,* Johns Hopkins University Press, Baltimore.

——, 1992. *China Country Economic Memorandum: reform and the role of the plan in the 1990s,* World Bank, Washington, DC.

——, 1993a. *The East Asian Miracle: economic growth and public policy,* World Bank Policy Research Report series, Oxford University Press, New York.

——, 1993b, 1996a, 1997a. *World Development Report*, Oxford University Press, New York and China Fiscal Economic Publisher.

——, 1995a. *Reform and the Role of the Plan in the 1990s*, World Bank Country Study, Washington, DC.

——, 1995b. *China the Emerging Capital Market*, World Bank, Washington, DC, Volumes 1 and 2.

——, 1996b. *China: reform of state-owned enterprises*, Report No. 14924-CHA, China and Mongolia Department, East Asia and Pacific Region, World Bank, Washington, DC.

——, 1997b. *World Development Indicators*, World Bank Publications, Philadelphia [CD-ROM].

——, 1997c. *Governments in a Changing World*, China Fiscal Economic Publisher, Introduction and Chapter 1.

——, 1997d. *China 2020: development challenges in the new century*, Washington, DC.

——, 1997e. *China Engaged: integration with the global economy*, World Bank, Washington, DC.

——, 1997f. *Sharing Rising Incomes: disparities in China*, World Bank, Washington, DC:Chapter 2.

Wu, H. and Wu, Y., 1994. 'Rural enterprise growth and efficiency', in C. Findlay, A. Watson and H. Wu (eds), *Rural Enterprises in China*, Macmillan, London.

Wu, J., 1993a. *Large and Medium Size Enterprise Reform: establishing modern enterprise institutions*, Tianjin People's Press, Tianjin.

——, 1996. 'Does China adopt a 'gradual' reform strategy?', in Gradual or Radical: the choice of China's economic reform, *Economic Science Publisher*, 1:1–10.

Wu, X., 1995. ' China's financial institutions', in Tam, Kit (ed.), *Financial Reform in China*, Routledge, New York:113–30.

Wu, Y., 1993b. 'Productive efficiency in Chinese industry', *Asian-Pacific Economic Literature*, 7(2):58–66.

Xia, B., 1995. 'Analysis of China's inter-bank money market', in O.K. Tam (ed.), *Financial Reform in China*, Routledge, New York:Chapter 4.

Xiao, G., 1991. 'Managerial autonomy, fringe benefits, and ownership structure: a comparative study of Chinese state and collective enterprises', *China Economic Review*, 2(1):47–73.

Xu, D. and Wen, G. (eds), 1996. *Reform of China's State-owned Enterprises*, China Economy Press, Beijing (in Chinese).

Xu, W., Jefferson, G.H. and Rathja, D., 1993. China data documentation, Transition and Micro-adjustment Division, World Bank, Washington, DC (manuscript).

Xu, X., 1998. *China's Financial System under Transition*, Macmillian Press, London.

—— and Wang, Y., 1997. Ownership structure, corporate governance and firm's performance: the case of Chinese stock companies, World Bank China and Mongolia Department Workshop, Washington, DC (manuscript).

Xu, Z. and Li, L., 1996. *Management History of China's Publicly Owned Enterprises, second volume (1966–1992)*, Shanghai Academy of Social Sciences Press, Shanghai (in Chinese).

Xue, M., 1981. *China's Socialist Economy*, Foreign Language Press, Beijing.

——, 1996. *A Recollection of Xue Muqiao*, Tianjing People's Press, Tianjing (in Chinese).

——, 1998. 'A recollection of the path of China's economic reform', *Economic Information*, 42:16–18.

Yang, J., 1998. *Deng Xiaoping Era: a recording of 20 years' reform and openness in China*, Central Translation Publisher, Beijing.

Yang, P., 1990. *Contract System: inevitable choice of enterprise development*, China Economy Press, Beijing.

Yang, Y., 1996. 'China's WTO membership: what's at stake?', *The World Economy*, 19(6):661–82.

—— and Huang, Y., 1997. 'How should China feed itself?', *The World Economy*, 20(7):913–34.

Yao, S., 1997. 'Profit sharing, bonus payment, and productivity: a case study of Chinese state-owned enterprises', *Journal of Comparative Economics*, 24:281–96.

Yin, W., 1995. 'Reform of state-owned enterprises and inflation: dilemma and policy choices', *Economic Research Journal*, 7:21–7 (in Chinese).

Yu, G. (ed.), 1996. *Evolution of Chinese economic theory 1949–1989*, Henan People's Press, Zhenzhou (in Chinese).

Zhang, W., 1994. 'A principle-agent theory of public ownership economy', *Economic Research Journal*, 4 (in Chinese).

——, 1995. *Entrepreneurs of enterprises: a contract theory*, Shanghai Sanlian Bookstore and Shanghai People's Press, Shanghai (in Chinese).

——, 1996a. 'Outlet of the state-owned enterprises', in D. Xu and G. Wen (eds), *Reform of China's State-owned Enterprises*, China Economy Press, Beijing (in Chinese).

——, 1996b. 'Promoting reform of the state-owned enterprises through understanding coordination, scientific planning and multiple-experiment', in T. Song and X. Wei (eds), *Multi-dimensional Thinking on Promoting State Enterprise Reform by 40 Economists*, Economics Science Press, Beijing (in Chinese).

——, 1997. 'Decision rights, residual claims and performance: a theory of how Chinese state enterprise reform works,' *China Economic Review*, 8(1):67–82.

Zhang, X., 1993. China's trade patterns and international comparative advantage, PhD dissertation, The Australian National University, Canberra.

Zhao, J., 1998. 'Review of foreign economy and trade in 1997 and prospects for 1998', in M. Heng (ed.), *Economic Situation and Prospects of China*, China Development Publisher, Beijing:195–219.

Zhao, R., 1988. 'An overall design for the objectives of reforming China's economic system', in G. Liu (ed.), *Studies on Models of China's Economic System Reform*, China Social Science Publisher, Beijing:52–94.

Zhao, Y., 1996. 'The nature of China's state-owned enterprises and its implications', in D. Xu and G. Wen (eds), *Reform of China's State-owned Enterprises*, China Economy Press, Beijing (in Chinese).

Zhou, S., 1996. 'China's enterprise reform and industrial development', in T. Song and X. Wei (eds), *Multi-dimensional Thinking on Promoting State Enterprise Reform by 40 Economists*, Economics Science Press, Beijing (in Chinese).

Zhou, T.H., Wu, Z., Fu, F.X. and Gao, S.Q. (eds), 1984. *Economic System Reform in Contemporary China*, China Social Sciences Press, Beijing.

Zhou, X., Wang, L., Xiao, M. and Yin, W., 1994. *Enterprise Reform: model selection and compatible design*, China Economy Press, Beijing (in Chinese).

Zhu, L., 1994. 'Inequality and non-farming income in rural China', in R. Zhao, K. Griffin, L. Zhu and S. Li (eds), *Distribution of Household Income in China*, China Social Sciences Press, Beijing:136–51 (in Chinese).

Zhucheng Municipality Government, 1996. 'Property rights reform in Zhucheng Municipality', in H. Ma (ed.), *Asset Restructuring in*

Enterprise Reform: case studies and theoretical analysis, Economic Management Press, Beijing (in Chinese).

He, J. and Yang, Y., 1998. The political economy of trade liberalisation in China, National Centre for Development Studies, The Australian National University, Canberra, mimeo.

Huang, Y., Meng, X. and Woo, W.T., 1997c. Lessons from China's state sector reform, National Centre for Development Studies, The Australian National University, Canberra, mimeo.

Li, S. and Zhang, W., 1997. Decentralisation, competition, and institutional change: privatisation in China, Department of Economics and Finance, City University of Hong Kong, Hong Kong, mimeo.

Wang, H., 1997b. 'An analysis of capital structure of China's state-owned enterprises', Institute of Economics, Chinese Academy of Social Sciences, Beijing, mimeo (in Chinese).

Index